"REMEMBER"

"*Remember that I am the Adversary, the Interloper*

Remember that I am war, strife, famine, pestilence, martyrs, great signs and silence

Remember that I am the Lord of the tribe, king of the jungle and hunter of great beasts

Remember that I am the Viper of the pit, the most cunning animal whose poison is the deadliest known

Remember that I am the second son of Adam and Eve

Remember that I rose up in front of god and slew my brother Abel out of greed

Remember it all, but if you should somehow forget some of it, just remember this 'My name is Cain and I kill people' "

—FROM THE NOTEBOOK OF DAVID BIRO

Other True Crime Cases by
Gera-Lind Kolarik
with Wayne Klatt
from Avon Books

FREED TO KILL

"I AM CAIN"

GERA-LIND KOLARIK
AND WAYNE KLATT

AVON BOOKS ◆ NEW YORK

"I AM CAIN" is a journalistic account of an actual murder investigation and conviction for the 1990 murders of Nancy and Richard Langert and their unborn child in Winnetka, Illinois. The events recounted in this book are true, although some of the names have been changed. The scenes and dialogue have been reconstructed based on tape-recorded formal interviews, police department records, and published news stories. Quoted court testimony has been taken verbatim from trial transcripts.

AVON BOOKS
A division of
The Hearst Corporation
1350 Avenue of the Americas
New York, New York 10019

Copyright © 1994 by Gera-Lind Kolarik and Wayne Klatt
Front cover photo of David Biro by Geoff Scheerer/*Pioneer Press*
Published by arrangement with the authors
Library of Congress Catalog Card Number: 93-90655
ISBN: 0-380-76624-8

First Avon Books Printing: April 1994

AVON TRADEMARK REG. U.S. PAT. OFF. AND IN OTHER COUNTRIES, MARCA REGISTRADA, HECHO EN U.S.A.

Printed in the U.S.A.

RA 10 9 8 7 6 5 4 3 2 1

Acknowledgments

We would like to thank former Winnetka Police Chief Herbert Timm, along with Lieutenant Joseph Sumner, Sergeants Gene Kalvaitis and Patricia McConnell, and Officers Billy Caldwell and Eddie Benoit. They and former task-force members John Fay, William Broten, and Kevin Keel spent hours detailing how the case was assembled. The late director of the Northern Illinois Police Crime Laboratory, Andy Principe, and technician Bob Wilson reenacted for us their work in turning a crime scene into evidence. Dr. Mitra Kalelkar of the Cook County Medical Examiner's Office helped recreate the crime for us also.

A fuller understanding of the case was also made possible by Bob Fusel, director of the Chicago Crime Commission; Peggy Anderson, a clerk in the Cook County Circuit Court; Roger Badesch, former director of advertising and public relations at Gloria Jean's Coffee; and Robert Glotz, security director of the Cook County Department of Corrections.

Members of these organizations have helped us on the condition that their names not be used: the Federal Bureau of Investigation office in Chicago, the U.S. Customs Service offices in Chicago and Washington, the Chicago Police Intelligence Division, and the Irish Northern Aid Committee.

Authors' Note

This is a look behind the headlines of a shocking double murder that had no apparent motive. A police department with just two dozen employees launched a million-dollar investigation that included inquiries at Scotland Yard and Interpol. Because the officers did not know where to start, the private lives of the victims and their families became part of the investigation, only increasing their grief. In time, the personal lives of the killer and his family underwent scrutiny and speculation as police tried to answer the question "Why?"

And so this account of the killing of Richard and Nancy Langert is very much the story of three families before and after the crime. No relative wished to provide information for this book. We understand their pain and respect their desire for privacy. But a number of friends of the victims and the killer shared their memories. Other personal information came from the trial, reports obtained through the Freedom of Information Act, and documents made available as a result of a civil suit filed by the Bishop family, the family of one of the victims.

Dialogue has been recreated only from these sources and interviews with at least one person involved. Names that have been changed are marked with an asterisk the first time they are used. Scenes reconstructed from physical evidence have been verified by police and medical experts as reasonable accounts of what may have happened.

We also wish to acknowledge the contributions of three journalists who provided assistance during the early stage of this research: Jessica Seigel, reporter for the *Chicago Tribune;* Dominick Najolia, photo editor of the *Chicago Sun-Times;* and Sharon Wright, reporter for WMAQ-TV. Special thanks to Gene Janowski, who transcribed hundreds of hours of taped interviews, and Sharon White, our photographer, whose photo ideas aided in presenting this case.

Special thanks to David Highfill, our editor at Avon Books, who suggested this book in the first place.

A Quiet Sunday Afternoon

April 8, 1990

A LIGHT BREEZE rolled in from Lake Michigan in picture-perfect Winnetka. Police activity in the Chicago suburb on this overcast Palm Sunday consisted of three speeding tickets, one petty theft, and a man from out of town caught driving with an expired vehicle registration. That was typical. In this upscale village trouble usually involved teens or people just passing through.

Mahlon Lee Bishop, a successful civil attorney, drove from his home in the secluded southern part of town to the eastern end, where his daughter Nancy and son-in-law Richard were living. Lee, who owned their townhouse, intended to put up some shelves in a bedroom closet. That would give him something to do while his wife attended a rehearsal for an amateur production at the community center. Besides, Lee and his wife wanted to make sure their youngest daughter was all right. The family had celebrated Lee's sixtieth birthday the night before, but Nancy was ill from her pregnancy and couldn't enjoy the festivities. And now, no one was answering the phone.

As Lee pulled up in the driveway, he saw the couple's two cars parked in front of their townhouse. Climbing out, he playfully tugged at the leash of the beagle Nancy and Richard had given him. The small dog eagerly walked ahead of its master to the front door of the one-and-a-half-story brick house.

Lee had a key, but as a courtesy he pressed the buzzer. When no one came to the door he opened it himself and called out from the threshold. No answer.

Perhaps they were at a neighbor's. He crossed the room and slid back one of the two large glass patio doors to let his dog run outside on the narrow patch of grass between the house and the six-foot wooden fence. Nancy and Richard were planning to move into a home of their own by the end of the month, so their belongings were packed in old boxes. A card table and folding chairs substituted for furniture.

Almost as soon as Lee closed the patio door, the beagle was beside him again with the excited look of a dog that had discovered something. Only then did Lee notice that some glass had been removed from the second patio door and the sections stacked on the ground. Richard wouldn't do anything like that without asking him, Lee was sure.

The faint sunshine kept the house dim, but a light still burned in the basement. His uneasiness mounting, Lee saw Nancy's purse on the floor, with several fifty- and hundred-dollar bills sticking out of a pay envelope. Her credit cards were scattered about.

The house had a terrible stillness. When a faint sound came from upstairs, Lee's throat went dry. He reattached the leash to his dog and went up the stairs, calling Nancy's name and knocking on the bedroom door. When he opened it, the Langerts' cocker spaniel ran out. That explained the sound Lee had heard, but not everything else. He grabbed both dogs and put them in the bedroom to keep them from distracting him as he continued his search.

He returned to the ground floor and started down the basement steps. That's when he saw Nancy. He could see her arm outstretched on the concrete floor near the bottom stair, her eyes open in death. She was dressed in the same clothes she had worn at the party the previous night.

With a feeling that what he was seeing couldn't be real, Lee took a few more steps and stopped when he saw a pool of blood and the body of his tall, muscular son-in-law. Richard Langert's hands were behind his back, his head to one side, his face caked in blood. Midway between the two bodies lay an axe.

Lee ran up the steps to call the police. Not wanting to disturb any evidence, he put a handkerchief around the receiver before touching it. He dialed 911. "I saw my daughter, my daughter and son-in-law are here and they're dead," he said, almost in hysterics.

"Okay," the dispatcher began. "I want you to stay on the phone with me. I'm going to put you on hold and then I'm going to come back and talk to you."

"Oh, God," Lee said. "How could this happen?"

The seconds seemed endless as Lee held the phone and struggled to remain calm. "Sir?" the dispatcher returned after notifying a patrol car and an ambulance. "They should be driving up in just thirty seconds." After all, the townhouse was right across the ravine bridge from the police station.

Half an hour later, newspaper and television news crews rushed to the scene of the only double murder in Winnetka history. Inside, officers found no sign of robbery or any other obvious motive. Although there was an axe, both victims had been shot. Richard, it seemed, was killed execution style.

But none of it made sense. Strangest of all was a clue on one of the metal shelves in the basement. Police found what they believed was a message that Nancy had written in her own blood.

I

An All-American Couple

". . . with His blessing, what God has joined, men must not divide . . ."

1

"Now Life Begins"

Saturday, May 23, 1987

SOCIALITES, TOP CIVIL attorneys, and white-collar workers flocked to the Kenilworth Union Church to celebrate the marriage of Nancy Bishop and Richard Langert. The L-shaped English Gothic church was built with a stark gray timelessness modeled after a country estate. Guests and pretty bridesmaids clustered on the church steps with the vast Lake Michigan in the background.

Before the ceremony, Nancy tugged at the waist of her fitted satin bridal gown in the small dressing room of the Congregational church. Pictures never captured the real Nancy. Her green eyes and continual animation gave her a loveliness that a frozen pose could never convey. Standing by the mirror, she gave a casual fluff to the brown curls flowing to her shoulders.

"I do think you should have worn your hair in an upsweep," her mother, Joyce, said as she placed the flowered crown of the veil onto Nancy's head.

"Please, mother, I want that natural look."

"All your bridesmaids look fine," Joyce remarked lightly while tucking in a few stray hairs. Joyce always wanted her family to look its best.

Nancy started to turn, but her mother said, "We're not through yet." She lifted a satin bag from the table and drew from it a strand of pearls she had worn at parties and family gatherings. She placed the pearls around her daughter's neck and said, "You must have something old. These were mine. Now they're yours."

Nancy's sisters, Jennifer and Jeanne, came into the room with a rustle of their lavender gowns and presented her with a tiny gift-wrapped package. The bridesmaids came closer to watch as Nancy opened the box and lifted out a gold ankle-chain with a little heart dangling from it. Nancy's eyes glistened. She hugged her sisters and mother.

"Don't cry," Joyce said, hugging her back. "You'll ruin your mascara."

This wedding had seemed unlikely not too many months before. Nancy and Richard had met while working at a spice specialties company, but the relationship was stop and go. Richard, who was still adjusting to a salesman's life after carefree days in college, was not so sure he was ready for marriage until Nancy's exuberance won him over.

Nancy was so determined to make this marriage work that she had them both sign a list of qualities she considered most important in a successful relationship: patience, understanding, love, and trust.

The bride's father, Lee, was a proud man this cool and rainy Saturday. It was hard enough to accept that his youngest child had turned twenty-three less than two weeks ago, and even harder to realize he was losing her. Nancy had been the mediator and the entertainer of the family, and the house would seem empty without her.

Lee, a heavy man with auburn hair and a double chin, was a member of the oldest law firm in Chicago. Isham, Lincoln & Beale was founded by Abraham Lincoln's son, Robert Todd, and its client list included the Chicago Bears and NBC. The firm had thirty-six million dollars in billings from its recent merger with Reuben & Proctor, but insiders were predicting that the legal powerhouse would collapse under its own weight.

Nancy had begun as a Daddy's Girl, but she and her mother shared a fondness for singing and often volunteered for charity work. The middle daughter, Jeanne, followed in her father's footsteps with her serious temperament and desire to be a lawyer. The slender, blonde young woman and her heavier older sister stood as maids of honor with two of Nancy's University of Kansas sorority sisters.

The three brothers of the twenty-seven-year-old bridegroom ushered guests to the pews while Richard stood in a side room looking as if he wished the ceremony were over. The brothers liked Nancy well enough, but they were unhappy Richard was marrying outside the Catholic faith. Richard's friends in Chicago had been warning him for weeks that trouble lay ahead because he was marrying into an upper-middle-class family. Once when he brought Nancy to a beer-guzzling pig roast, his friends could see how uncomfortable she was.

Richard was six feet, two inches tall and weighed two hundred and fifty pounds, much of it muscle. He had straight black hair and relatively small eyes that made him look as if he were squinting. His size might have been intimidating, but his glasses made him look more approachable and let people relax around him.

Although Richard looked like a natural for the gridiron, he preferred baseball. He played on the Illinois High School championship team at Brother Rice High School. From there he went to Lewis University but disappointed his family by dropping out. Although bright enough to earn a degree like his brothers, Richard preferred socializing with his Chicago friends. He seldom did without his weekly golfing, and Nancy could match him in an aggressive game of tennis. When the family held a combination engagement and Christmas party the previous December, Lee raised a glass to the pair and thanked Nancy for giving him the son he never had.

Now Richard's parents, quietly as usual, were watching him begin a life on his own. The Langerts felt a mixture of joy and loss. The father, Robert, an accountant nearing retirement, had his hand on his wife's arm as the plump woman cried without caring who saw her.

The bride looked lovingly at Richard as Dr. Gilbert W. Bowen pronounced that "with His blessing, what God has joined, men must not divide." The newlyweds kissed with their hands intertwined. Nancy beamed and the bridegroom, less comfortable showing emotion, managed a smile as they turned to face the applause and flashing cameras of three hundred guests.

Outside the church, Lee hugged his wife with a "Well, it's done" expression. Nancy's two sisters passed around little bags of rice. The women among the guests kissed Nancy on the cheek, and the men received a strong grip from Richard as they shook hands. Most of the guests knew that the Langerts and the Bishops were not lending the couple any substantial financial support, so they handed the couple envelopes with checks inside.

After snapshots were taken on the church steps and under the stone arches in the graveyard, everyone headed for a reception at the Kenilworth Club. The nearby hall had a 1920s elegance under its arched beams. Salads, fruits, and finger sandwiches were laid out along the U-shaped buffet table, and caterers brought out a tiered cake topped by a pastry of lavender flowers.

As disk jockey Robbie Wilson played "We Are Family," Nancy and Richard took the hands of the two Bishop sisters and three Langert brothers. The other guests moved back to give them room. The Bishop daughters and the Langert sons then took the hands of their parents and brought them into the dancing circle.

When the song ended, Lee returned to the table as everyone applauded and had another drink. Mopping his face from time to time, Lee went around the hall making sure everyone was having a good time. He joked with a friend, saying, "Now life begins, my dog is thirteen years old and my last child is married off."

The older guests headed home and friends of the bridal party took over the dance floor for rock and roll.

The newlyweds spent their honeymoon skiing in Colorado, then settled down in a single-bedroom apartment in the tidy western suburb of Willowbrook. Nancy and Richard were fun to be around, and they behaved like a team. But Richard had his serious side. What meant the most to him was someday becoming a success, and he was old fashioned enough to think hard work alone would be enough. Using his contacts in the industry, he and a friend started SpiceTech Limited in west suburban Maywood. Lee Bishop incorporated the small firm and served as its attorney.

As chief salesman, Richard spent long hours on the road, but he couldn't understand the strain his absences put his wife under. From what friends could gather, though, sex wasn't all that important to him. To Nancy, it was the spark of life.

Nancy was born in Evanston, a suburb between Winnetka and Chicago. Her personality blossomed after the Wilson Certified Foods company assigned Lee to its offices in Oklahoma and the family moved there. Lee became a director of the Oklahoma City YMCA, the Oklahoma Symphony Orchestra, and the Last Frontier Boy Scout troop. He also kept up with his business contacts as a member of the Oklahoma City Golf and Country Club. The family then moved to Dallas for awhile before returning to the Chicago area. In these years, Nancy went from being Daddy's Little Girl to Mommy's Little Girl, though she always kept close to Lee.

While Nancy was still in grade school, Lee bought a house on Indian Hill Road, in one of the wealthiest areas of the community. Everything about the family now had the air of security and permanency.

With Nancy's good looks and soprano voice, she won the coveted role of Maria in the New Trier High School production of *West Side Story,* and friends still talked about her performance well after she graduated.

During a summer break from the University of Kansas, she found a job at Saratoga Specialties, a spice and chemicals company in the Chicago suburb of Elmhurst. Lee was the senior vice president, Robert Langert was the comptroller, and Richard was a salesman.

Richard was so smitten by this lively girl that after she returned to college, he ran up eight hundred dollars in long-distance bills calling her.

Friends thought the two young people were made for each other because of their sense of humor and optimism. But that spirit didn't always carry over into their marriage. Most of the tension had to do with how quickly they spent their money, since neither Richard nor Nancy knew the first thing about managing finances.

Nancy was also unprepared for the impact of her husband's long working hours. Marriage had brought her a loneliness she never knew before. She tried to fill her time by working at a veneer company, visiting her parents in Winnetka, and taking part in productions with her mother at the suburb's Community House. Joyce not only had featured roles, she also did promotional work for the theater group.

Joyce Bishop was a lovely woman with red hair and sharply carved features. She had musical training and moved about with grace. While not effusive with her three daughters, she watched over her family with a careful eye and empathetic heart. Knowing what it must have been like for the "baby" of an active family to find herself suddenly alone so much, Joyce started making inquiries about apartments in the northern suburbs.

That way, Nancy could live again by the low hills along Lake Michigan rather than in the flatlands of the western suburbs.

Joyce also set in motion social events that just might help her husband now that his career was being threatened by the impending collapse of his law firm. She believed that Lee would be better on his own rather than as one of 235 lawyers at Isham, Lincoln & Beale and Reuben & Proctor. So she sent out invitations to a dinner party at the family home for his business associates and their wives.

There was no direct way to reach the house. Instead, a winding road in a golf course led through woods dotted with mansions. The Bishops' colonial-modern home was simpler than some of its neighbors, but it had a small stable, painted white with black trim to match the house. The stable had not been used for years.

The living room was done in faded greens and gold, with a large sofa behind a coffee table. Family photos were mounted above the stairs leading to the den: Joyce performing in plays during her teenage years, Lee smiling his understated grin, and shots of the three girls growing up with ribbons in their hair and wearing velvety dresses with lace collars. In the master bedroom was an oil painting of the entire family.

Lee's well-worn easy chair faced the parlor hearth. When he was relaxed, he let his pipe lay nestled in his mouth. When he was nervous, he sucked on the stem. On this night he was sucking on the stem and trying to look relaxed at the same time.

The evening was no casual affair. The attorneys, most of them well into their sixties, arrived in suits and their wives in semi-formal dresses. A little out of place were two family friends, *Mary and *Gary Gasglow. Joyce quietly admitted to inviting them to bring a little fun to the party.

After the formalities of dinner, Joyce explained why she had all the guests bring a throwaway gift they might have found around the house. She held up a pair of dice and rolled one of them. Anyone who rolled the same number could pick one of the wrapped gifts and pass the die to someone else. Soon everyone was laughing as guests opened unwanted presents such as a stuffed owl that had gathered dust in some closet. By the end of the party, middle-aged and elderly men were joking with one another as if they were law students again.

In the side rooms, the wives spoke of mismangement at the law firm and how the rumored collapse was threatening many long careers. A few said their husbands were smart in planning to get out while they could. "Oh?" Joyce asked with a peaceful expression.

In April 1988, newspapers were carrying stories about the demise of Isham, Lincoln & Beale and Reuben & Proctor. By then, the law firm of Palmer, Bishop and Wardell had just opened in northwest suburban Schaumburg. As part of his work, Lee became a registered agent for a number of new companies. He had to take his clients where he found them.

2

Day Of Wrath

WINNETKA IS BUILT largely on a rolling plain from Indian Hill to Hubbard Woods. Although the shoreline mansions eighteen miles from Chicago have high walls blocking off Lake Michigan, the rest of the suburb has a friendly, open feel.

The village was established in the 1850s as a railroad community for those who could afford to get away from the smokestacks and crime of the city. The name is said to be from an Indian word meaning "place of beauty," although the first blacksmith wanted it called New Trier, after the German town overlooking the Rhine. New Trier lingered as the name of the township and the village's major high school. The village was so quiet that in the 1880s, a teenage girl opened her second-floor window in the middle of the night and screamed "Fire!" just to see people get excited.

Movie producers have used the community for stories of pleasantly well off yet hardworking families such as those in *Ferris Beuller's Day Off* and *Home Alone*. Some of the more modern homes in the four and a half square miles of Winnetka seem like intrusions on the spirit of the community, but most streets have a quiet order. Residences set back from the sidewalks display generous lawns, giving the streets an almost parklike appearance. The City Hall on Green Bay Road looks like a city hall, and the Swiss-chalet-inspired row of shops at Elm and Chestnut looks designed for a miniature train.

Since the village was founded, there had been only three murders—two separate ones in one day by robbers from out of town in 1884, and the shooting of a patrolman in 1957 by a man who then turned the gun on himself. Sometimes a year goes by without a robbery. The police force of twenty-five commissioned officers and ten noncommissioned personnel seemed more than adequate for anything that might happen in the community of thirteen thousand. New Trier High School is about the only place with anything going on, with cars and school buses driving back and forth every morning and afternoon.

Since 1976, the police department had been headed by Herbert Timm, a former Chicago officer who could pass for a banker because of his careful grooming and dark suits. He usually jogged in the morning before having a leisurely breakfast at a restaurant. The middle-aged police chief had a methodical mind, and in his free time could often be found in "Scotland Yard," a small bookstore specializing in mysteries, a fully costumed statue of Sherlock Holmes standing guard in the front window.

The tranquility was disrupted on May 20, 1988, when a tormented professional babysitter named Laurie Dann went on a murderous rampage. Police in several North Shore communities knew of Dann's growing unpredictability, but there was nothing they could do. Officials estimate that if all her attempts had succeeded, she would have killed fifty people.

Dann's rage smoldered after Marion Rushe said her services soon would no longer be needed because the family was moving to New York. The former Laurie Wasserman, now overweight from an overuse of prescription drugs, had been fairly popular with boys when she went to New Trier High School. By the time her marriage to Russell Dann ended in separation, she was so unstable that he feared for his life. Two years later, Laurie enrolled at the University of Wisconsin in Madison but never went to class. Sometimes she would ride campus elevators for hours according to a schedule she had written out.

Dann awoke early on May 20 to begin her systematic destruction. Her first act was injecting a solution into sixteen packages of food destined for people she cared for before the relationships crumbled or because they had done something she didn't like.

After this, Dann went to the Rushe house and offered to take Marion's two boys to a carnival. With them in her car, she used bottles of flammable liquid to set a small fire at the Ravinia Elementary School in Highland Park. She also gave the two Rushe boys milk laced with arsenic, but it tasted sour and they dumped it out when she wasn't looking.

Half an hour later, Dann tried to enter a Jewish day care center with a gasoline can but a guard refused to let her in. She took the boys home and kept up a conversation with their mother. As Marion started to wash clothes, Dann set the carpeted basement stairs on fire with her can of gasoline, then locked the woman and her two sons inside. The family barely made it out through a narrow window before fire fighters arrived.

Dann then walked into the Hubbard Woods Elementary School with three guns. She dragged a six-year-old boy into a washroom and shot him with a .22-caliber Beretta. A teacher thought the explosion was a science experiment until the wounded boy dragged himself back into her room.

The babysitter left her largest gun, a .357 Magnum, in a washbasin and returned to the corridor. She entered a class and ordered a substitute teacher to put the children in a corner. The teacher struggled with her, but

Dann shot five of the students. All survived except eight-year-old Nicky Corwin.

Winnetka Sergeant Patricia McConnell—an attractive woman with a mop of curly hair—was wearing her undercover "civies" of jeans and a sweatshirt when she received a report of shots fired in the school. She left the drive-in window of a bank to speak to the other children in Nicky's class, mainly to calm them down. Next she drove around the neighborhood with the substitute teacher to see if they could find "the crazy woman." Repeatedly the teacher muttered, "I wish she had shot me and not my children, I wish she had shot me."

Chief Timm's second in command, Lieutenant Joseph Sumner, was kept busy deploying officers as a telephone company crew installed additional lines. Breathless inquiries from newspapers across the country, as well as in England, Germany, and Austria, kept the phones ringing.

By then, Dann had invaded a stucco house and was keeping a gun on Phil Andrew, a university student. She stared out the window for a moment, then calmly turned and shot him in the chest. The young man staggered away and left Dann alone inside.

Police agreed to let Laurie's father, a wealthy accountant, speak to her outside the house. But it was too late. Laurie Dann had gone upstairs and shot herself to death in a children's room.

Sergeant Patricia McConnell that afternoon received a call from the local post office about packages of food that Dann had dropped in the mail. She took them to the Northern Illinois Crime Laboratory and discovered that they had been injected with arsenic.

The Laurie Dann tragedy came three days before Nancy and Richard Langert's first wedding anniversary. A celebration was out of the question; the entire Chicago metropolitan area was in shock. The couple, still living in Willowbrook, could barely believe that something like this could happen in the orderly town where Nancy had spent almost half her life. For the first time, people began locking their doors. As one resident said, "Today, Winnetka lost its innocence."

For Winnetka police, there were more than just Dann's crimes to consider. She had been prescribed a drug that was then unattainable in the United States without federal Food and Drug Administration authorization, but it was used legally in Canada and Europe for obsessive-compulsive personalities. The drug helped two-thirds of the patients, but the packages carried warnings that the medicine could cause delusions or suicidal depression. Even so, studies showed that the medicine was unlikely to produce violence even in combination with other drugs.

But it remained undetermined how this drug might have influenced Laurie Dann. Timm's department worked with the Illinois Department of Professional Regulations, the Medical Disciplinary Board, the U.S. Department of Health and Human Services, and the office of the Inspector General to learn how she obtained it. The officers also assisted the FBI and the U.S. Postal Service.

No small suburb is equipped to handle such a complex series of crimes. Yet the often harsh news media had nothing but respect for the way Winnetka handled the crisis. At one point, three hundred police officers, fire fighters, and other emergency personnel from numerous suburbs were involved. In one day, Timm's department had emerged from its isolation. Timm authorized a videotaped documentary on the case for any small police department wanting to learn how a major case is handled. As he saw it, his officers were now ready for anything.

3

Dreamtalk

LAURIE DANN'S OUTBURST haunted everyone on the North Shore. Sergeant Patricia McConnell appeared calm when talking to community groups about it, but from that day on she became a chain-smoker. She was put in charge of a task force of eighteen detectives from neighboring suburbs to retrace Dann's movements step by step. The work McConnell supervised was so thorough she was commended in a letter written into the Congressional Record and was named Illinois Police Woman of the Year. But the community was concentrating on ways of preventing violence.

Although Chicago retains notoriety from the Capone era, its suburbs are the center of a national movement to outlaw guns at a local level. Of the first five communities in the United States that adopted such ordinances, four were around the city.

Winnetka residents, often using children as recruiters, collected twelve hundred signatures on petitions for a referendum on whether to ban handguns from the village. United States Appeals Court Justice Richard Cudahy stood up at a public hearing and told the divided audience that despite the pleasure he took in owning a .357 Magnum revolver, the safety of his children, who attended Winnetka schools, came first. "I'll be glad to contribute my handgun to Chief Timm," Judge Cudahy said. Three-quarters of the audience burst into applause.

Youngsters spent their school lunch periods cutting out opened hands from construction paper, writing the word "vote" across them, and tying string around the index fingers. Hundreds of these reminders hung on front doors throughout the village as the April elections approached.

A week after the referendum was approved, supporters packed a meeting room to see how the village board would decide. Ten children dressed as if for a birthday party sat in the front row. When the board unanimously voted to make Winnetka the sixth community in the country to outlaw firearms, the children walked onto the stage and, with Winnetka showmanship, gave each member a rose.

That spring, Lee and Joyce Bishop took the newly-weds on a visit to England and Ireland. Jeanne went along but seemed to be in her own world. Standing with her sister and parents at the changing of the guard outside Buckingham Palace, she mocked the guardsmen as "little boys who will be sent over to Ireland to kill innocent people."

When the family returned, Joyce lovingly put together a vacation scrapbook. The front cover featured a sunny travel brochure, although many of the snapshots showed the family trying to smile as drizzle fell around them.

Nancy wanted to do something to show her appreciation for everything her parents were doing for her and her husband. Since Lee's dog had died of old age more than a year before, she and Richard went to a pet shop and bought him a beagle. "Here," Nancy said as she gave her father the puppy, "we don't want you to be lonely now that all your children have moved out." Lee was so pleased he hugged her.

In autumn, Joyce found a small apartment in
Winnetka for the young couple. The nondescript, two-
story white building was at the corner of Tower and
Green Bay roads, the two main cross streets of the village. The strong-minded Bishops had a tendency to turn
important decisions into family matters, even
apartment-renting. Jeanne went over the lease to make
sure it specified that minor repairs would be made. The
rent was nearly eight hundred dollars a month. Nancy
and Richard didn't know how they could keep up the
payments, but they signed the lease anyway. Then
Jeanne videotaped the apartment as a proof of condi-
tions.

The young couple thought they wouldn't be like
those husbands and wives who fight all the time, but
that was what began to happen. Strain from their con-
flicting work hours increased spats over bills, but
Nancy never backed down. In life as in their tennis
matches, Richard enjoyed the way she stood up to him.
They were not the only people living beyond their
means in the quaint suburb. As a former resident says,
women on the North Shore can wear designer clothes
and torn underwear at the same time—"It's all facade."

Something else was troubling Nancy. Out of guilt,
she confided to friends that she felt so alone when
Richard was away that she was drawn to a salesman
where she worked. They had a couple of drinks, but the
salesman didn't want to sleep with a married woman.
Nancy became more involved in community theater, but
she found herself spending some time with one of the
other actors, another salesman. But this time, it was
Nancy who ended the affair; she loved Richard too
much.

With her growing maturity, Nancy felt the only way
to show Richard she was sorry and that the affair was
truly over was to tell him about it. At first he felt be-
trayed, but over the next few weeks he realized the
strength of his wife's honesty, and it brought them

closer. To their friends, it seemed as if Nancy and Richard had fallen in love with one another all over again.

The Langerts entered marriage feeling they weren't ready for children. But when Nancy missed her period and her doctor told her it was a false alarm, she felt disappointed. She began to think that having a baby was what they needed, if only Richard could find a job that would give them the resources and freedom to do so.

Nancy's sister Jeanne had moved back in with the Bishops after a brief marriage to oral surgeon Louis Clarizio. They had dated while she studied law at Northwestern University in Evanston and began to have an interest in reports of British abuse of political prisoners in Northern Ireland. Joyce even set up a meeting in Winnetka's Community House so her daughter could speak about it.

Jeanne and Clarizio moved to New Hampshire, but the doctor soon realized she was no longer the woman he had fallen in love with. As she worked for a law office in Portsmouth, she became involved in an Irish-American organization, the Brehon Law Society, that was defending IRA members being held in the United States. Soon she was taking calls from Joseph Patrick Doherty, an Irish nationalist whose imprisonment in New York City on immigration charges was becoming an international issue.

Dr. Clarizio was Catholic and Jeanne was Presbyterian, yet he found himself asking her to give up defending the rights of Catholics in Belfast, Dublin, and Londonderry. She made frequent visits to those cities and gave speeches in Boston, Philadelphia, and at the 1986 dedication ceremony for the museum at Ellis Island. Louis felt he was being treated like a stepchild in his own home.

During one of their quarrels, Jeanne said that if Louis was so angry with her he should tear up their wedding picture. Louis couldn't, she still meant too much to him. But finally in May 1988, he packed his clothes in his BMW and moved out of their condominium. A week later, Jeanne moved on her own to the Sise Inn hotel to see if her husband would prefer to live at their home without her.

When she drove back in her Volkswagon to pick up her clothes, she found that Louis had changed the locks. Jeanne contacted a locksmith and returned to her rooms only to find that all of the pictures of her and her family has been stacked face down as a final rejection. Her response was to take a wedding picture from its frame and tear it up as—she would later say—"a visual image of what he was doing to both of us."

After the final break, the salty winds of New England no longer interested Jeanne. She returned to her parents' home on Indian Hill Road and sought openings in Chicago law offices. She was hired by the Loop firm of Mayer Platt and Brown. All this time, her divorce proceedings continued unresolved because Dr. Clarizio was holding onto a journal that she had kept from one of her visits to Europe and Ireland.

Jeanne never revealed why the journal was so important to her.

Winnetka was just another place to sleep for Jeanne, but Nancy loved its friendly boutiques. She and Richard were still having trouble comprehending the relationship between spending and available funds. They were able to pay their rent on time every month but other bills had to wait. Not all their money went for essentials, however. Richard abhorred drugs, but he was hooked on sports betting. He borrowed money from friends to take him from one bet to the next. On some Fridays, Richard would go to Nancy's office at the veneer company to pick up her paycheck rather than wait for her to bring it home.

By July, Nancy and Richard realized there was only one solution: move into the Bishops' home. The house on Indian Hill Road became busy again. Soon after the Langerts moved in, Joyce decided that it was time for them to grow up. Her first act was to take away their credit cards. Then she told them the facts of life—that if a creditor gives you a bill for four hundred dollars, you can stay out of trouble by sending a minimum monthly payment as small as ten dollars until you are able to increase the amount.

Next, Joyce established separate files for payments due and showed the couple how to use a pocket calculator to distribute available funds. She also drew up a budget for them. Joyce even put them on a weekly allowance from their paychecks, explaining that this was how she herself was able to keep family spending in line and put three girls through college.

One Saturday evening that summer, the family went with the Gasglows for a concert at the Ravinia indoor/outdoor music theater in nearby Highland Park for an orchestral concert of show tunes. Lee smoldered as they sat in traffic near the gate and finally he said, "That's it." Chomping on his pipe, he made a U-turn and headed back.

Once they were home, Nancy and Richard brought out picnic baskets of grapes, imported cheeses, and goose liver pate. Then, on the patio, the families played Trivial Pursuit from 7 P.M. until past midnight. Lee kept winning as Richard dropped one empty Pepsi can after another into the garbage.

Nancy preferred performing over intellectual challenges. Sometimes she and her mother were able to sing in the same productions at the Community House, but the young woman wanted a straight dramatic role to show her growing maturity. At another theater, she won the grueling lead in *Extremities*, the story of a rape victim who turns on her attacker and terrorizes him.

Joyce would never appear in a play like that. She loved the stage, and there was theatricality in everything she did—even the way she wrote memos in red

ink and signed them with a heart under her name that
meant "love."

Some production members told her to be less aloof
as she rehearsed the starring role in *Mame*. "Joyce,"
said the director, "wear a pair of blue jeans, sneakers.
Mellow out." At the next rehearsal, she wore neatly
creased white designer jeans to go with her ever-present
pearls.

The musical director found at the tryouts that Joyce's
trained soprano voice was too polished in a part written
for a belting alto. But Joyce loved the challenge. She
stood before the packed audience as Auntie Mame and
declared that "life is a banquet, and most sons of
bitches are starving to death." For her, it was the role of
a lifetime.

Life changed for Nancy and Richard in the late summer of 1989. A family friend learned of an opening in
the sales department at the rapidly expanding Gloria
Jean's Gourmet Coffee company. He suggested that this
might be the kind of job Nancy was looking for. The
owners, Gloria Jean and Ed Kvetko, were immediately
struck by Nancy's efficiency and liveliness, and they
quickly hired her. Soon she became a sales representa-
tive. Her duties involved arranging business contracts
with franchise owners and helping set up new stores.

The company, then located in northwest suburban
Arlington Heights, was the sort of success story most
entrepreneurs dream about. Gloria Jean Kvetko, a
friendly dark-haired woman, had quit school after
eighth grade. She owned a beauty salon but persuaded
her husband, a construction contractor, to buy a small
gift shop in Long Grove. The gifts didn't make much of
a profit, but customers kept coming back for the imported coffee that was only a small portion of the business.

The Kvetkos read up on the subject, got a sense of
the market, and realized that although coffee drinking

in general was declining, shoppers would be willing to pay anywhere from six to twenty-five dollars a pound for specialty flavors. They established the business with a single store in 1979. Five years later, the Kvetkos decided to expand by selling franchises, most of them in strip malls. The couple also set up a training school for managers, called "Coffee 101."

It seemed that every time the Kvetkos hired a new employee they had to make another corridor in their labyrinthine office building. Ed joked to Nancy that one of his tests for future franchise holders was finding the way from his office to the front door. Nancy's job was to handle preliminary questions from prospective franchise holders, send them a company brochure, make sure they received it, ask if they had any questions, and turn the account over to a salesman. The Kvetkos felt they had found just the person for the job. She asked the proper questions, she asked them the right way, and she had a warm, friendly phone voice.

Before long Nancy became the darling of the office, with a sunny "Hi" that could cheer up anyone. Pizza delivery men who came in while she was away would ask, "Where's emerald eyes?" As she took on added responsibilities, she helped set up new stores and attended opening parties in Colorado or New York.

But Richard's small company, SpiceTech, was having financial problems despite Lee's efforts to keep it solvent. Nancy told her husband not to worry, she might find him a job at Gloria Jean's. In November, she brought him to the warehouse and called out to one of the men on forklifts, "Ed, this is Richard!" Her husband looked up at a friendly middle-aged man in blue jeans and thought it was some office worker Nancy knew. Only when Kvetko came down and traded power handshakes with him did the "gentle giant" of the Langert family realize that this was his future boss.

"Look around and see if you can make yourself useful," Ed told him. Richard fit right in. In a few minutes he was repairing machines and making suggestions for increasing efficiency. After a few hours, Edward told him that he was hired. "I can only offer you a little over four dollars an hour," he said, "and it's just part-time and at night."

"That's all right."

"Are you sure this is the job you want?"

"I really do," Richard answered.

The work didn't pay as well as Richard's full-time job at SpiceTech, and occasionally he put in twenty hours a day at his two jobs, but it was all part of Nancy's long-range plan for them to have the kind of life they wanted. Starting at the bottom could even be an asset, since Richard was learning all the details of production and distribution.

As a gift for Richard's birthday a few days after he was hired, Nancy surprised him with a frisky cocker-spaniel puppy she named after something he loved— Pepsi!

Richard was still working nights at Gloria Jean's when their anniversary came around in May. They hadn't celebrated their first anniversary because of the Laurie Dann rampage, and Nancy was feeling a little depressed around the office because she wanted to do something special but couldn't afford it.

"Why don't you take the morning off and spend a little time with your husband," Gloria Jean suggested. "Look, your folks will be away. You two can be alone."

"What's the use, we can't buy presents."

"You can afford paper and scissors, can't you? Be romantic. Think of how nice it would be for Richard to come home and see a surprise. Be creative."

Nancy sped home, excited by the possibilities. Whatever she did must have worked. When Richard arrived at the warehouse that night, the grin on his face spoke of more than his usual good humor.

Ed Kvetko liked Richard's openness and the way he could throw himself into his work. Kvetko persuaded him to quit SpiceTech and made him vice president of production, supervising the company's packaging warehouse. That meant more than a bigger paycheck—Richard would at last be working days so that he and his wife would have nights together.

The Langerts' combined income was now fifty thousand dollars a year. They felt they might even be able to buy a home in a few years. This wasn't just dreamtalk; Gloria Jean's was expanding so rapidly that they could rise with it. Nancy was so happy she began talking about having a child. At closing time one day, she told friends she had to get home because she and Richard were trying to make a baby.

4

"This Is Going To Be Our Year"

The Bishop house was a fun place to be in when Nancy and her husband were around. Sometimes Richard jokingly imitated his father-in-law lowering himself into the easy chair. Then he commanded, "Nancy, bring me a Pepsi!"

"Yes, master," she would say, run into the kitchen, and return with a can of cola. Adopting a servile pose, she would say, "Here, my master."

"Now sit at my feet," King Richard would order, and he'd pat her lowered head.

Once when Nancy and her mother strolled down a row of shops in town, Joyce looked wistfully at a display of frilly dresses for little girls. Her daughter playfully whispered, "We're working on it."

Although Nancy had cut down on spending, she still loved whiling away hours in stores. One afternoon, Gloria Jean Kvetko took her to a newly opened shopping center. Nancy was struck by a man's long leather coat. Richard was such a John Wayne fan that she bought it for him on impulse.

He was more than pleased. A transformation occurred when he slipped on the coat. "Come here, little lady," he said in his John Wayne voice, "you deserve a little kiss."

Still, the Langerts were aware that everything they bought set back their plans to live on their own. Gloria Jean suggested that an extra house she and Ed owned in Prospect Heights would be perfect for the young couple. The man who had been leasing it was moving out, and the Kvetkos needed to rent the space.

Nancy loved the four bedroom, ranch-style home. She and Richard were worried that they wouldn't be able to afford the payments, but with their new budgeting skills they worked out a plan. At the annual Bishop Christmas party, Nancy said that next year everyone would be invited to their new home on Countryside Lane.

For New Year's Eve, the Kvetkos invited the Langerts to celebrate with them at a restaurant and tavern in Long Grove. As they waited for midnight, Nancy—still thrilled about the prospect of their new home—put her outspread hands to her cheeks and sang the theme song from the television show "Green Acres."

At the stroke of twelve, everyone whistled and cheered in 1990.

At 12:15 P.M. on January 9, a call came over the Illinois State Police Emergency Radio Network about a holdup at the First Nationwide Bank in Wilmette. The robber had handed a note to a teller, then shoved close to three thousand dollars into a shoulder bag. Within minutes, squad cars from nearly half a dozen suburbs were running their lights and sirens in a search for the getaway car.

Inside the modern, single-story Winnetka police station Officer Eddie Benoit (pronounced ben-WAH) looked over a map to see if he could guess where the bandit might be heading. The husky black policeman was born in Mississippi but had lived in Chicago's northern suburbs since he was thirteen, when his mother moved to find work as a maid.

Minutes after the first bank robbery, a silent alarm went off at the Harris Bank of Winnetka, four blocks from the station. Benoit was running to his car before the dispatcher could ask if he wanted to respond.

A bank guard led Benoit and two other officers to a pair of shocked middle-aged tellers at the drive-in booth. They told the policemen how a young man had spray-painted the lens of the security camera and snapped a bolt off the door while his accomplice waited behind the wheel. The two men fled with more than thirty thousand dollars.

Descriptions of the robber didn't match the one from the earlier bank heist. Many of the officers assumed that the heists had been committed by a team. The older and taller man could have pulled off the First Nation-wide robbery, then driven the car for his partner in the Harris holdup. After awhile, the FBI put the case in its inactive file to look over whenever there was another bank robbery. But Winnetka police couldn't let it drop.

For weeks, Benoit and Sergeant Patricia McConnell went to shops with a composite sketch of the bandit whenever they had half an hour or so free.

"Officer Patty"—as she was called—and her four sisters and brothers had been among the few white children in their South Side of Chicago neighborhood. Their mother was a teacher in the area and their father was employed by the Park District. Pat majored in English but found working part time as a J.C. Penney security officer more to her liking. She quit college and became Winnetka's first woman police officer.

McConnell jokingly called the suburb the "Emerald City of the North Shore." Since everything closed before the last commuter train passed through, she would drop by at a 7-Eleven store in Wilmette for late-night coffee. That was how she met and fell in love with Wilmette policeman Matthew McConnell. They were married in the fall of 1983 and had a baby in the autumn of 1987.

The arrival of Kristen meant that Pat and her husband had to rearrange their hours at the neighboring police departments so one of them would always be home with the baby. Rather than slowing down, Pat showed such dedication that Chief Timm made her the chief of detectives in 1988, at a time when many large police departments across the country did not even have women in plainclothes investigations.

The men in the office had been living in a world in which women were police secretaries, dispatchers, and meter maids. They had trouble showing respect for a young woman with a cheery disposition, lipstick, and dangling earrings. Sometimes when she spoke to them about procedures or asked questions about their reports, they would just nod their heads and pretend to be listening. After all, they thought, her rank was just politics.

Pat lacked the military discipline of her counterparts who had served in the armed forces. Her informality made it easy for the men to underestimate her. She used her desk more as a shelf and an extension of her purse than as a workplace and kept an acrylic nail repair kit in a "fanny pack" because she bit her fingernails when she was nervous.

One day, McConnell—still unable to let the Harris bank robbery case go—rolled her swivel chair to the filing cabinet and began pulling out folder after folder, reading only the descriptions of the offenders. She found what she was looking for. The bank robber Pat was tracking fit the general description of a man who had snatched a purse on November 7 at the Village Toy Shop on Elm Street. When he was discovered in a back room, the man apologized and claimed he was looking for a washroom. An employee checked a few minutes later and found that her purse was gone.

Criminologists would have told McConnell that bank

robbers have personalities considerably different from purse snatchers. Besides, there had to be millions of white men about five feet seven and around twenty years old. But to Pat, the thief was her best bet. Seeing that an AT&T calling card had been in the stolen purse, she thought: I bet he's dumb enough to use it.

Eddie Benoit picked her up at the station and drove her to the toy shop. The two officers showed the employee sketches of various suspects, and she pointed to the one of the bank robber. Pat called AT&T, and in a few hours lists of phone billings came over the station's fax machine.

The card had been used to make a number of calls to hotels and motels in the western suburbs. The two officers visited them all and showed employees the sketches. Yes, yes, the employees said, that man checked in with his girlfriend. In one hotel the couple had asked for the $445-a-night presidential suite but had accepted a cheaper room. At each location they paid cash.

Working with the FBI and a Cook County drug investigation team, McConnell and Benoit learned the name of their suspect. He and his girlfriend were arrested as they came out of yet another motel. Patty felt the exhilaration of seeing an arrest grow out of a hunch. Sometimes cases go unsolved because they are simpler than they seem.

In early January, Nancy and Richard took a break from the coffee company and stayed at a friend's cabin in Galena, a picturesque town straddling the steep hills of northwestern Illinois. When they came back, Nancy was hoping she might be pregnant. She joked with her parents that they wouldn't have to see her blow up like a balloon because she and Richard would be in their own house by summer.

Their plans to move out helped the Bishops reach a decision they had been putting off for some time. Joyce and Lee loved their large house on Indian Hill Road, but they had to be realistic now that Lee was not making as much as he did at Isham, Lincoln & Beale. Besides, their daughter Jeanne now had an apartment in Chicago, and Jennifer was living on a farm near Kankakee.

On January 15, the Bishops signed the papers for a townhouse in the eastern part of Winnetka for a little over $275,000. The home was in an ideal location. All the trees were bare, but in a couple of months the nearby Village Green Park would come alive. The Community House, where Joyce spent much of her spare time, was less than half a mile away. The Chicago and North Western commuter station was just across the Cherry Street bridge, and the location was especially safe because the police station was close by.

The Bishops wouldn't be able to move in until late April, so Joyce asked a friend of hers, Sue Bardon, to redecorate the townhouse for them. Sue had gone back to college to study interior design and was delighted at the chance to prove what she could do.

Little by little, the house was taking shape. One night as the family discussed the new home, Nancy asked her parents, "Why don't we stay over there until we can move to Prospect Heights? Then you two can have this house for yourself again."

"But all that bother just for a few weeks," Joyce said.

"We could keep everything in boxes," Nancy suggested. "We won't disturb anything."

Joyce looked at her husband, and Lee said, "I don't see why not, if that's what you want."

The Langerts moved into the townhouse, bringing no furniture other than a bed, a card table, and a couple of folding chairs. Nancy remarked to Gloria Jean that the place wouldn't seem so barren if only it had something like a recliner chair to make it look like a home. Mrs. Kvetko surprised the couple by lending them a credit card to order one on the promise that they would pay her back.

Nancy was still hoping for a baby as if in a hurry to complete the American dream before she was twenty-six. On a Friday in early February she excitedly told Gloria Jean at work that she had taken a home pregnancy test and "I really am. I did it, I did it!" She was almost dancing in excitement, but Gloria Jean advised her to see a doctor just to make sure.

Late that afternoon, Joyce was rehearsing her role as Vera the perfectionist in the musical *Stepping Out* when Nancy came down the aisle smiling. Mrs. Bishop could tell from her glow what the doctor had said. Mother and daughter hugged, Nancy cried, and the whole cast burst into the Hallelujah chorus.

A new house, a new baby, a new life. Nancy could hardly believe that all this was happening. She told Gloria Jean, "This is going to be our year. Nothing can go wrong now."

In addition to Lee's work as a registered agent for a number of firms, he and his longtime friend *Joseph White were developing a business that would recycle wood and building materials in the blue-collar western suburb of Foster View. They didn't intend to operate the plant themselves, just set up the project and sell the package to someone with the capital to build it.

The location chosen was near Chicago's Midway Airport. The partners applied for the permits, bought land from the Santa Fe Railroad, and supervised the architectural drawings. All nonrecyclable wastes would be sent to landfills approved by the state.

The partners had put two hundred thousand dollars into the venture, hoping that by the end of the year it would be worth millions. But distrustful residents demanded public hearings.

Lee, planning on quick money to get him through financial straits, hadn't expected opposition. After all, the

Chicago area had become one of the largest recycling centers in the country. No toxic or chemical wastes would be accepted, and there would be no incineration. The partners even offered to implement a free curbside recycling program if the village approved the project.

Joe's wife, Mary, wrote newsletters on her desktop computer, delivered releases to community newspapers, and arranged for a coffee buffet in the village hall after the hearing. But Lee was tense as he sat in the back of the auditorium on a night in late February. A member of Greenpeace raised his hand and asked a lawyer hired for the project about groundwater cleanup for any leaks. Other questions from the audience concerned the loss in property values for homes within a mile of the balefill.

Lee felt the project was doomed. White came down the aisle as the questioning continued and asked, "Are you sick?"

Lee stood up and said, "They don't let me smoke in here. I'm going out and smoke my pipe."

He left through a back door and walked to the Whites' Oldsmobile. When he returned to shake hands at the reception, he smelled of scotch.

Driving Lee home, White told him not to worry. The final decision was still a month away, and by then the board would realize what an opportunity the plant would be. There were eighty-five recycling companies around Chicago, and all those communities were thankful for the jobs and tax revenue.

This wasn't the only reason Lee was on edge that winter. He also worried about *Nathan Calabrese, a business client who had an unsavory reputation. Richard clearly didn't like the man and wished he would stop showing up at the home.

Less than two weeks after the public meeting on the recycling plant, two men burst into Calabrese's home in northwest suburban Palatine while his wife and her sixty-seven-year-old mother were inside. One of the men—who was around sixty and kept a scarf around his face—pulled duct tape over the older woman's mouth. When she ripped it off, he put a gun to her head and threatened, "I'll kill you if you try anything like that again!"

The aging mother-in-law grabbed the gun, and in the struggle pulled a few hairs from his head. He started slapping her and demanded, "We want our money, where is it, where is it!"

The younger man, wearing a white mask, came downstairs with Calabrese's wife and repeatedly struck her with his fists. At last she went to the top of the refrigerator and gave them a few hundred dollars from rent from a building the family owned. The two men then fled into the rain and fog.

The mother-in-law had to be treated at a hospital for lacerations on the back of her head. As police questioned her there, she kept changing her descriptions of the intruders, and the officers felt the whole family was being uncooperative. For one thing, professionals wouldn't terrorize two women in the middle of the day for rent money.

Calabrese's daughter, *Marisa, went to the police station to answer questions. But when the detectives asked her to bring her father down, she hedged. "It's not that he won't come to the station," Marisa said. "It's just that he's a very busy man and has difficulty getting time to do anything not involved with his work."

Too busy to help police find the men who assaulted his wife and her elderly mother? That was strange. But all the detectives could do was drop the case as if nothing had happened.

Nancy and Richard left for a skiing trip to Colorado in early March. At O'Hare International Airport, Gloria Jean gave Nancy a black maternity dress. The young woman was so eager to see what she would look like in a couple of months that she put it on in the airport washroom and gazed in the mirror.

Two weeks later the Forest View village board approved the recycling plant. Joseph White said to his wife, "Oh my God, we pulled it off!"

The final permit was signed on April 4, 1990. Lee felt that he wouldn't have to worry about the financial status of his business or his family again. "Things are going so well, it's scary," he said.

Nancy and Richard had three days to live.

5

Someone Is Waiting

A YOUNG CHOKECHERRY tree and a windbreak of maples and pines grew at the side of the townhouse facing Cherry Street. The attractive brick building had a tall sloping roof that opened onto a driveway. The outward appearance was deceptive, since the Langerts' front room looked like a warehouse with virtually all their belongings in boxes.

Although Nancy and Richard still worked long hours at the coffee company, they still had time for others. They occasionally babysat for the teenage sons of family friends. Richard would play ball with the boys, joke around, and tell them that messing with drugs was stupid. The brothers thought he was the "neatest person in the world."

In March, the Langerts attended the christening for one of Richard's nephews. They had bought a present to give the boy but had forgotten it, and the box stayed in the townhouse, still in its gift wrapping.

When one of the Kvetkos' grown sons invited people from the office to go target shooting, Richard went along only because he had his reputation as a "fun-loving guy" to protect. He hated guns, but he borrowed a .22-caliber pistol his father-in-law had not used in years and went with the others to the outdoor range. Afterward, Richard handed the gun over to Ed Kvetko and asked him to keep it for awhile, since Ed was a collector. The boss put the weapon in a box and a few days later tried to give it to Nancy.

"Keep it," she said.

"But it's your father's."

"Well, buy it for a dollar, then."

"Nancy!"

"I'm scared of guns."

"Then I'll keep it for you," Ed said. "Just tell me when you want it back."

At around this time, Joyce threw a party for the cast of *Stepping Out*. She seldom cooked, so this was a bring-your-own-dish affair. Since there was a break in the cool weather, Richard started a grill outside with a chef's apron over his coat.

Nancy's job was to take salads from the refrigerator and find room on the tables for everything. At least once she sneaked a kiss from her husband as she took plates of meat from him. Joyce was talking proudly about her two pregnant daughters, since Jennifer was also expecting a baby in the fall.

But not long after the party, Joyce received a call from Jennifer's husband in Kankakee telling her that the young teacher was in a hospital. Jennifer had had a miscarriage. Jennifer was all right, but for Joyce it was as if a member of the family had died.

The miscarriage was like a shadow passing over Nancy. Until now, she hadn't considered that something might happen to her own unborn baby. To make matters worse, her morning sickness wouldn't go away. Nancy switched doctors, but the new one also assured her everything was fine and that the baby could be expected around October 6.

Jeanne Bishop continued going to Ireland twice a year, some of the trips paid for by American Protestants for Truth About Ireland. She was now one of seven directors of the small Philadelphia-based group, which conducted fact-finding missions and reported back on human rights violations. Richard said privately he thought his sister-in-law was "naive and nuts" about this commitment.

In 1985, Jeanne and 125 members of the Northern Irish Aid Committee (Noraid) flew to Ireland for the August "marching season." They found Belfast a city with a beautiful natural setting yet gripped by the bleakness of more than six decades of military occupation.

Thousands of marchers greeted the Americans, but loyalists sneered at the "terror tourists." The visitors stayed at the homes of nationalist families as arranged by the political wing of the IRA, the Sinn Fein. They saw the sentry posts at the barricades, the walls charred by petrol bombs, the lean look of hunger, the litter of stones thrown between Catholic and Protestant children, and the seemingly impervious families who accepted civil warfare as a way of life.

In 1988, Jeanne attended the trials of accused terrorists in Belfast and Londonderry. Afterward she told two hundred people at a Boston church that Irish strife as a conflict of religions was a misconception, that the British government was forcing Catholics into violence.

By the spring of 1990, Jeanne was one of many Americans working to free IRA soldier Joseph Patrick Doherty from the Metropolitan Correctional Center in Manhattan. He had been arrested in Belfast for taking part in a shootout that killed a British army captain in an elite undercover anti-terrorist unit. Before Doherty could be sentenced, he and seven other IRA members used a pair of smuggled guns to get past ten feet of steel mesh fencing outside their jail and run to freedom. Catholics all around Belfast lit bonfires in celebration of the new folk hero.

Doherty fled to America and worked as a bartender at an Irish tavern in New York City. His arrest there posed a problem in the Reagan administration's attempts to show unity with Margaret Thatcher's administration. By international treaty, he could not be extradited because he had been a political prisoner in the United Kingdom, but the State Department decided that granting Doherty protection would set back the U.S.'s hard line against international terrorism.

Federal Judge John Sprizzo spent nine months considering the case before ruling in December 1984 that Doherty could not be deported. On the other hand, Sprizzo held, the prisoner could not be freed from the American jail because he had entered the U.S. illegally. And so the years dragged by as Doherty remained in a legal limbo.

When Nancy went to New York for a Gloria Jean's franchise party to open a coffee shop on Long Island, Jeanne came along and took her to speak with Doherty through a partition. But Nancy never could understand Jeanne's all-consuming passion for what seemed to her a foreign cause.

At the Gloria Jean's warehouse, Richard was starting to worry about the job he had worked so hard to win. The Village of Arlington Heights had a policy of enforcing zoning laws whenever there was a complaint. And someone complained that workers at Gloria Jean's had just unpacked a coffee roaster in a warehouse close to a subdivision of more than six hundred homes. The roaster had been approved by the Illinois Environmental Protection Agency, but the residents feared their air would smell like a percolator. They also didn't want to hear sounds other than sparrows in the morning and crickets at night.

A rumor circulating around the office the first week in April was that if the roaster couldn't be assembled, the company would have to close the warehouse and Richard might be out of a job. He tried to keep up his usual good cheer, but his co-workers could see the strain. More than his job was at stake. There were a career, the new house, and the baby to consider.

On Friday, April 6, Nancy went to the First National Bank of Mount Prospect to deposit their two paychecks. She put one thousand dollars into their account and kept five hundred dollars for expenses.

The next morning, both Nancy and Richard drove to work as usual. Sam, the engineering manager at the warehouse, spent a few minutes helping Richard install spark plugs in his auto on the company lot. Nancy left after a few hours to visit a family friend, *Helen Cleary. Richard arrived there at around 2 P.M. after finishing some computer work in his office.

He relaxed and talked about how his father-in-law was going to make a lot of money soon with his recycling plant. Richard also spoke about some friends he wished Lee would drop, but he didn't mention Nathan Calabrese by name. To Mrs. Cleary, the couple had never seemed happier.

The Kvetkos had just returned from a trip to Anchorage and were trying to call Nancy and Richard at the townhouse to say they had bought tickets for the Chicago Cubs opener at Wrigley Field. Gloria Jean also wanted to set up a hair-cutting session. The former beauty-shop owner would cut Nancy's hair in the kitchen of her Long Grove home, using the oven door as a mirror. When she finally reached Nancy by phone, the younger woman didn't have time to talk because she and Richard were going out to celebrate Lee's birthday.

The couple put their cocker spaniel in an upstairs room to keep him out of trouble and picked up the Bishops on Indian Hill Road. The four of them drove to Jeanne's apartment on Chestnut Street near the Water Tower Place vertical mall on Chicago's Near North Side. Since Jeanne had been in Ireland on her father's birthday, April 2, she had decided to hold a little party for him at an Italian restaurant a few blocks west of her place.

Before leaving Jeanne's apartment to make their 8 P.M. reservation, the family had a little wine and cheese as an appetizer. Jeanne handed her kid sister a present from Ireland. Nancy opened it and pulled out a sweater for herself and some clothes for the baby. The two young women giggled and the family piled into the car for the five-minute drive to Bellagio's.

A tuxedoed maitre d' led them from the end of the long bar to the restaurant section in the adjacent room. Jeanne had reserved two intimate corner tables. Nancy was trying to downplay how sick she was because of her pregnancy. A family friend recently had tried to console her by telling her "when you're hungry all the time, it's a boy. When you're real sick all day long, it's a girl." No one noticed that Nancy left her plate untouched. Jeanne kept talking about her encounters in Ireland, but she acted as if something were still on her mind.

Nancy slipped Jeanne some money under the table to help pay for the meal. A waiter brought a birthday cake with a single candle. Lee was a trifle embarrassed that at age sixty he should be treated like a schoolboy, but he blew out the candle as his family sang "Happy Birthday."

Joyce was concerned about her daughter's sickness. When the plates were taken away, Joyce suggested that Nancy and Pepsi, the cocker spaniel, spend the night back in the house on Indian Hill Road. After all, Richard was supposed to house- and dog-sit that night for a neighbor spending the weekend in Florida. But Pepsi was ill as well, and Nancy didn't want to expose the Bishops' beagle to whatever the cocker spaniel had.

Richard dropped Jeanne off and headed for Winnetka. As the Bishops climbed out of the car outside their home, Joyce said one last time, "Nancy, please stay with us tonight."

"No, Mother," she replied. "I want to be with Pepsi and in my own bed."

Richard then drove to the townhouse. He intended simply to drop off his wife and the gift from Jeanne, take Pepsi for a walk, and go to the neighbor's house. There was no way for him to know that someone was waiting with a gun.

6

"Oh My God!"

April 8, 1990

WHEN LEE AWOKE at 6:45 that Palm Sunday morning, Joyce was already getting dressed to sing in the choir at the Congregational church in Kenilworth. She called the townhouse at 7 A.M. to ask if Nancy was feeling well, but no one answered. She thought that perhaps Nancy and Richard were sleeping a little longer because of last night's party and would join her at church.

Lee enjoyed having Sundays to himself. He dressed in a blue jogging outfit and told his wife he would take the beagle for a walk in Thornwood Park.

"If anything happens, Lee, you know where to get me," Joyce said. After the service, she would go to the Winnetka Community House for another rehearsal of *Stepping Out* and be back home in the late afternoon to make a Sunday dinner for Lee, Nancy, Richard, and herself.

After his wife left, Lee drove to the park off Sheridan Road. The cool lake breeze and warm land air created a fog that didn't burn away with the morning sun. Lee grabbed the dog's leash and climbed out of the car.

At around 11 A.M., a neighbor who had been looking

out her window called police to report that a suspicious man was rummaging through a garbage container in the park. Officer Huck stepped out of his squad car and found Lee by a trash barrel that contained a few full bottles of liquor.

The embarrassed attorney apologized and explained that his wife wouldn't let him drink at home, so he had stashed some bottles there for his strolls with the dog. Officer Huck warned him against such public behavior and sent him on his way.

The shore fog was gone by afternoon. Joyce was still worried about Nancy's sickness but no one answered the phone. She called her husband from the Community House, and Lee promised he would go over there since he had to do some work on closet shelves anyway. As he drove, he thought that perhaps Nancy had suffered a miscarriage, like Jennifer, and that Richard had rushed her to the hospital. But as Lee pulled into the driveway he saw that both Richard's and Nancy's cars were still there.

He let himself in and realized immediately that something was wrong when his dog came trotting through an open patio door. Then he saw the scattered credit cards, the money, and the purse on the floor. He sensed a new and ominous presence. Lee went upstairs, knocked on the door, found only the cocker spaniel, and knew he had to go into the basement.

Lee was sweating as he started for the steps. He found himself breathing in uncontrollable gasps when he saw the bodies sprawled on the floor. He rushed up the steps to dial 911. The woman at the control board wrote down the address, alerted a patrol officer, and asked Lee what had happened.

"I just walked in," he said. "I'm the owner of the place and I saw my daughter. My daughter and son-in-law are here and they're down in the basement and they're dead."

"When was the last time you saw them?"

"You can ask a lot of questions!"

"I will, sir. I have officers on the way but I need a little bit more from you."

"Well, I saw them last night."

"Now, I want you to stay on the phone with me. I'm going to put you on hold, then I'm going to come back and talk to you, okay?"

"All right."

As Lee held on, the dispatcher set everything into motion: "Four forty-two, forty-three, respond with four-forty to 722 Oak. Hello, Metro Fire Department and ambulance call. Ambulance, come to 722 Oak. Possible two DOAs."

Lee sighed into the receiver "Oh my God, how could this happen?"

The dispatcher told him "Sir, they should be driving up in about thirty seconds."

An officer called in on the police radio, "This is twenty-nine. Responding to assist the ambulance."

The dispatcher said, "We have a person still on the scene. Bishop. 722 Oak. He's calling from that location."

"Forty-eight's on location."

"Four-forty, do you want the ambulance to respond into the house?" asked the dispatcher.

"Negative Winnetka, negative."

"Ten-four."

At the time the call came in, nothing was expected to happen in the village. Chief Timm was vacationing in Florida with his wife and teenage daughter. Officer Patricia McConnell, the head of investigations, was with a number of other top American policewomen visiting the Soviet Union. That left Sergeant Frank Siwak as the commander on duty. The six-foot-three officer had been in the department for fourteen years, but with his youthful looks could pass for a recruit.

When Siwak heard the call come in, he said, "I'm going there too."

As the flashing lights of two squad cars turned the asphalt driveway red, Lee walked from the front door in a helpless daze. "I found my daughter and her husband dead in the basement," he said. "I'm Lee Bishop, and they're Nancy and Richard."

Siwak gently took Lee's arm and led him to the patrol car. "Are you alone?" the officer asked.

"Yes."

"Mr. Bishop," Siwak said, "I'm going in. Officer Pat Lyons here will take your statement. Just try to be calm. I'll be right back."

Like most officers in the Winnetka department, Siwak's only experience with a homicide had been the Laurie Dann case. He drew his gun and entered swiftly but cautiously through the open door. With his eyes darting for possible hiding places, he noticed a slug lying on the floor near the basement stairs.

Siwak kept his back to the wall as he went sideways down the curving steps of the small basement. He didn't think this could have been a home invasion. Things like that didn't happen in Winnetka. One possibility was that someone had killed the couple in a jealous rage, and that the person might be unstable enough to take a shot at him as well.

As Siwak reached the bottom step, he could smell death mingled with the iodine-and-copper odor of blood. The basement was in disarray, but not as if there had been a struggle. The two bodies were separated by a pool of blood several feet in diameter. The only visible wound on Nancy's body was at her elbow. Richard's face was distorted, and the caked blood from the ears, nose, and mouth told Siwak that he must have been shot through the back of the head. His glasses lay shattered. The bodies apparently had been there for hours, yet because of a lack of ventilation Siwak could still faintly smell gunpowder.

The sergeant held his semiautomatic pistol close to his side so he could aim at any angle as he carefully looked at areas not reached by the basement light. Watching the shadows, he slowly knelt on one knee and touched Nancy's throat to verify from the carotid artery that there was no sign of life.

Now he had to make sure the house was safe for detectives and evidence technicians. Siwak inched his way sideways up the basement stairs to search the upper level. When he reached a closed door, he shouted, "Police, come out! Police!" At one room he heard some movement, and he slowly backed away until he was at the front door.

Once outside, Siwak turned and ran to his car. "We need more personnel out here," he said into his transmitter. "Contact the director of operations and all officers who are off duty. I need evidence technicians. Notify the medical examiner's office and have paramedics out here."

Officer Joe Pellus arrived in his one-man squad car. "Come on, Joe," Siwak told the younger man, "we have to check this house. I have a closed door upstairs and I heard something."

Pellus had no time to ask questions. They ran into the house and went silently to the upper level. When they reached the closed door, Pellus gripped the knob, ready to give the door a jump kick above the lock. Then Siwak would rush in.

Pellus jerked the knob back and the sergeant pushed the door open for a clear view. Lee's dog and the cocker spaniel ran out of the room as if they were shot from a cannon. So much for the mysterious noise. Pellus grabbed the dogs, and Siwak jumped in to make sure the room was empty. The officers brought the pets back in to keep them from trampling the evidence.

There was one more possible hiding place, the attic. Pellus handed the sergeant a foot-long Mag light. Not only was the beam powerful, but the lens end of the aluminum flashlight made a formidable club. The sergeant lowered the ladder from a rope attached to the ceiling and climbed into the opening as Pellus covered him. Siwak adjusted his beam to throw a wide light across the storage space, looking for movement or shadow. He saw nothing but boxes and dust.

"Okay here," Siwak called out and started back down the ladder. "Joe, stay inside. I need you to preserve the scene. We've got to start bringing more people in here."

Siwak was glad to get out of the house for a few breaths of fresh air. Occasionally in his career he had wondered how he would react if he ever had to investigate a murder. Now he knew.

The sergeant went to the driveway and removed the mobile phones from the two police cars. He slipped into his own auto and called his office to say, "I am setting up a command post here in my squad. I have my two-way and now three mobile phones. If you haven't already, contact Gene Kalvaitis, Joe Sumner—"

"We can't find Joe," the station officer said.

"Then find someone who knows where he is. Also get Eddie Benoit, Bobby Caldwell . . ." The sergeant continued naming officers from the Laurie Dann investigation and other major cases. "I also need Schimian to videotape the house, and I want someone from the state crime lab out here before the bodies are carried out."

At that moment, off-duty Lieutenant Joseph Sumner was mixing plaster and placing ceramic tiles in the shower of his mother-in-law's home. He had taken his pager off to keep it from being damaged and had not heard its piping. In time his brother called him on the phone and told him of the murders. Sumner's hands were still caked with plaster as he called Siwak from the mobile phone in his car. The sergeant told him that no one was sure how the victims had died because there was a bullet on the floor and yet an axe lay between the bodies.

Officer Lyons drove Lee to the station just across the

Cherry Street bridge and half a block south. The policeman led him to an empty room and suggested that he sit down. "Coffee? Soda?"

Lee stared into mid-air. "No, I must tell Joyce, that's my wife." He reached for a phone and dialed the house on Indian Hill Road. No answer. "She must be at the Community House. She acts."

"Okay, no problem," Lyons said. "How about if we go there?"

"Yes, that would be good. We can go there." Joyce usually drove down Lincoln on her way home from rehearsal, passing by the townhouse. Suppose she saw police cars outside? No mother should learn of her child's death that way.

The overcast sky was dimming the late afternoon when Lee and Lyons arrived at the Community House. The interior was like a large hotel. As they walked down the wide hallway, they passed some people playing cards in a side room. Lee pushed open the door of the theater and saw a few cast members practicing on the bare stage. The amateur dancers turned, startled that Lee's face was red as if he had been crying.

"Where's Joyce?" he said.

"What's wrong, Lee?" asked Jackie Steiner, one of the actresses. "Lee, is there something wrong?"

The director came over and said, "Joyce just left. Is there anything I can do?"

Instead of answering, Lee walked back across the rows of seats and went to the large reception desk at the other end of the hall. His hand shook as he dialed his home again and kept the line ringing.

"Let's go to the station," Lyons said. "You can call from there."

At police headquarters, Lyons took Lee to a rear interrogation room and asked in his usual gruff tone, "Is your wife always so hard to get a hold of?"

"Maybe she's at church," Lee responded. "The pastor is a friend of ours . . ." Lee didn't know that Joyce had taken another route home so she could pick up a roast for dinner.

The department's short, dark-haired social worker, Elan Adler, quietly introduced herself and sat down as Lee dialed again. When he reached his wife, he said, "Joyce, there's been a terrible accident. I'll be right home. It's Nancy and Richard."

"Lee, what happened?"

"I'll be there in a minute."

"Tell me, I want to know!"

"Stay there," Lee said and quickly hung up.

Joyce was standing outside the two-story, white frame house when the police car drove up. Lee walked toward her and stopped to keep a barrier between them for what he was about to say. "Nancy and Richard have been killed."

"What are you talking about?" Joyce looked at the blank faces of the policeman and the dark-haired woman, both strangers to her. "Lee—what do you mean?" Joyce asked hesitantly.

"They've been shot."

"I don't know what you're talking about," she said with a shake of her head.

Seeing the distraught Mrs. Bishop completely deny what she was hearing, Adler identified herself as the police social worker and suggested that everyone go inside. Once there, Lee called Richard's parents and broke the news of the tragedy.

Jeanne Bishop was in the Fourth Presbyterian Church near her Chicago apartment when a secretary told her she had a call. The minister who had married the Langerts, Gilbert Bowen, asked Jeanne to stay on the line and gave Lee the receiver.

"Nancy and Richard have been killed," Lee said. "They have been murdered. They found an axe down there. Dr. Bowen is going to pick you up."

Like her mother, Jeanne refused to believe what she had heard. But ten minutes later, as reality settled in, she began to weep. She and Nancy had been more than sisters, they were friends. The church secretary consoled Jeanne and drove her home.

II

"Four Or Five Scenarios"

7

The Riddle Begins

April 8, 1990, 6 P.M.

OFFICER EDDIE BENOIT learned about the murders when
he was paged while grocery shopping with his wife. He
drove to the townhouse, signed in with his name and
star number, then was handed a pair of plastic gloves.
As the hefty African-American officer stood on the carpeted steps, he muttered, "My God, what do we have
here? Someone really did a number on these two."

Siwak was outside to see if he could find anything
without stepping on footprints or other evidence. There
was still light, but he used his flashlight to lift shadows
from the walkway by the stockade fence. Lying on the
wood-chip path was a man's black leather glove. Rather
than remove it, he noted its location for the evidence
technicians.

Officers inside the townhouse saw how the killers
must have entered. Sections from one of the overlapping patio doors had been scored with a glass cutter and
removed with a suction cup or folded-over tape. The intruders simply could have reached in and slid the door
back. The sections were stacked nearby. The killers
even left hints about how they left. The chain-link
fence between the wood-chip path and the railroad ra-

vine had a broken top pipe, as if someone had vaulted over it.

The intruders had left several hundred dollars, the couple's stereo, and a Discman compact disc player. It was as though they had entered the house with murder in mind.

An officer with a video camera took long shots of the house, then moved into the rooms and basement. Never before had the officers seen so much blood. Two Winnetka officers came in with a 35-millimeter camera and an evidence kit consisting of a sterile bottle, an eyedropper, small bags, cotton swabs, and file cards. The bullet slug on the floor upstairs was the first piece of evidence photographed. An officer used a tape measure to show its distance from the door.

Minutes later the still camera flashed a picture of Nancy's right arm extended past her head—her fingertips covered with blood. The police photographer crouched closer and took a shot of the reddish smudges on the axe handle. Then he took pictures of an overturned utility shelf.

Watching the officer straddling Richard's legs to take a picture of the man's face, Benoit remembered for a split second an event from his time as a rookie in north suburban Skokie. He had been sent to a home where a man had stabbed his grandmother thirty times and slashed his own throat. The man lay dead on the snow, blood from his throat frozen into the icicles hanging from the trees. Red icicles. Benoit would never forget it.

Once all the photos were taken downstairs, officers wearing thin yellow plastic gloves moved around the bodies almost on tiptoe to avoid disrupting evidence. One of them carefully added distilled water to dried blood on the gray floor and used an eyedropper to place it in a vial. The officers had no idea whose blood it was. Everything bagged was logged in on the evidence sheets.

"I think we may have some drugs involved here," Benoit said as he stood halfway up the basement stairs. He was sketching the position of the bodies in relation to the stairs and the overturned shelf so that detectives could make sense out of all the pictures being taken. He looked closer at Nancy's outstretched hand. She seemed, in death, to be pointing at the shelf.

A Cook County medical examiner's car pulled up, and investigator Tony Ortiz passed through the police lines. Benoit briefed Ortiz as the investigator slipped on his surgical gloves. He went to Richard first. The victim's eyelids were puffy from hemorrhaging caused by the bullet as it entered his brain, and his face was covered with dried blood from his ears and nose.

"No apparent exit," the medical examiner's investigator said as he stood over the stiff corpse. He grabbed Richard's belt and raised the body at midsection. The victim's right arm remained to the side, and there was a clink of metal as a pair of loose handcuffs slid down his left wrist. That drew the officers' attention, but Ortiz was more interested in locating wounds.

The medical examiner's investigator lowered the body to the concrete floor and felt around the black hair. "Ahh, I found it," he said. "Shot in the back of the head at close range."

"Execution style?" an officer asked.

"Could be." Ortiz now had his finger inside the wound. "From the angle, it looks like he was shot while he was on his knees. No exit wound, so the bullet is still in there."

"The slug we found was a .357 Magnum."

"That could have done it," Ortiz said.

Lieutenant Joseph Sumner had a question. "Why did the cuffs come off so fast?"

"Looks like our killer panicked in cuffing or undoing the cuffs and couldn't get them off fast enough to take with him," Ortiz speculated. "Or our victim got real mad and snapped them off. He looks strong, and they're cheap cuffs."

Ortiz pulled up Richard's blue sweater and felt with two fingers for bullet holes or broken bones, anything to suggest a struggle. "Nothing here," he said.

Officers in the basement and those peering down from the stairs tried to imagine how the murders occurred. Richard Langert probably died as soon as the bullet tore through the back of his skull. But wherever Nancy's wound was, her death did not look like a professional hit. "She might have been shot trying to run up the stairs," said one of the men.

"No blood here," Benoit told him.

Two of the officers came up with this theory. The killer surprised the couple as they came in. Nancy was still wearing her heavy coat when she and Richard were forced into the basement. After she was shot, the weight of blood saturating the coat made it too heavy for Nancy to make it up the stairs. She pulled off her coat but was then too weak to reach the steps.

6:40 P.M.

Sergeant Gene Kalvaitis's wife woke him and said that Lieutenant Sumner wanted to talk to him. Kalvaitis, who worked the overnight watch, was still a little groggy when he picked up the phone. "Yeah, what is it?"

"We got two murders on the East beat," Sumner said. "Man and wife, wife's pregnant. We don't know what we've got, but it doesn't look like robbery. We have plenty of men down here but we want you to start putting everything together."

"Sure, I'll be down."

The slender, sandy-haired officer pulled on his brand-new yellow coat and went to the station to get a handle on what was happening. The reality of the double murder didn't hit him until he drove across the bridge over the commuter tracks and saw police cars filling the driveway of the townhouse.

Kalvaitis bypassed the swarm of reporters and news crews by walking through the alley. Sumner met him halfway.

"Gene, you know what we need," the lieutenant said. "I want you to get a team together. Pull the phone records, get background checks, everything. Don't worry about manpower, we're getting people from all over. Find out who knew this couple and has a gun permit. Remember, we got two families involved. That means twice the work."

Kalvaitis stooped down by the open patio door and studied the glass sections by standing at every angle. "Why did the killers cut the glass?" he wondered out loud. Sumner couldn't answer him.

Gene went in and saw boxes of clothing and dishes. "This place is a mess," he said.

"The girl's father says they moved in a couple of months ago and were moving out soon, so they more or less were living out of boxes rather than fix up the place."

"Anything taken—TV, VCR?"

"We don't think it was a burglary. Look over here, see the money on the floor? We think the wife was trying to pay someone off."

Kalvaitis stopped halfway down the stairs, taken aback by what he saw. Ortiz was examining Richard's body. The mingling puddles of blood now stretched more than four feet. Kalvaitis wasn't disturbed by the violence as much as the youth of the victims. He had served in an artillery unit in Vietnam. He knew death close up. He never got used to it.

When Kalvaitis returned upstairs, Benoit showed him the marriage contract found on a table along with two gift-wrapped boxes. Officer Shimian, who had been studying the evidence, gave him a rundown of what the officers were speculating. After the intruders unlocked the side door, one of them apparently pulled up a chair near the patio wall. The officers guessed this because the chair or a foot broke a piece of glass. Then the men waited for Nancy and Richard to come through the front door.

"Then why is this marriage paper out?" Gene asked.

"We think the killers got bored, found it on top of one of the boxes, and took it out to read," Sumner said. "You know, for his own amusement."

That is cold-blooded, Kalvaitis thought. Anyone breaking in for drugs or money wouldn't be this careful yet leave hundreds of dollars on the floor. The killing of the husband had all the earmarks of a hit. Yet cutting double-pane glass rather than prying the door off its track suggested someone unfamiliar with burglary.

"Something is wrong here," he said.

6:45 P.M.

Ortiz, the medical examiner's investigator, went to Nancy's body, wedged between the wall and the bottom step. At age thirty-one, he had worked on six hundred murder scenes, and there was no horror for him. Yet he could not help being affected. On some corpses, the eyes are half-open. But this woman's lids were all the way up, giving her cloudy stare a disturbing intensity. Unlike her husband, Nancy's mouth was slightly open as if she had died with a gasp.

"It took her a time to die," Ortiz told the officers. "Look at her eyes. That's tache noir. See those horizontal lines across them?" Most of the officers couldn't. "Her eyes were exposed—open—as she was bleeding to death. That goes away in time." He drew her lids down so that the young woman might seem at rest.

Since only the wound in her elbow was visible, he unbuttoned her blouse and ran his hand down the green camisole until he found a hole through her abdomen and another in her lower back.

"Those blood smears on the axe must be hers, then," Benoit said. The killer had a gun, so he wouldn't need a hatchet, and Richard was handcuffed from behind. "Maybe she was shot as she was trying to attack them."

"It could have happened that way," Ortiz said.

Sergeant Siwak came down the stairs with a troubled expression. "The parents say the girl was pregnant about three months," he announced in a somber tone. Benoit and Sumner had the same thought: they were dealing with three murders, not two. "There's something else," Siwak added. "The victim worked at that Gloria Jean's coffee company."

"Oh-oh," Benoit said. "I knew it, there's got to be a Colombia connection."

Evidence expert Ron Schimian lifted the four-by-five-foot utility shelf to help form an idea of how Nancy fell. Reddish-brown streaks became visible as light hit the gray bottom shelf. No, not streaks but actual letters or a drawing, each mark a couple of inches long. "Look at this," Schimian said. "Isn't that blood?"

"The only one who could have left it was the woman, since the husband died instantly," Lieutenant Sumner said as he walked over. That explained why there was so much blood on Nancy's outstretched hand; she had dipped her fingers into it so that she might leave a message. But what could it be?

The officers jostled for a closer look, careful not to touch anything. They saw what appeared to be a straight line, either an "I" or an "l"; then a sort of rounded figure, possibly a heart or bow or a letter such as "B" or "R"; and a "U" or an incomplete "O." The policemen looked to one another for an explanation, but no one could even offer a guess.

7 P.M.

The dispatcher was busy calling in extra officers from nearby suburbs. Officer Mike O'Connell from

Glenview was the first to arrive. Going wherever he was needed in or out of the house, he heard a lot of speculation he couldn't agree with, such as hitmen arriving on the commuter train. O'Connell had been part of the Laurie Dann investigation, and he knew that cold-blooded murder is not always rational. "Remember, Gene," Mike told Kalvaitis, "it might be some nut. They don't have to have a reason for anything, they just do it."

An evidence technician was carefully dusting a dark powder of iron filings on the metal chair handles. Once a print was found, it was photographed and lifted with sticky paper.

Officers at the station had been trying to reach Chief Timm, but he and his family were having dinner in Pompano Beach, Florida. Finally Timm returned to his room, saw the telephone message light, and called in to ask what was happening. The dispatcher had him call Lieutenant Sumner about a double murder.

"It's a husband and wife, Herb," Sumner said from his mobile phone on the basement. "No motive, but they both work for a company that imports coffee from Colombia."

"Oh, jeez."

8:47 P.M.

Kalvaitis and another officer drove back to their headquarters to see what they could do there. Gene, with his instincts for organization, thought the station had become a zoo. Officers and civilian personnel were busy answering calls from throughout the Midwest. Reporters complained that they were getting little information, not understanding that police at this point had little to give. It was the Dann case all over again.

Jeanne Bishop arrived and was led to her father in the back of the station. Kalvaitis asked them, "Can either of you think why anyone would want to kill them?

Has either of them or anyone else in the family received a threat?"

Jeanne sat in a tight silence.

"No, no threats," Lee said. "No reasons, absolutely none."

Kalvaitis and another detective asked a few more questions, all the time watching to see if the family's expressions matched the words they were saying. The detectives sensed that Jeanne was keeping quiet intentionally. But Kalvaitis—knowing nothing about her Irish activism—thought that might be the shock of the murders setting in.

Adler, the social worker, apologized for interrupting and said that "Mrs. Bishop insists on going to the house. She wants to see Nancy and Richard."

Kalvaitis shook his head. Police didn't need anyone else disturbing the scene, and there was no need to add to the parents' grief. Adler continued, "She says she must see them for herself to believe what happened. She sounds like she can take it. I think we should let them."

Kalvaitis looked at Lee and his daughter. "Do you really want to go?"

"Yes," he answered. "We'll go with Joyce."

When the family arrived, television equipment was bathing the townhouse in a white light. A fire truck from the police/fire department headquarters was providing its own light on the narrow patch of grass along the side of the house from the ravine to the driveway. It was now 9 P.M., an hour before the main newscasts. Two men from the M.H. Scott Funeral Home in Glenview entered the basement with a pair of black canvas bags. First they wrapped a white towel around Nancy's face, covering her blood-soaked hair, then eased her into a body bag and carried her up the stairs to a stretcher.

Joyce had been telling herself that none of this was happening, but now she slowly began to accept it. She wondered how these two young people could have their lives taken from them so senselessly. She froze as she saw the stretcher wheeled toward her. Nancy's pale face and lips showed through the plastic, and some of her hair was exposed under the towel. Joyce was in control of herself again. She brushed her daughter's forehead tenderly as her husband and Jeanne held onto her arms.

Joyce had cried at her daughter's performance in *West Side Story* but she didn't cry now. Benoit had never seen a family like this before. No tears. They kept their emotions in check almost completely. Adler wept softly as she watched. The two dogs kept barking at the commotion of the officers moving through the house until Benoit grabbed the beagle's leash and carried the cocker spaniel to the Bishops outside.

Lee's partner in the recycling venture was among those trying to get past the police line. When White was finally let through, Lee seemed relieved to be with someone he knew. "I'm here if you need me," White told his partner, and Lee put a hand on the man's shoulder. White moved to comfort Joyce, but she walked by in a concentrated daze.

State police brought in a trained German shepherd to go through the house for drugs, but the dog found nothing. Outside, police photographed the black leather glove Siwak had discovered on the wood chips. Under the glare of the firetruck light, a line of officers with notepads inched forward to look for anything on the grass, sidewalk, or driveway. One officer looked over the fence and saw a footprint, but it was too faint to make a good cast. The police instead measured and photographed it.

9:40 P.M.

Officers went door to door asking neighbors if they had seen or heard anything unusual. An elderly woman in the adjacent townhouse said she had heard a shot and some loud voices, maybe a woman saying "Don't do it again," but she had assumed it came from the television set. After all, murders don't happen in Winnetka.

Richard's parents and eldest brother, Robert Jr., arrived at the police station from their home in southwest suburban Oak Lawn. The three of them were in shock as they were led to a side room for routine questions about when they had last seen the couple, and whether Richard had any enemies. Lieutenant Bill Gallagher told the family that the Bishops were at the house, and Delores Langert cried for them as well as for the victims.

Ed Kvetko was listening to music through earphones when his wife ran into the bedroom screaming, "Nancy and Richard are dead!" All she had heard on a news break was that a young Winnetka couple had died, then she called the police and learned that the victims were the Langerts. The Kvetkos assumed the couple had been killed in a car crash, until they turned on the ten o'clock news. They held onto each other, neither saying a word.

April 9, 2:30 A.M.

After all the evidence was logged and collected, police locked up the townhouse and began to write up reports and enter data into computers. By now, Sergeant Kalvaitis had so much trouble concentrating that Lieutenant Sumner told him to go home for a little sleep so he would be fresh when the task force began work at 6 A.M. Gene would be off the street and in civies until the case was solved.

Sleep wasn't much on Gene's mind now; he just wanted to change his clothes and clear his head. The case wouldn't leave the sergeant as he drove through the empty streets to his home in Lake Zurich, half an hour away. The nearly full moon shone like a dime in the unclouded black sky. He kept remembering things he had seen on the floor, in the living room, and in the basement. Something isn't right, he told himself once more. The officers had written up what they called a kick-ass report. It stated all the facts but they didn't add up to anything.

Gene's wife, Pam, awoke as he let himself in. "I'm going to be in charge of the task force," he told her. Pam knew what case he meant. She channel-hopped newscasts whenever there was a Winnetka story.

Her husband took off his yellow coat and muttered, "Where the hell do I go from here?"

8

Without Apparent Motive

Monday, April 9, 8 A.M.

BENOIT AND BALDING Sergeant Jimmy Brewer of the evidence section turned off the Eisenhower Expressway that Monday morning and drove through rush-hour traffic to the Office of the Cook County Medical Examiner. The modern building was part of Chicago's medical center complex of private and public hospitals, clinics, and testing laboratories a little west of the Loop.

Carrying video equipment and an evidence kit, the officers identified themselves at the reception desk and were led to the autopsy room where Dr. Mitra Kalelkar would be performing the postmortem examinations in half an hour.

The bodies had been brought in through the rear doors Sunday night, weighed on a large scale, and taken to the next room for x rays of the bullet wounds. The photos were developed overnight as the victims— still in body bags—were kept on racks in the refrigeration unit. By the time the bodies were taken out in the morning, Nancy's eyes had opened by themselves and stared blankly at the attendants wheeling her down the cinder-block corridors.

Dr. Kalelkar, a short woman with black curly hair,

had come from an aristocratic family in India. She had been with the medical examiner's office for eleven years, and she well remembered the smell of decay that pervaded the old morgue. This new facility was designed to ease the grief of relatives in public areas, and the building had increased ventilation in the work sections. But despite the restful mustard color of the autopsy room, it still had the odor of preservative and disinfectant.

The pathologist came in with a blue surgical gown over her skirt. Sergeant Brewer took some scrapings from the hands and nails of the victims in hope of finding a strand of the killer's hair or something to identify his blood type. Dr. Kalelkar cut Richard's clothes with a pair of shears and had her assistants hose down the dried blood. Next, she made a Y-shaped incision from his shoulders to his groin. The pathologist also used the semicircular blade of a motorized Stryker saw to cut through the crown of Richard's head. There was a faint cloud of bone dust as the saw, the size of an ordinary electric drill, worked a circle around the calvarium, the domelike portion of the cranium.

The pathologist memorized all the details for her report, but she pointed out to the two officers information she felt might be helpful. Glancing at the X ray on a screen above the slab, she carefully removed the slug from the subcutaneous tissues of Richard's scalp, and the blunted copper jacket of the same bullet from the right frontal lobe of the brain.

A twenty-cubic-centimeter syringe was used to draw blood from Richard's heart. Kalelkar rinsed the syringe and reused it to remove urine from his bladder. The sample would be sent to one of the labs in the building to be screened for the presence of drugs.

Benoit was making a videotape, but he could see that Dr. Kalelkar objected to having everything she said recorded. He turned off the camera and took notes so his department would have something to work with until copies of the autopsy reports were ready. Less than an hour from the time Kalelkar started, she told the officers what the medical examiner's investigator had already determined: Richard Langert was killed by a single bullet in the back of the head that fractured his skull and extensively lacerated his brain.

Richard's body was wheeled off to the side, and Nancy's was placed on the slab. Benoit was taking her fingerprints when he jerked in alarm. "Her hand moved!" the officer said, and felt a little foolish when no one else looked scared. Could he have imagined it in the eeriness of the setting?

"It happens, sometimes," the pathologist said. Rigor mortis leaves in stages, and its effects vary with the victim and the circumstances of death.

One gunshot wound consisted of a clear hole through the rear of the left elbow. Another was through her stomach and two loops of her small intestine, as well as the kidney and right lobe of the liver. Kalelkar removed the slug from the right side of her back. The second bullet had cut a slightly downward path, fracturing the right portion of her tenth rib before being deflected and burying itself under the skin in the right side of her back.

Benoit winced as Dr. Kalelkar removed the amniotic sac, containing the couple's unborn child. The officer had never seen a fetus before. He could see the feet, the tiny hands, the head. He didn't want to cry, and he was glad that being behind the camera made everything less real. Still, he had to lower the camera a moment to regain his composure. He knew he should take some close-ups, but he couldn't. Even big, tough Eddie Benoit had difficulty with this part of his job.

The bullets had not struck the womb, meaning Nancy's death had stopped the heart of her unborn child. The fetus weighed thirty-six grams, and it was too young for its sex to be determined.

After the autopsies, Sergeant Brewer took charge of

the clothing, the recovered bullets, and a vial of blood from each of the victims. Then he and Benoit drove back to Winnetka without saying much of anything.

That afternoon Jeanne Bishop, representing both families, walked to the reception desk of the medical examiner's office and showed her driver's license as identification. She sat still on a sofa until the "intake" man came through the double doors and called out "Langert!"

Jeanne rose from the chair, went through the orange-red doors, and took the two steps to the identification room. She sat on a small sofa and stared at the television set anchored to the ceiling. The closed-circuit camera showed Nancy's face, looking nothing as it had in life. "Yes, that's my sister," Jeanne said quietly. The screen went blank for half a minute. When the camera showed the disfigured face of Richard, she just looked at the intake man and nodded.

Sergeant Kalvaitis didn't even try to sleep after coming home before dawn that morning. He lay in bed until a little before six, took a shower, drank some coffee, and headed back to the station. The place was still disorganized. All shifts had to be rearranged to create the task force, and half a dozen officers on loan from other suburbs were trying to familiarize themselves with the case.

No one involved was getting any sleep, but Kalvaitis waited for what he considered a decent hour before calling the Bishop home and asking Lee for wedding albums, address books, and anything else that might be used to trace acquaintances. He also called the state's attorney's office and requested subpoenas for the phone records of all calls from the townhouse in the twenty-four hours before the bodies were discovered, and for six months from the Bishops' house and the headquarters at Gloria Jean's Gourmet Coffee.

Kalvaitis then took all the task-force officers to a

classroom downstairs, where an Illinois Bell crew was setting up extra jacks and laying out new lines. Several policemen walked in with typewriters and put them on the metal tables. Gene gave the men a briefing before leading them in a line of cars in the morning drizzle. The officers needed to get a feel for the place that photos couldn't provide.

When they returned, Lieutenant Sumner asked Gene to talk to a couple standing in the lobby. "We are very close friends of Nancy and Richard," the woman said in a trembling voice, "and we know something we felt you should know."

Kalvaitis quickly took them to an empty office, brought Detective Robert Kerner in, and closed the door. The woman, who lived in another suburb, asked the officers, "Are you aware of the threat that Jeanne received?"

"Jeanne?" Kalvaitis asked, making sure the woman didn't mean the murder victim.

"Jeanne's very much involved in the Irish Republican Army. I mean with activities involving the IRA."

Yes! Kalvaitis thought. When he had asked Jeanne the night before if anyone had received threats, the young woman seemed to tighten up before his eyes.

Gene lit a cigarette and sat back in his chair. "What kind of threats, and how is she involved in the IRA?"

"She's all heart and soul into it; has been for a few years," the woman said. "The FBI contacted her a few months ago about a threat. Shouldn't I say 'alleged' threat? Because of all that's going on you can't be sure, can you? Someone said if Jeanne ever went back she would be killed. But she went back anyway."

The friend began to cry, and her husband placed his arm around her.

"It upset Nancy, and she told us about it," the woman continued. "But it doesn't make sense, does it—to kill Nancy?"

"How did Jeanne react to the threat, was she worried?"

"I guess not," the woman replied. "It's not like she was involved in anything illegal. She just arranged visas and things like that."

"Do you know of any enemies Nancy or Richard had? Business people, or maybe lovers?"

"They were a happy couple, everybody liked them," the woman said. "She was looking forward to the baby, to the new house . . ." Her voice trailed off.

The husband told the officers, "That's all we know, really." Then he led his wife outside.

Chief Timm made notes on the plane trip from Florida to sort everything out. Business ties to Colombia. Husband shot execution style. The axe. The overturned shelf. The indecipherable message in blood. Corner house. House by the railroad station. The more Timm considered everything, the more he was sure big money had to be involved.

A Winnetka officer met Timm at O'Hare Airport and drove him home. Timm dropped off his bags and went to the station. When he arrived, Lieutenant Sumner was talking to Lee and Joyce.

"I can't believe that somebody took my baby's life just down the street," Nancy's mother told Timm as he sat in on the interview. "You can see the house from here!"

"Mrs. Bishop," Timm said as he stood with his arms crossed against the window, "we're going to turn over every stone that needs to be turned over, and we will step on whatever toes we have to." The couple understood that. "We may have to ask some very unpleasant questions of you and your family. We apologize in advance, but we have to get at the bottom of this. We're certain you feel the same way."

Lee nodded and Joyce said, "Do whatever you have to. We're going to cooperate fully with you."

"Then I would suggest that for a very long time you don't say anything to others. Let us handle the media. We don't want certain things to be revealed, and we want to be very careful about that." He especially meant the writing in blood.

"You don't have to worry about us," Lee said.

After the Bishops left, Sumner drove the police chief over to the guarded townhouse so he could look over the basement and the killers' apparent escape route. The officers told Timm where all the evidence had been, including the $513.

The bodies were returned to the funeral home and Joyce said she wanted immediate cremation, without consulting the Langerts even though their Catholic religion was against the practice. As Lee helped make the funeral arrangements, Joyce kissed her youngest daughter good-bye. A tear dropped from her eye and lay upon Nancy's face as if the young woman were only sleeping.

That evening, Joyce was too upset to eat. "How will I get through every day—every birthday without Nancy? Every Christmas?" No one could answer her.

More than a dozen friends and neighbors arrived, many bringing homemade cakes and other food as a way of easing the pain. Salads, breads, and a pan of lasagna were already on the dining room table as Joyce greeted the new arrivals. She looked well in her simple brown dress and strand of pearls, but her expression was vacant.

The visitors spoke in hushed tones as they clustered in side rooms and the kitchen. Nothing is so wrenching as murder without an apparent motive.

At the police station, Benoit called the medical examiner's office on a routine inquiry concerning the testing and learned of the cremations. He rushed the news to Kalvaitis, and the sergeant was so angry he slammed his fist onto the desk.

"Damn it!" he shouted. "I called that office this

morning and ordered them not to release the bodies no matter how much the Bishops insisted on it."

"Don't get upset," Benoit said, "it's too late now."

"I wanted a DNA test on that fetus to make sure Richard was the father." But that wasn't what really was upsetting Kalvaitis. This was his second run-in with the Bishops in forty-eight hours. He was sure that things wouldn't change from here on in.

Tuesday, April 10, 4 P.M.

On Tuesday afternoon, about thirty friends formed a continual stream through the Bishop home. Lee walked slowly and in a stoop, and Joyce looked as if she wanted to cry but couldn't. At one point she sat at the piano and picked at the keys as if to call up memories. She reached for one of the photos on the piano—the one with Richard and Nancy at their Christmas and engagement party. Richard was smiling into the camera and Nancy looked radiant in her green dress and red corsage. With her finger, Joyce traced the outline of Nancy's face and lingered a moment. Then she returned to the sofa without a change of expression.

"We know, Joyce," one of the women said. "Let it out."

"How can you know?" Mrs. Bishop asked. "How can you possibly know?"

In the kitchen, a longtime family friend asked Jeanne how her mother was holding up.

"The doctor gave her tranquilizers, but I don't think she's eaten anything," Jeanne said.

"She has to eat," the friend remarked and poured some of her homemade chicken soup into a bowl.

"I don't think my mother will eat it."

"At least we'll try," the friend said. She brought the soup out on a tray. Tears welled up in Joyce's eyes, but the soup brought her back. In a moment she was going around the house talking to visitors again.

Lee had been at the police station all this time to learn of any new developments. The officers told him that the FBI had been contacted because of the possibility that the murders were an IRA assassination. He came home so upset his wife immediately asked, "What happened?"

"I don't want to talk about it right now."

"I want to know, Lee."

He pulled her into the kitchen and said, probably louder than he intended, "I've learned some things that are going to blow this thing wide open, but it doesn't concern you or me."

"What do you mean? My kid is dead, everything concerns me!"

"I don't choose to tell you at this time," Lee said, his raised voice making the guests uncomfortable.

Joyce followed him up the stairs to the family room, lined with books and leather furniture. Here were trophies and photos of the family playing tennis. A place of comfort and memories.

A family friend who had followed Joyce part of the way, to see if she could help, heard her ask Lee, "Just what did you mean by that remark? What did the police say?"

Lee refused to answer. "I'm the man, I take care of everything," he said. "You don't need to be bothered by it."

After a few minutes, Joyce walked back down the stairs so shocked her friend had to lead her to the sofa.

In the evening, Robert and Delores Langert came over. Lee greeted them in his way of hugging them without their bodies touching, and the two fathers clasped each other's arms. The short, plump Mrs. Langert's eyes were red from crying. No one quite knew what to do or say next as the four parents stood facing each other.

The Bishops' minister, Dr. Bowen, dropped by to speak privately with the two families. All the other guests left, passing on quiet words as Joyce saw them out the door. The Langerts were about to leave with Richard's cocker spaniel when Lee asked about the services. "I'll bring the ashes," Bowen told him. The Langerts were stunned and turned to the Bishops.

"Yes," Joyce said to the question the Langerts could not ask, "we had it done." That was that. The couple stared at her, unable to comprehend that decisions were made about their son without consulting them. "We want their ashes buried behind the Kenilworth church," Joyce added. "It is lovely there. You will see that the setting will be tasteful."

Robert could do nothing but put his arm around his wife and leave. They could not be as controlled as the Bishops in the face of tragedy. Delores wept as the door closed behind her. Lee retreated to his chair with a pipe, sucking hard on the stem and gripping his glass of scotch.

Since the two families had avoided answering questions from reporters, Jeanne issued a statement to the news media on behalf of the Bishops and the Langerts:

Nancy and Richard were the light of our lives. They were good and innocent people. They loved life and had everything to live for: a loving family, a happy marriage, and the anticipation of their first child and home. We will love and miss them the rest of our lives. The part of our hearts that can feel anything but grief goes out to every family that has suffered a similar loss. It is one no one should have to endure.

Our heartfelt thanks to the people who have expressed concern and offered their prayers. Our comfort lies in those prayers and in the knowledge that Nancy, Richard, and their baby are in the arms of God.

As part of the groundwork for the investigation,

Kalvaitis began placing evidence photos in an album and making the hour-long tape of the crime scene available to newly assigned task-force members.

Gene also agreed to let two close friends of Nancy pick up the personal belongings at the townhouse for the Bishops and Langerts. But one of the young women called in a panic from inside the home. "We're trying to get out the front door but they're shoving cameras in our faces. They're all over the place." It sounded as if the house were under siege.

The reporters and camera crews swarmed around Gene as he left his car and went to the door. "There's nothing going on, believe me," he told them.

The door opened and out came two scared young women. The sergeant wanted to swing his two-way radio at the cameramen. Instead he just led the woman to the auto. When someone shoved a microphone at him, he snarled, "I've got absolutely nothing to say," then slammed the car door.

April 11

Under a light snow that fell from the overcast sky, more than eight hundred people filled the pews and aisles of the Kenilworth Union Church that Wednesday. Two-member police teams cruised streets around the building, one officer driving and the other taking down license plate numbers to begin a list of contacts.

Dr. Bowen stood behind the hand-carved pulpit and spoke of his personal feelings, as well as those of the Bishops. "This is a time not only for grief but also anger," he said. "Let us be clear about where the guilt and responsibility of this awful act rests. It rests in one place. It rests upon a human being or human beings out there who chose to do unspeakable evil. And who deserve our anger and rage, who deserve the justice of God and society, who deserve some internal misery and pain for their misdeeds."

Bowen added that God gave mankind free will, including the freedom to choose evil. "And some do, to the loss of their humanity and the pain and suffering of others."

Referring to the insular nature of the North Shore, Dr. Bowen said the community is "not removed from the evils of the larger world . . . for inevitably, sooner or later, the world comes to visit us and our own."

The Congregationalist minister asked the mourners, with Easter only a few days away, to remember the gift each of them had received from Richard and Nancy, "the gift of these two very special lives. Jesus gave himself up in trust in his dark hour, confident that death and evil do not have the last word."

There was a numbness in the air that the TV crews were unable to capture. The entire Langert family wept, but the Bishops sat straight.

Officers watching the crowd from outside tried to be discreet. They knew that occasionally a killer attends the funeral of his victim. It's part of his fantasy of getting away with the crime. For all these officers knew, he could be in the church at that very moment.

At the wishes of the two families, the mourners were allowed to express their condolences in a reception line that was formed in a large parlor inside the church. A friend seeing the Bishops' lack of outward emotion thought, "It's not real." Just tea, tiny sandwiches, and utter self-control.

Among those paying their last respects were Joan Biro, the wife of a former business associate, and her teenage daughter Nancy and son David. Because all the pews were filled during the service, they had watched it on closed-circuit TV in another room.

In the afternoon, Jeanne went to the police station and sat with perfect posture in a side room, her mourning-black designer dress offset by pearls and a gold bracelet. Kalvaitis started right in by saying, "We understand you received a death threat. Did you, Miss Bishop?"

She took a breath and knew by his tone that he wasn't asking just a general question. "Well, I did," she snapped. "But there's nothing to it. I mean, it was totally ridiculous."

Detective Robert Kerner snapped back at her, "Why didn't you tell us that last night?"

Jeanne didn't like his tone, and she refused to answer.

In a more controlled voice, Kalvaitis asked, "What do you mean 'ridiculous,' Miss Bishop? Can you tell us what's going on here?"

Jeanne shook her head as if wondering why the officers were so interested in her when it was her sister who was killed. "Last November I got a call from the FBI about someone in Ireland saying that if I return, I may be killed or injured, but I give no credence to this. I have no belief in this at all."

"You weren't scared?"

Giving Kalvaitis an iron-hard look, she said, "I told them to send me what they had, and"—here came a strange smile—"they never did."

"The IRA kills people," Kalvaitis said.

"Not in this country, and not like that."

"You and your sister look alike."

"Not that much."

"Then why was she killed?"

"That is not why she was shot."

"You can't tell me why she was killed?"

"No, but it wasn't that."

"You really don't know?"

"No, I don't, but it had nothing to do with me or what I do."

From her expression, Kalvaitis couldn't tell whether Jeanne Bishop was being honest or holding back something.

9

The Drug Connection

Tuesday, April 10, 10:20 A.M.

THE DAY BEFORE the funeral, Gloria Jean and Ed Kvetko offered a ten-thousand-dollar reward for information leading to the arrest and conviction of the killer or killers. Before the day was out, the Bishop family matched the offer with ten thousand dollars of their own.

The reward announcement came as teams of task-force members were being deployed to explore every conceivable motive. Detectives Tom Welter and John Garza were assigned to follow up any leads they might find at the coffee company, where Gloria Jean still kept a photo of Nancy on her desk as if the young woman had been her own daughter.

"There was so much love," Mrs. Kvetko told the officers. "When you meet someone and all of a sudden there's something more in you than before, that's like what it was around them."

The muscular Garza asked the Kvetkos if they could see where the victims worked.

"Sure," Ed answered and led them to Nancy's office. "You don't know how bad I felt about having their gun. At first I thought they were killed by some crazy teenager looking for drugs and not knowing what Richard and Nancy were like, so maybe if they had the gun this wouldn't have happened. But when I heard about the handcuffs and everything, forget it; I knew the gun wouldn't have made a difference."

Nancy kept her desk clear of papers and personal clutter. "She was very organized," Kvetko said and pointed out how neat her handwriting was. It was as if she still had been trying to please her grade school teachers.

Garza pulled Nancy's chair back and picked up her desk calendar to see if anything on her schedule might hold a clue. He found it strange to think that she had sat at this desk last Saturday, unaware that everything would soon come to an end.

Tall, thin Welter told Kvetko, "We'll need their phone lines so we can check every call that went in and out from their desks for at least all of last week."

"We have twenty-five lines here," Kvetko said. "Nancy and Richard could have gotten calls on any of them."

Welter knew what that meant: a subpoena from Illinois Bell that would translate into hundreds of pages. Each name would have to be entered into a police computer to be checked for any criminal record.

Next to a desk photo of Richard was a Precious Moments statuette of a sweet-faced pregnant woman that Gloria Jean had given Nancy when she presented her with the black maternity dress. There also was a bottle of grapefuit juice Nancy would sip from, hoping to keep her unborn baby healthy, and the flat shoes she wore when her feet swelled from water retention.

"Are you looking for anything in particular?" Kvetko asked.

"There was something written when she died," Garza said. "Maybe her handwriting samples will help us figure it out."

The officers not only looked through the drawers,

they searched under the desk for anything that might have fallen, or perhaps a key taped to the underside.

"When we come back this week we'll need access to her computer terminal," Welter said.

"Sure," Kvetko replied. "We're not touching anything. Do you want to see Richard's desk? It's in the warehouse half a mile away."

The officers looked at each other and nodded.

As they went to the parking lot, Welter casually asked Kvetko if he owned a gun.

"Yes, I collect them," the businessman said fondly.

Hundreds of burlap bags were on one side of the warehouse, and men on yellow forklifts were hoisting still more. A chill came over the officers when Ed said that seventy percent of the coffee came from Colombia.

"Did Richard work in here?" Garza asked. The U.S. Drug Enforcement Administration had told him at a seminar that many smugglers believed coffee hid the scent of some drugs.

"When a shipment came in, Rich opened the bags before the beans were sent to be roasted," Kvetko said.

"Who else did that?"

"Just him."

"Did he open any bags Friday or Saturday?"

"The last time must have been about a month ago," Ed answered.

Kvetko's pride in his business showed as he brought Welter and Garza to the large roaster. "This cost $320,000, but because of ordinance problems it's just sitting here."

"This gourmet coffee business is very competitive, isn't it?" Garza asked.

"Oh, yeah," Ed said.

Garza was wondering where the money for all this equipment came from. He was not aware that the gourmet coffee industry then accounted for twenty percent of all coffee bought in the United States.

"I guess there are a lot of trade secrets to the coffee blends and the roasting," Welter said.

"For the special blend, it's a science. But once you get the right combination, you got it."

The officers went through Richard's desk, turned over his chair, and went through the file cabinets, hoping to find something leading to a drug connection, perhaps even packs of cocaine.

"Rich was totally against drugs," Kvetko said.

Welter had his own idea about why Richard was killed. "Say, Ed, if someone who knew the secrets took off on his own, bingo, he could make a million dollars, couldn't he? I mean, how could anyone prove he stole the secret recipes?"

Kvetko wasn't sure what Welter was implying, but from then on he seemed a little less open in his answers.

When the detectives came across a list of importers, Garza said, "We need to know exactly where you get your coffee from, who gets it, and who sets up the shipments."

Kvetko was insulted.

"There could be things you don't know about, it happens all the time," Garza explained. "You run a business, you don't inspect every single bag. There could be things Richard didn't know about, either."

"Okay."

"And did Richard fire anyone or have problems with them?" Welter asked.

"He fired a woman a few months ago and she made a threat, but you hear things like that all the time."

When they went outside, Garza spoke to some loading-dock workers in Spanish, but they couldn't help the detectives. By then it was nearly 3 P.M., and many of the drivers and warehouse workers were out on shipments. The investigators returned to the building and talked to the office workers. One cried as she told them how much Nancy had been looking forward to having a baby. Nancy even asked about writing a will to make sure the baby had something if she died young.

An executive at the firm turned over to Garza tapes of answering machine calls made to his home when he was out of town in late February. An unidentified male caller was heard saying he was going to jump off the eighth floor of a building and that he also was going to kill the executive's wife. The call ended in a wordless scream. Whatever the conversation was about, it wasn't the murders.

The wholesome image of the victims and the fact that the murders occurred in Winnetka was making the crime a guessing game for the entire Chicago area. Not even the FBI, working with an employees list, could turn up promising leads. Kalvaitis was convinced the motive was a juice loan because of the recent home invasion at the house of one of Lee's clients. But Timm insisted that he concentrate on the coffee business for now. Extortion was not likely to end in the murders of two innocent people, but a narcotics deal might.

One day a *Chicago Sun-Times* reporter phoned Gloria Jean about a tip that a hitman had killed Nancy and Richard on orders from a rival coffee company. The caller supposedly had named a man who "has done this type of thing for other franchises." She notified Welter and he began tracking the tip down, absurd as it was.

There was an even more off-the-wall report. A man said his friend, "John Doe," had overheard a conversation at a skinhead bar on Chicago's North Side. John Doe claimed he was at a table next to three men named Butch, Spike, and Weasel. While they were discussing the Winnetka murders, one of them said he knew for a fact that the shootings were a hit paid for by the company because Nancy and Richard were planning to quit.

Garza was making background checks on the Kvetkos. Ed's former wife, a suburban school teacher, shivered as she told the detective in her home that Ed had a temper. She wasn't the only one who had told police that, so Garza and Welter made a surprise visit to the Kvetkos' home in Long Grove.

The intentionally quaint northwestern suburb required that all new buildings at the crossroads have early nineteenth-century architecture. When the detectives arrived, Long Grove was in its annual Victorian Days.

The Kvetko house was the most beautiful Garza had ever seen. The spacious cottage-style home had a huge fireplace between two windows. All the cabinets were built of cherry wood. Yet the detectives were surprised to see Gloria Jean doing the cleaning herself.

Over a container of Chinese food split four ways, Garza and Welter talked to the couple about a rumor that Ed had gone to a mall on Chicago's Southwest Side to have a talk with an employee about some missing money. Welter had been told that Ed accused the manager of skimming profits and waved a gun in the young man's face. Kvetko denied taking his gun out, but he told the officers he had fired the manager and changed all the locks at the corporate offices.

Garza and Welter apologized for the intrusion and let the matter drop. But they well knew that anyone along the packing line in the company could have been involved in drug smuggling.

On April 17, Welter called the U.S. Customs Office in Chicago and gave agent *Susan Hatfield the names of seventy Gloria Jean's employees to check for any records. The computer showed that a few had "minor involvement," but nothing to indicate they would know about the killings.

Welter called the office again two days later. This

time his voice had a sense of urgency. Ed Kvetko had just notified him that the next shipment to the Paragon Coffee Trading Company in New York was expected to arrive that day.

Hatfield, a woman in her early twenties, used her desk computer to issue a stop order on the transfer of the containers. The possibility of smuggling drugs through imported coffee was by no means farfetched. Just that January a shipment authorized by the same distributor in Colombia had been stopped in Buffalo before the vessel could anchor in Canada, and a search had turned up five kilos of cocaine. Everyone aboard from skipper to cook told inspectors, "We don't know how it got there," and nobody was charged. Paragon and Gloria Jean's were not involved, and there was no evidence that even the distributor had known about the drugs.

The large gray ship—due in New York on April 19— didn't arrive until the twenty-sixth. The forty-ton, stainless-steel containers from various consignments were stacked nine deep under the deck and four on top. Waiting on the dock were ten uniformed inspectors from the Customs Enforcement Team and a pair of German shepherds. A customs officer went on deck with his clipboard and told the captain, "You know we're going to search this, don't you?"

"Go ahead," the captain answered. Inspections were fairly common, but not ones that might be connected to a double murder a thousand miles away.

Some of the longshoremen paused from loading crates to watch the huge containers being "devaned." A giant yellow crane hoisted the containers headed for Gloria Jean's and lowered them dockside. The crew unlocked the back doors and removed the ventilator covers. Inside both containers, three rows of dusty brown sacks were crammed almost to the loadline. As the inspectors watched, random bags were cut open and the dogs were "run over" them. Nothing.

The same thing happened with a shipment that arrived the next day. When Agent Hatfield got back to Garza and Welter, the detectives realized they were no closer to the killer than the day the bodies were found. One motive down, at least four to go.

10

The Syndicate Connection

April 8–14

THE LANGERT MURDER case arrived at the Northern Illinois Police Crime Laboratory in little brown evidence bags on Sunday night, April 8. The crime lab occupied the entire top floor of the Highland Park police station four miles away. A Winnetka officer had the watch commander unlock the door, then laid the bags on a desk. At 8 A.M. Monday, the small staff set to work on the handcuffs, axe, clothing, metal trays, and floor scrapings.

Over the next few days, the one-room serology department found that smears on the axe handle were consistent with Nancy's blood, but not Richard's. There also was no trace of blood of any other type on the handle. That could mean Nancy had picked up the axe after being shot, but for some reason she didn't strike anyone with it. At the time, no one considered that Nancy might have used the axe to pound on the metal shelf for help.

The privately operated facility, serving more than forty communities, was established because the Chicago police department had stopped helping the suburbs under the weight of its growing number of drug cases, and state technicians in Joliet were always backlogged.

The laboratory offices were filled with computers and specialized equipment, but not everything needed to be truly state of the art. Near the entrance, a young woman in a white smock used an ordinary steam iron in hopes of bringing out latent prints on the marriage contract. The technician slowly moved the iron an inch above the paper, but no swirls emerged.

Another technician used an eyedropper to put chemicals on a swab that would turn blue-green at a trace of blood on any of the evidence. For amounts too small to make an enzyme test possible with a swab, the technician used dozens of thread tips to study absorption. Each quarter-inch-long tip was then glued to a card with ordinary nail polish. In time, the Langert file would contain approximately 360 of those thread tips.

In the trace evidence section, a fluoroscopy test showed that the slug found on the floor carried tiny streaks of white paint, but no blood or tissue. The staff was not there to make assumptions, but this would be consistent with a warning shot. No one considered that the bullet might have been fired by accident.

Middle-aged Bob Wilson of the crowded ballistics office didn't have much to do on the case for now other than to check the general characteristics of the slugs against his thick book of manufacturers' specifications. Usually crimes that came in didn't personally affect Wilson one way or the other, but the riddle in blood disturbed him. Here was a young woman—dying beside her husband, her baby dying within her—using up her life to leave a message that no one could read. Wilson felt he owed it to her to understand these murders.

From time to time, Lieutenant Sumner dropped by and talked over the case with the lab director, Andy Principe, a former cop. Sumner didn't expect any dramatic findings, he just wanted something positive to tell reporters.

But as head of the task force, Sergeant Kalvaitis operated differently. Every morning he would check the bulletin board and throw away half a dozen messages from the news media asking for interviews. He was convinced the less the media knew about the investigation, the better.

Patty McConnell was enjoying her trip to Moscow. The police let her ride along in a Russian patrol car so she could see how the officers handled drunks and petty thieves. But this was her first time away from her family, and she missed her husband and young daughter. It took thirty-six hours for a telephone operator to patch a call through, but at last McConnell could tell Kristen how much she wished the girl could be with her. Her husband, Matt, also a policeman, came on the line and said, "Patty, you missed a big double murder the day after you left."

"Where?"

"In Winnetka!"

"Who did it? Why? Did they catch anybody?"

"Everybody's talking about it, it's the biggest case ever . . ." Then the line went dead.

Due to a phone problem between Russia and America, there was no way of finding out more. Patty put down the useless receiver. The biggest case ever to hit Winnetka, and she was thousands of miles away.

On the fourth day of the investigation, Chief Timm gave a pep talk to the officers as they returned from their assignments. The former classroom had seven desks, four telephones, three computers, a police teletype, a fax machine, and a photocopier. A new lock had been installed to make sure no unauthorized personnel saw the reports.

Some of the officers were from less affluent suburbs, and Timm wanted to remind them that Winnetka was able to pay for as large an investigation as this case needed. "You have carte blanche," he told the men. "I'll give you anything you want within reason, just get this thing solved. Talk to anyone you want, I don't care how much money they have."

On Thursday, April 12, Kalvaitis stood on a chair and posted a list of every name his men could turn up—a list five feet long. Gene called this the "tree of contacts" for file number 90-02352.

As Benoit sat waiting for the briefing to begin, he refreshed his memory by going through index cards that recorded calls from the public. He did not get much sleep in the past few days, still troubled by the bodies lying in their own blood. Richard's death was quick and didn't disturb him as much as Nancy's and her unborn baby's.

The cards he thumbed through ranged from the mundane to the ludicrous. Someone suggested that a Chicago policeman's handcuffs—taken in a burglary of a locksmith's shop—might be the ones found on Richard. Not true, the killer had used cheap ones from Taiwan. Another card came from Officer Bobby Caldwell, who reported seeing sixteen-year-old David Biro, a local troublemaker, walking down the street Saturday night. So what? One caller reported overhearing a bookie tell a trader at the Chicago Mercantile Exchange he would end up "like the Winnetka couple" if he didn't pay up.

Questioning people in the neighborhood also had failed to turn up anything useful. A young woman who had been cleaning her house reported seeing a teenage boy walking or running down the slope of the railroad ravine just past the Langert home sometime between eleven o'clock and midnight Saturday. Maybe so, but police couldn't verify it, and teens were always on the embankment.

Unlike a typical murder, there was nothing coming in to indicate a personal motive. Everyone police had talked to said the victims had no enemies, that they were "squeaky clean." The couple had spats, but they stayed in love.

As the chairs filled up on this Thursday, the room began to smell of coffee and cigarettes. Officer John Fay, the humorist of the group, taped the quote of the day to the podium: "Loose Lips Sink Ships." The joke was that some of the outside officers were complaining that Timm might be giving out too much information. The police chief had become used to the news media during the Laurie Dann investigation, and now he drew more attention to the case by saying things such as the police had recovered "an article of clothing." Kalvaitis felt that once the killer heard that, he would throw his remaining black leather glove into the garbage.

This was the first homicide investigation for William Broten of the Northbrook police. While waiting for the morning briefing, he studied the album of scene photos, waiting for a clue to jump out at him.

The tension and frustrations of working in the task force had to be broken up with a little humor. Early in the case, Fay and a few others began designating mock specialties for each of the seven members of the team. The one that got the biggest laugh was naming Ed Reynolds the "deviate sex expert," because he was a strong traditionalist and had four children.

Kalvaitis tapped his knuckles on the podium and began with a "Good morning" that meant: Listen up! "Day Four and we still have no motive on why Nancy and Richard Langert were killed. What I'm going to do now is bounce around motives. Come on, fellas," Gene added with a smile, "we're all cops—we go to the movies." The sergeant lit a cigarette and threw out an obvious possibility—"Burglary."

"Naw," Broten said. "An execution, a professional hit."

"It couldn't be a burglary," Northbrook detective Kevin Keel put in. "You could look right through the patio doors and see there was nothing worth taking."

"Yeah, and not too many burglars come with handcuffs," Benoit called out from his seat.

"Besides," Kalvaitis said, "burglars wouldn't leave five hundred dollars in cash on the floor, I don't care how scared they are. So how about home invasion? Something surprised them and they panicked."

No one seemed interested. Robberies like that just didn't happen on the North Shore. But Benoit had another idea. "I got a call this morning that Rich was into gambling. I think someone was trying to get him to pay but something went wrong."

Lieutenant Sumner stuck to his belief that the killings were an IRA hit. "I'm calling a friend of mine in Scotland Yard to check on the sister," he said. "Maybe someone mistook Nancy for her, or she had something of Jeanne's they wanted and she wouldn't give it up."

Officer Keel had his own idea. Unlike most of his colleagues, he was no newcomer to violence. Several times he had seen fatal victims of robberies or drunken fights as a railroad security guard. "I know this is far out," he tossed off with a shrug, "but this isn't our community, so I got to ask: who's your nut case here that could pull off something like this?"

"Does this look like an average nut case?" Kalvaitis said. "I mean, look at what they used: glass cutter, gloves, handcuffs."

A few heads nodded, and there were no more suggestions.

"Is that it, then?" Gene asked. "Okay, I'm now giving you guys the chance to work out your theories. One of you has to hit the jackpot. Benoit, take Brotman and work on your idea about Richard's gambling. And pick up those telephone subpoenas downtown. Fay and Reynolds, talk to some of Nancy's friends who were at the wedding and see if she had a lover on the side. Let's get her medical files. Kevin, go to Elmhurst and check out Saratoga Specialties, they both worked there. Get anything you can from the files. Welter and Garza, keep on Gloria Jean's. It's a big company, and all big companies have secrets."

With a dismissal gesture, Kalvaitis added, "Okay, everybody, be back by seventeen-hundred hours [5 P.M.]. And please keep those mobile phones on."

The mood was just too tense for Fay. As all the officers were leaving, the skinny detective put his hand to his mouth and quacked in a Donald Duck voice, "Roger, Wilco, and out."

Benoit and Brotman made the forty-minute trip to the Illinois Bell Telephone building in Chicago's Loop. They came out with binders a foot thick showing calls from the townhouse as well as the homes of Jeanne, the Bishops, Richard's parents, his brothers, and Lee's business associates.

The two officers then drove to the nearby offices of MCI to question a man who had gone to college with Richard. *Ralph Klein met the officers in a business suit and assured them that when he saw the newscast about the murders, he couldn't believe it.

Benoit spoke up. "Did Richard ever . . . You know, was he gay?"

"No way, not Richard," Klein said as if wondering why the officers would be asking such a question. "I was his roommate, he never did anything like that."

"We just had to ask," Benoit said.

"Was he a heavy drinker," Broten asked, "or did he take drugs?"

"His only 'vice' was that occasionally he would bet on sports."

"So much that he would get himself into serious debt?" Broten asked.

"Not when I knew him, but I wouldn't be surprised." Klein's voice turned a little snide. "Nancy lived on the North Shore and liked that high-living lifestyle."

The detectives thanked him and left. One thing they had learned in their careers was that people never really know their roommates.

The head of the privately funded Chicago Crime Commission, John Jamilo, volunteered his assistance. He felt the home invasion against the Nathan Calabrese family had occurred too close to the murders for coincidence.

The commission contacted the Illinois Secretary of State's office, and soon the fax machine in the task-force office spat out the names of half a dozen businesses that listed Lee as the legal officer. There was always the possibility that some of the firms were used to launder mob money, but all the companies appeared legitimate. Calabrese alone remained questionable. Benoit proposed that the murders could have been a warning to him.

The place to start looking into Nathan Calabrese's criminal background was an aging police station on the West Side. Constructed in an era of horse-drawn paddy wagons, the Maxwell Street station was as close to a haunted house as anything in Chicago. It was big, brooding, and its bricks were the color of dried blood. As soon as Brotman stepped out of the car, he was struck by how familiar the building seemed. "Wasn't 'Hill Street Blues' made here?"

"Just the opening," Benoit said, "but wait 'til you see inside."

When its precinct offices were transferred to a modern building, the station was kept open as the vice investigations headquarters for the entire city. A plainclothes sergeant in the gambling section unlocked a drawer and pulled out the Calabrese file for them. Calabrese was a reputed bookie who had been picked up in a major narcotics raid the year before, and in 1975 he was charged with aggravated battery, but the complaint was dropped three months later.

Benoit then called the Palatine station to let them know he and Brotman would drop by to pick up the file on the March home invasion and anything else they might have on the Calabreses. Benoit, who once was sure there had been a drug connection in the murders, now believed that organized crime was the only explanation. Who but a mob killer would ignore five hundred dollars from a defenseless young woman?

The two detectives returned to the Winnetka station and told Kalvaitis there was nothing to report. And yet Calabrese's name kept popping up as they looked deeper into his background. A suburban pizza parlor he ran had been bombed in 1980, but that was blamed on the previous owner.

Benoit also learned that Lee had handed Nathan a bill for one thousand dollars for legal services, and Calabrese refused to pay more than a few hundred dollars. But it didn't make sense for anyone to kill Nancy and Richard for that.

Someone then mentioned that perhaps Calabrese had arranged a mob loan for the Langerts to buy the house in Prospect Heights. The possibility intrigued Chief Timm, who was telling reporters that the task force was working on "four or five scenarios." But police studying copies of the couple's income tax forms found that they would have been able to afford the rent the Kvetkos had set for them.

The possibility of a mob or loan-shark connection wouldn't go away. As the days dragged on, Benoit was learning how many friends Richard owed money to, including suburban policeman *Charles Kregger. He and Richard had been roommates in college, but Richard thought nothing of pulling out of a condo-buying deal they had arranged. Kregger was still angry as he spoke about it.

"Everyone I introduced Richard to said he stiffed them out of money," Kregger said. "I mean a lot, like four hundred dollars for baseball tickets and using credit cards for rent-a-cars. He even sent a guy a check for his wedding, and it bounced. I had to track him down and make sure he started paying me off little by little."

Benoit tried not to show his excitement at finding someone who had both a gun and a motive. But, upon reflection, not enough of a motive.

The questioning of Richard's acquaintances continued over the next week. College friends told police Richard loved to gamble on sports. But a "big gambler" who went to bars with him a few times told police he never knew Richard to wager more than he could handle.

The only new physical evidence came from Bob Wilson of the Northern Illinois Crime Laboratory. He couldn't get much information from the police photos, so he visited the townhouse several times to study the scene on his own. He wanted to find out how a slug could end up on the floor. Some officers said it must have been fired from the basement, meaning the slug traveled upward, but Wilson theorized that the shot might have come from the direction of the patio doors.

The balding man got on his knees and made a cast of the bullet hole on the baseboard with a tube of Mikrosil, a Swedish product used for making small impressions. Once he learned the "directionality" of the hole, Wilson ran strings from the white board. There was no way of determining exactly from what point the gun had been fired, but the strings showed all possible locations, from mouse level to overhead. The angle seemed too steep to be natural.

The baseboard then became just another piece of evidence to photograph, log, and store.

Every evening, officers came into the station team by team to report what they had learned and type up their reports. Sergeant Kalvaitis had never been on a case like this. Everything was bizarre, and with so many possible motives there seemed no way to concentrate the resources of the task force.

Gene Kalvaitis's frustration was showing in his personal life. Pam never knew what her husband would be like when he came home. Some days his mood would be up and he would lie on the floor playing with their dog, Blitz. Other times he kept to himself and just stoked the fireplace or sat in front of the television set without really watching it.

Most disturbing to him was the enigma of the patio door. Half the actions taken by the killer were professional, and half were amateurish. Gene kept mulling over what one of the officers had said at the scene, that the killer could have just chosen the townhouse on a whim. That meant the case might never be solved.

"What's bothering you?" his wife would ask from time to time.

"Nothing."

"You can tell me what's wrong, can't you?"

"I don't remember," he would say just to keep her from asking again. If she tried to reassure him by rubbing his back or kissing him, Gene would say, "You're hanging on me." But she knew that sometimes he needed a hug.

Until the bodies were discovered in Lee's townhouse, Niagara Recycling Manufacturers was considered a hot property. Lee had even moved out of his Schaumburg law office to operate from the corporate headquarters on the fringe of Chicago. Although Lee and his partners had permits from the Illinois Environmental Protection Agency, the project was still under-financed, and the Whites were having money problems of their own.

Lee originally had invested ten thousand dollars in the project. In February, after having Joseph White sign over the business to him, he secured additional people who came up with one hundred thousand. Then the village of Forest View signed the permit on April 4, only three days before the murders. There was no reason to suspect a connection, but police had to ask.

When Detective John Fay and another officer visited White's home while Joseph was away, it was clear his wife was still upset over the murders. Mary followed them through the large house and answered whatever they asked until Fay said, "Do you mind if we take a look at the names of other business associates of your husband, so we can see if they worked with Mr. Bishop, too?"

"Yes, I do mind," she said. "I can't go in his room and pick through those things. He is my husband." Her tone seemed to say: How dare you suspect Joseph, we are dear friends of the Bishops!

After the officers drove away, Mary cried.

As the police continued their investigation at the various businesses Lee worked for, rumors spread that he must have mob ties. It didn't matter that none of the inquiries about loan sharks and the syndicate led anywhere. All the potential buyers who had virtually been lining up suddenly stopped inquiring, leaving just the bill collectors.

When something like that happens, developers usually go out and re-sell the project by assuring potential buyers that the Mafia was in no way involved. But Lee could not think of business at a time like this. There was nothing in his life to prepare him for what was happening.

Lee had grown up in the central Illinois town of Pekin with its grain elevators and clatter of trains from fifteen railroads. He was essentially a simple man looking for contentment. There wasn't the drive in him anymore to turn situations around. He had poured all his energy and all the money he could scrape together into a project that was now just a vacant lot and stacks of paper.

Business associates would see Lee at work every morning, still the laid-back lawyer he had always been. But by afternoon they would find him brooding alone inside his car in the underground garage of the Chicago office building. The impact of the double murders was victimizing more and more people as the ripples continued to spread.

11

The IRA Connection

Saturday, April 14

ALL THAT FIRST week after the murders, Jeanne Bishop slept and ate little as she stayed with her parents on Indian Hill Road. She would think every morning, "Why should I brush my teeth? Why should I put on my makeup?" As the family was packing away Nancy's things and she saw some of her sister's grade school drawings, Jeanne didn't care if she lived or died.

The sun was starting to show through the clouds that Saturday when the FBI called and asked her to come down to the Winnetka police station. She didn't want to talk to federal agents without an attorney, but she was too run down to think about that. Besides, perhaps they had turned up something new.

Her hope ended when a policeman took her into a small room with Sergeant Kalvaitis and two FBI agents, including *Howard Ryan. Ryan, a short, husky Irishman, was from the bureau's international terrorism squad, and his specialty was Northern Ireland. Many people in Chicago's Irish community considered him a traitor to the cause.

Jeanne had learned not to trust Ryan the previous November, when he assured her that she was not under investigation even though her father was told by a friend at Illinois Bell that her phones were being tapped.

Now Ryan told Jeanne that authorities were working on the theory that someone from the IRA wanted to carry out the death threat from last fall and had mistaken Nancy for her.

"First of all, we don't look alike," Jeanne said. "My sister was fifty pounds heavier. Her hair was darker. Her nose was smaller, and her chin was stronger."

Ryan and agent *Sal Rossi looked at Jeanne as if humoring her.

"For another thing," she continued, "I was in that house only once in my life. So why would the killer go there? Anybody could look up the address of where I work in the phone book and follow me home. And have you ever heard of the IRA killing an American? And even when they make mistakes, they always claim responsibility. I mean, this whole thing is ridiculous."

"A waitress at the restaurant says she thinks you made a phone call at the restaurant that night."

"She's mistaken. I went to the washroom. The washroom is next to the phone booth."

"You asked for change."

"I didn't make a phone call," Jeanne insisted.

"It's just a theory we're investigating," Ryan said impassively. "Did you know Nancy was in fear of her life when she went to England with you and her parents last year?"

"That's nonsense," Jeanne said.

"Someone at the coffee company where she worked told police she had asked about making a will before she left."

"She also talked about a will when she found out she was pregnant. It doesn't mean anything."

"How can we be sure of that?"

"I don't even know why I'm talking to you," Jeanne

said, "you're just an arm of the British government."
Ryan had heard it all before.

"Why are you upset, Jeanne? We're trying to help
you."

She held back her temper, but from then on she said
as little as possible until the two agents gave up. When
she returned to Indian Hill Road she called a friend of
hers, attorney Jerome Boyle.

Like Jeanne, Boyle had become interested in the Irish
cause through the appearances of the late Sean
McBride, the 1974 Nobel Peace Prize winner. McBride
had been a foreign minister for the Irish Free State and
felt the only way to stop violence in the North would be
to end economic inequalities and the widescale practice
of favoring Protestants in jobs.

Boyle, a tall and thin man, had a gift that made many
Irish-Americans adept as politicians and coaches. He
could guess the enemy's game plan. "It's an old tech-
nique," he told Jeanne about the purported threat. "It's
used in Ireland all the time. They must be thinking,
Here's a sweet girl trying to do some do-gooder works,
and if you push her she's going to fall apart."

"They want me to name my contacts."

"That's it, and then they'll put the pressure on those
people. They're just using what happened to get at you.
Don't tell them anything. And, Jeanne, if you feel ready
to fold, hold on a little longer and talk to me or somebody else about it."

Later that Saturday, Winnetka police and the two FBI
agents asked Lee and Joyce to come to the station. The
agents outlined their theory and told them their daughter was obstructing the investigation. Joyce, holding
onto her husband's arm, looked into the faces of the
two agents and said, "If our daughter won't speak with
you, neither will we."

After they left, one of the policemen wrote in his
supplemental report that it was apparent Jeanne's "po-

litical beliefs are more important than identifying the Offender/s."

Jeanne and Boyle discussed the murders over the weekend. Boyle scoffed at the theories of a professional hit just because of the handcuffs and the fact that the townhouse was near the train station. If the killers were high-paid hitmen, they certainly would arrive by car rather than be seen by dozens of people on a train.

"Then who do you think did it?" Jeanne asked.

"Some kid," Boyle answered to her surprise. "Yeah, some local teenager, that's all."

On Monday, Boyle accompanied Jeanne to the station for a second meeting with the FBI agents. This time Jeanne answered only in brief sentences. Annoyed, Ryan said at last, "You want to solve the killings, don't you? All we want is to know the people you talked to on your last trip, so we can run down this threat."

"You've got the informants," she said, "talk to them."

"Look, maybe the threat is bogus, but we won't know for sure unless we track it down. Do you know how it's going to look when police say you aren't cooperating?"

"I am cooperating. I'll tell you everything about my trips, and I'll let you have my passport, but I'm not going to name the people I met."

Boyle stepped into the pause. "I believe my client has said everything she cares to. If you want to speak to her again, we would appreciate it if you contacted me first." As they rose to leave, Boyle turned to Ryan and added, "Howie, I think it goes without saying that I don't want to see on the TV news tonight, 'IRA implicated in the Winnetka killings; sister refuses to cooperate.'"

"Of course not," the FBI agent said. "That violates all our rules and procedures. We would never do that."

And they didn't, but Jeanne was still distrustful. She warned her family that they might be under surveillance for awhile. Then, at Boyle's suggestion, she filed Free-dom of Information requests at the FBI offices wher-ever she spoke against the British mistreatment of prisoners and convictions based solely on "super-grass" (informant) testimony.

By Thursday of the second week, police agreed among themselves that they had gone as far as the physical evidence could take them and that now was the time to smoke out anyone who was hiding some-thing. That meant unveiling their most dramatic piece of evidence.

One of the officers "leaked" to a reporter that Nancy had left a message in her blood. When Timm was asked for confirmation, the carefully groomed police chief said two of the letters were decipherable and that the private crime lab was magnifying the third to check it against Nancy's handwriting.

"It appears she was trying to tell us something," Timm added. "It's possible she was trying to leave someone's initials. It's a piece of the puzzle, and we want to see how it fits in."

The newspeople took that to mean police were close to an arrest. What Timm really said in police doubletalk was that the task force had reached a blank wall. Not one of the three letters or drawings was clear. A blowup photograph of Nancy's message was hanging in the task-room office as a daily reminder of how far the de-tectives really were from cracking the case.

Monday, April 23

The local FBI office received Jeanne's Freedom of Information form on Monday morning, April 23. Within hours, reporter Carol Marin of the local NBC station called Chief Timm about Jeanne and the IRA.

Oh, no, he thought. For the first time, he was at a loss for words. After a pause, Timm said into the receiver, "Before you put anything on the air, I want to talk to you. But not over the phone."

All this did was give Timm some thinking time. In the afternoon, Kalvaitis said this wouldn't be one of those items heard at 10 P.M. and forgotten by 7 A.M.; the news would be picked up by papers in all countries with a large Irish population, from Canada to New Zealand. Gene even warned him that letting the lead out now could undo everything his task force had gained so far.

Timm phoned the FBI, and Ryan exclaimed, "Jesus Christ, this can't come out!" The agent said the police could not possibly know what was at stake. He hinted that disclosing the theory could endanger some useful people in Chicago and New York as well as in Ireland itself.

"You don't have to tell me," Timm said, understanding the fragile network of informants any law-enforcement agency needs. He also felt the Langert case was now at a critical stage because of the recent disclosure about Nancy's writing in blood. Anyone thinking about coming forward now might suddenly think twice.

A little before six that evening, Timm and Lieutenant Sumner arrived at the WMAQ studio in downtown Chicago. Carol Marin, a red-headed woman in her early forties, led the officers to a side room where the producer and executive producer were waiting for them. After outlining what she knew about Jeanne's visits to Doherty, she said, "I also know that one possibility about the message on the shelf is that it spells IRA."

"Please don't air this," the police chief requested in his usual monotone. "We have reasons for asking you not to say anything about this part of the investigation, because it's very, very sensitive at this particular time."

"Well let me tell you something," Marin said. "The word is on the street, and if I say it or not, somebody's going to come out with it. Now, I want to know how this information was leaked."

"You're asking me?"

"Do you think it was the FBI?"

"That's something I can tell you right now," Timm said, "absolutely no. The FBI wants no part of this coming out. They are as concerned as we are."

"Then you are confirming what we have?"

"Your information is pretty good."

"Would you care to clarify some things?"

Timm shook his head and stood up. "I'm not going to give you any more," he said, and left with Sumner.

There was nothing they could do but return to Winnetka and wait for another round of calls from reporters asking for confirmation and elaboration. That had happened when the news broke about the mob connection, the drug connection, and the disclosure of Nancy's cryptic message.

As Kalvaitis feared, the IRA story made international news. The next day Joyce Bishop, poised as ever, strode into Timm's office with a framed picture from her home on Indian Hill Road. "I want to show you something," she said.

"Mrs. Bishop—"

"Please, I'm Joyce. All this stuff on the news isn't going to bring them back. *We'll* remember them."

"Okay, Joyce. You know, I apologize for this coverage. It's very unpleasant for both of us. We couldn't downplay the Irish aspect because the FBI thinks there's something to it."

"The story is preposterous, and you know it," she said.

"Well, it's the lead they have to follow."

She put the photo on the police chief's desk. "Look at their faces," Joyce said. "It's not about the mob or the IRA. It's about love, that's what it's all about. It's about the love of this girl."

She snatched the picture back and went out through the door.

Upon reflection, Timm thought that perhaps the Bishops were right, maybe they were hitting the IRA factor too hard. Kalvaitis had been asking for authority to let his men investigate the possibility on their own, and Timm thought now was time to give him a flat no.

"Gene," he told the sergeant, "I have a feeling you've become more concerned with Jeanne Bishop than with Richard and Nancy. Let's drop it for now, and let the FBI do what they want. You're in charge of this investigation, but I don't want you to forget who's in charge of this department."

"I understand," Kalvaitis replied and left smoldering.

Gene was so angry that he stared straight ahead and punched the cinder-block wall with the side of his fist as he passed by. He didn't even feel the pain. When he entered the task-force room, he shoved a metal chair against the table and shouted a "Damn it!" that could be heard throughout the station.

Timm heard the slamming and banging downstairs and decided to put a stop to it. He called Gene on the phone. "Look, I understand," the police chief said. "Jeanne Bishop is a very strong person. But that doesn't mean you have to blow this out of proportion. Until we get something more definite, this is just one aspect of the case."

The other officers could see that Gene needed to cool down. About ten of them took him to a Bennigan's restaurant in Northbrook and, as a joke, told the staff it was his birthday. At the end of the dinner, the waiter came out with a cake adorned with a candle, and the officers sang "Happy Birthday" through their laughter.

Jeanne's toughness was covering how upset she really was. One day she found herself following a young woman for blocks down Monroe Street in Chicago's

Loop, hoping the stranger wouldn't turn around and break the illusion of seeing Nancy one more time.

Jeanne continued working at her law office in the skyscraper canyon of LaSalle Street and attending functions at the stately Fourth Presbyterian Church a few blocks from her Near North Side home. She also frequently attended meetings in the Chicago Irish community. Every session drew a mixed group of the well dressed, blue-collar workers, a few radicals, and what Boyle called "a lot of old ladies in sneakers."

Everywhere else Jeanne went, there was the tension of suspicion. She took a week off when her boss said the staff was afraid about terrorist letter bombs. As she was preparing for an August tour of Britain with her church choir, the director asked her to book a separate plane because another member was afraid of getting hurt from an assassination attempt.

Through the Freedom of Information Act, Jeanne learned that despite what the FBI had told her, the Boston office had been keeping a dossier on her since 1986. United States Customs alone had 130 pages of reports about her. Yet nothing in all those documents indicated that she had ever done anything illegal, or that her sister's murder could be connected to her activities.

Sergeant Kalvaitis felt certain the murders were connected to Northern Ireland, but he had no idea what the federal agents had gathered. The only thing the FBI ever gave police was a typewritten text of the supposed November 1 threat on Jeanne's life. On a day when Gene couldn't contain himself, he went to Timm's office and thrashed the matter out with him.

"Look, Herb, the FBI is mainly interested in Jeanne's contact," Gene said. "They're not helping us one bit. Don't you think we should dig up what we can on our own?"

At last Timm relented, if only because the IRA connection was the only motive that remained. "Okay,

Gene, work that until you can't work it any more. Then come back to me and we'll figure out what to do next."

The hard part, Kalvaitis knew, would be overcoming suspicions that the police might be acting on behalf of the FBI. The federal government had stepped up its infiltration into the local Irish community when postal workers at a Dublin sorting station noticed in July 1986 that some mail-order merchandise from Chicago was slightly water damaged. They opened the box and found seven .357 Magnums and a Barretta M-82 sniper rifle capable of destroying aircraft and armored support vehicles.

Not knowing how else to start, Gene assigned two Irish members of the task force to see whether this was a blind alley or not. Kevin Keel, a slender man with close-cut auburn hair, set everything up by calling all Irish organizations to see who might be willing to talk. Then he and Fay made their first stop at Shamrock Imports in the bungalow belt of Chicago's Northwest Side.

The officers gave a casual glance at the shelves of dolls in Irish folk costumes and tins of wafers as Maureen O'Looney looked at them from behind the counter.

"Good morning to you," she greeted in her gentle brogue over a traditional Irish music recording. O'Looney had been part of the Irish conflict ever since her childhood in the 1930s, when British soldiers raided her family's cottage and tore up floorboards in search of guns. Eventually the British killed her father, but Maureen couldn't carry on his belief in violence as a solution.

O'Looney knew why the officers were there. Everyone in the Irish community knew about the murders. "Jeanne is a very fine woman," O'Looney said. "Though she's a Protestant, I'd vouch for her. Why should the IRA want to kill her or her sister, and like that? It would put them in disgrace, it would."

One of the regular customers called out, "Tell them about the threat you got."

"That was years ago," she said.

"Not so long ago," the regular replied, and continued browsing through Irish newspapers.

"I was told they were out to get me," O'Looney said. "I'm not sayin' there wasn't any threat, just that there wasn't anything to it."

"What about those rallies Jeanne goes to?" Keel asked.

"In Chicago you mean? You can call them rallies; they are get-togethers to let everybody know what is going on in Ireland. That's the only way. You can't believe what you read in the Irish papers and hear on the radio, the British control that too. Jeanne tells us exactly what is happening and keeps our spirits up."

"Do you know anything about that shipment of guns from Chicago a few years ago?" asked Fay.

"Do you think I would?" she asked with a smile. "I'm a bit smarter than my age."

"Hasn't there been any trouble, then?" Keel asked.

"My car was broken into, and things taken, you can call that trouble," O'Looney replied. "It's *Mike Haggerty and his people. He's spying for them." She meant Haggerty was working for the FBI, or maybe the CIA. "They talk to me, what do I care, but you can't trust them."

The officers found O'Looney congenial, but not very helpful. Later they spoke to Mike Morley, who ran a local cable television show on Irish news. Jeanne had been on his program a couple of times. He told the detectives that she was "committed and levelheaded, and certainly not fanatical."

The officers also went to a couple of Northwest Side Irish bars, including *Mead's. This nondescript building was one of the places where the FBI kept a watch because a few patrons were suspected of involvement in Irish deals. Haggerty occasionally went there, but his appearance made some people draw to the other side of the bar as if he were contagious.

Fay and Keel came to feel that Haggerty might really be part of some illegal activity for a government agency—until an Irish lawyer set them straight. A few years ago, the lawyer said, the FBI told Haggerty that a threat had been made on his life. Terrified, he named names. When Haggerty won election as head of an Irish-American group, the loser spread the word that Haggerty was an informant not only for the FBI but the CIA. From then on any time there was a burglary, theft, or beating in the community, people like Maureen O'Looney blamed it on Haggerty.

Whether that was true or not, Fay and Keel felt getting Haggerty to open up was their best hope. After the civil engineer hung up on them, the officers decided to drive out to his home. With their auto creeping through rush-hour traffic, Keel punched Haggerty's number on his car phone. The detective spent fifteen minutes wearing him down before he agreed to talk with them about his activities for the cause.

Haggerty lived with a stewardess in a gorgeous apartment in the Gold Coast, less than a mile from the Loop. When the officers arrived, he turned on his personal computer, fed it disks, and let them scan all the information. Just as Keel and Fay had suspected, there were no secret IRA contacts. No secret plans. No conspiracies. The officers might as well be looking at the minutes of a P.T.A. meeting.

12

"The Answer Is Here Somewhere"

May 3–June 28

ONE NIGHT IN early May, Detective John Fay kissed his wife, Annie, as she lay sleeping. A thought jolted him before he realized what it was. With the shadows falling on Annie's face and her mouth partly opened, she looked like the body of Nancy Langert lying on the basement floor.

John was the rookie of the task force. The Glencoe juvenile investigations officer was used to jobs such as looking for clues in Nancy's New Trier High School yearbooks and working on the "spaghetti bowl" of telephone records.

His clowning around at the task-force meetings was just a way of not showing how deeply affected he was. The former seminarian was troubled by the case as well as by some of the tensions in the Winnetka department, and not only between Kalvaitis and Chief Timm.

Patty McConnell had returned from Russia two weeks after the murders and knew that bad feelings would result if she took over the investigation in midstream. Timm sat down with McConnell on her first day back and said she could play an important role by handling other cases that needed follow-ups.

McConnell didn't go into the task-force office during briefings or when the members returned in the late afternoons. Instead, she would drop by when Kalvaitis was alone with the silent phones, and he would let her read the latest reports. She also helped out in a couple of minor interviews.

Timm had been down to the task-force office only a few times. He would look at the "tree" of names, the motive notations, and the blown-up photo of the message in blood. Once, he said half to himself, "The answer is here somewhere."

With all the manpower anyone could ask for, Timm let his officers run down whatever lead that crossed their minds. Detective John Graham checked up on a rash of burglaries at upper-income-bracket homes near forest preserves and railroad tracks in nearby suburbs, but those thieves never resorted to violence.

Benoit teamed up with Ed Reynolds to find out if any other couples had been murdered under similar circumstances in the last few years. The officers went to Ottawa County, Michigan, and looked over the files on the 1987 killings of Ricky and Gail Brink. The officers were struck by the uncanny similarities. The Brinks were shot to death when they returned home from a party on a Saturday night. Gail even resembled Nancy, with a triangular face ending in a strong chin, and Ricky was a large man who, like Richard, "wouldn't hurt a fly."

In addition, the Brinks had been married a year and a half, and they had moved into the home near Holland, Michigan, only about a month before they were killed. There was no apparent motive, and to Benoit it seemed as if someone just wanted to kill two young people because they looked happy.

When that trip led to nothing, Reynolds dusted off his "jilted lover" theory, based on nothing more than the fact that the Langerts' marriage contract had been left out in the open instead of in the storage box where it usually was kept. For awhile, Reynolds even thought he was on the killer's trail.

When he and Benoit went to the Bess Hardware Store to trace the handcuffs found on Richard, they were told that a strange young man had bought two pairs about a week after the killings. He was described as tall, thin, in his mid-twenties, and dressed in black. Strangest of all, once he bought the handcuffs he played with them in his car for a few minutes before driving off.

But the more Reynolds thought about it, the less he believed in his own theory. Why would a killer buy handcuffs a week after the murders? Reynolds dismissed the stranger as some disturbed person fantasizing he was a killer. Just a harmless kook.

For a few days some detectives thought Reynolds's "jilted lover" idea might be right. This came after Fay and Keel went to the northern suburbs to reinterview a woman who had stood up at Nancy's wedding. The third-grade teacher noticed the officers in the hallway as she was wiping chalk from the blackboard. The detectives came in, sat on children's desks, and asked if there might be something she hadn't told them the first time around. The teacher looked away and told them softly, "I don't want to betray Nancy's memory."

"There was a lover, wasn't there?" Keel asked.

"There was, but he was nothing to her."

The young teacher explained that the affair with *Jeff Mozer occurred when Richard still worked nights. Mozer had been a well-paid salesman at the veneer company where Nancy was working, and he was involved in community theater with her. The affair supposedly had been over for a year.

The detectives dug into Jeff's background and learned that he had taken a plane to Georgia just two days after the bodies were found. On May 9, Fay and Keel landed at the small airport in Brunswick, Georgia, and drove a rented car across the causeway to St. Simons Island. Mozer was helping his family establish a fastener business in the lush country of Spanish moss and palmetto palms.

Jeff was gangly, had glasses, and was not particularly good looking. "I was expecting to hear from you guys," he said as he walked toward their car, "but I didn't think you'd come all the way down here."

"We just want to talk to you privately," Keel said, and opened the door.

They drove him to the sheriff's office in Brunswick, where he behaved as guilty as any killer. Jeff kept rocking in his chair to work off his nervousness. "I know it looks suspicious, me leaving just a couple of days afterward," he said, "but I didn't do it. I don't know anything about it."

"We didn't say you did," Keel assured him.

"My moving down here was planned weeks in advance. Ask anybody."

After the officers calmed him down, Jeff said he and Nancy had gone to bed four or five times, always when Richard was away and she was lonely. Perhaps Jeff's not being attractive made it easier for her, the officers thought. She wouldn't have to worry about feeling emotionally unfaithful to her husband.

"Did you love her?" asked Keel.

"What would have been the point? I was a port in the storm, just someone to talk to." The parting was amicable. Jeff said Nancy ended the relationship, apparently so she could go on with her life.

The officers had no reason to doubt Jeff. There was nothing to do but thank him and take him back to his factory. After he was gone, Keel laughed and said, "That guy was as nervous as a whore in a church on Sunday."

When Sergeant Kalvaitis saw a chance to return to field work after weeks of investigating by phone and supervising reports, he took it. The task force felt that

someone should see what could be learned from
Jeanne's former husband, Dr. Louis Clarizio. Gene and
Detective Robert Kerner flew to New Hampshire and
met him in a hotel lobby.

Clarizio, a good-looking man in his middle thirties,
felt he had to be cautious with all this talk of mobsters,
drug smugglers, and Irish assassins. He studied their
badges and police identification before saying, "Okay,
let's talk."

Over coffee in the doctor's large condominium, he let
the officers go over eight albums of photos Jeanne had
left behind. "Take what you want," he said, "I don't
want to look through them." Clarizio still seemed to be
in love with her.

As the officers were going over the snapshots,
Clarizio asked, "Would you like to see her diary?" That
drew their attention. "In her rush to get out, Jeanne left
her journal here. She made such a fuss about it in the
divorce proceedings my lawyer had me make a copy."

Kalvaitis glanced over the seventy-five photocopied
pages detailing Jeanne's visits to Ireland. Yes, this in-
deed was something they wanted to take back with
them.

The officers thanked Clarizio and drove to their hotel, thinking all the time that they had struck gold. They
studied the journal that night and saw mentions of safe
houses and people who were killed, sometimes with explanations. Suppose Nancy had a similar journal of her
sister's somewhere in all those boxes in the townhouse,
or the killer just thought it might be there . . .

On their way back to Illinois, the officers rented a car
between flights and went to the Philadelphia-area home
of Rachel Hoffman, who had founded Protestants for
Truth About Northern Ireland and was close to Jeanne.
Since the woman had agreed by phone to give them an
interview, Kalvaitis made a mental list of questions as
he drove. Hoffman answered the door and, without a
word, handed them a card stating, "If you want to talk

to me you have to contact my attorney." She closed the door on them.

The two men stood stunned with their badges still in their hands. As they walked back to their car, Kalvaitis muttered "Damn it!" and kicked the dirt.

The task force they returned to was slowly losing its enthusiasm. Some of the detectives felt that the scatter-shot method of approaching any case never worked. "You start to have blinders," one of them said. "Every group has got their little investigation going and thinks that this has to be the key."

The officers by now had run down all the news-making speculation, and there remained the remote pos-sibility that the motive lay in the life of Nancy's eldest sister. Fay and Keel drove south of Chicago to inter-view Jennifer and her husband, Malcolm Jones, in their farmhouse near Kankakee.

Malcolm was an imposing man, not tall but with a red-bearded muscular beefiness and an aura of pent-up energy. Sitting on the couch, he and Jennifer described how they met and Fay asked Malcolm to describe his marital problems. "We've been told there were argu-ments," Fay added.

Malcolm looked at his wife and replied, "Various verbal disputes. We are in marriage counseling."

"Did you ever strike your first wife or Jennifer?"

"No, never." But a source had described the marriage as "explosive."

"You shot a gun, didn't you?" Keel asked.

That was a sore point for both of them. Malcolm, whose brother was a police dispatcher, wasn't allowed to complete a course to become a policeman because he had fired a revolver during one of his quarrels with his wife.

"I didn't fire at her," Malcolm said. "I fired just to scare her. We were in the garage. I got the gun back from the police and no charges were filed. It was a Smith & Wesson Model 66. .38 caliber." He stressed that fact, since the newspapers had said the murder weapon was a .357 Magnum.

"What happened to the gun?"

"I gave it back to my brother after the murders. I just didn't want it around the house anymore."

"Why not?"

The powerfully built man paused and said, "Nightmares."

After the interview, police had to track down the gun. Malcolm had given it to his brother who, in turn, sold it to a policeman in Indiana. The Winnetka police had to issue a subpoena for the weapon to be tested at the Northern Illinois Police Crime Laboratory. As expected, the bullet fired into a test tank didn't match the slugs recovered from the bodies.

But Bob Wilson of the crime lab was excited about something else. After weeks of studying the photos in his cramped office surrounded by guns and microscopes, he concluded that Nancy had been shot only twice. He drove to the Winnetka station and went over his theory with Chief Timm and Kalvaitis, demonstrating how Nancy might have been standing for the bullet to go through her elbow and then into her abdomen.

Police now had a piece of information only the killer would know. "All the papers say she was shot three times," Timm told Gene. "I think we should keep it that way."

The case was eating away at Chief Timm as he saw the task-force members coming back with less information every day. He trusted Kalvaitis, but he wanted an outside opinion. Without notifying Gene, he called in a homicide expert he knew to look over hundreds of pages of reports. The expert came away saying the task force had done everything it could, and that he couldn't make any recommendations for what to do next.

In the final week of May, Kalvaitis decided to invite all the Bishops to the station, including Jennifer and her

Nancy and Richard Langert in 1989.

Left to right: Winnetka Police Chief Herbert Timm, Lieutenant Sumner and Sergeant Gene Kalvaitis.
(Photo by Sharon White)

Left to right: In the Task Force office: Eddie Benoit, Sergeant Gene Kalvaitis, John Fay, and Bill Brotman.
(Photo by Sharon White)

Detective Sergeant Patricia "Patty" McConnell walking along the railroad tracks behind the townhouse where Nancy and Richard Langert were murdered.   *(Photo by Sharon White)*

The back patio entrance of the townhouse at 722 Oak Street where the killer entered and waited for Nancy and Richard.

(Photo by Sharon White)

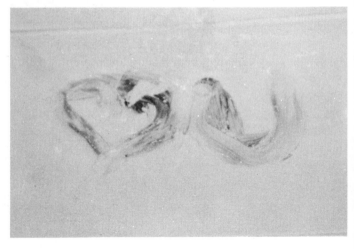

Nancy's final message scrawled in blood as she lay dying.

(Photo by Sharon White)

The gun that killed Nancy and Richard Langert.

(Photo by Sharon White)

Ballistic expert Bob Wilson of the Northern Illinois Crime Laboratory.

(Photo by Sharon White)

The Biro home at 765 Willow Road in Winnetka, Illinois. David's room is on the third floor. *(Photo by Sharon White)*

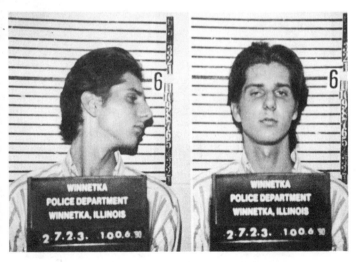

David Biro's mug shot at the time of his arrest.
(Winnetka Police Department Photo)

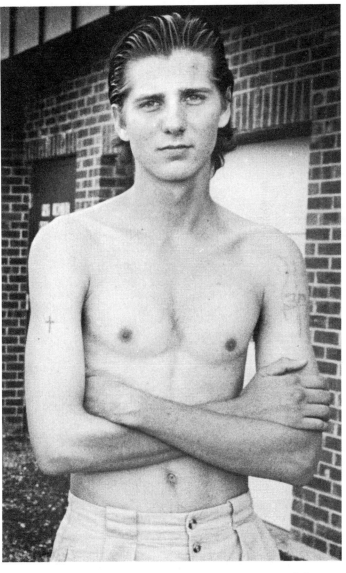

David Biro photographed in September 1990, as part of the New Trier Cross Country Track Team.

(Photo by Geoff Scheerer/Pioneer Press)

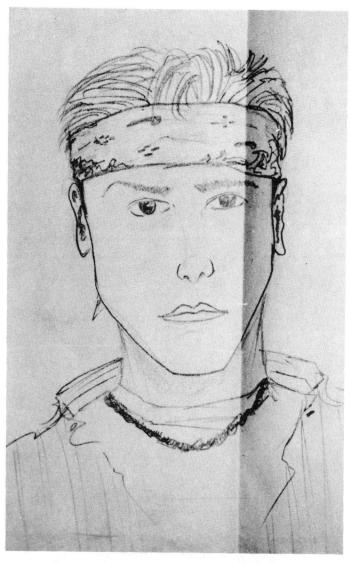

Self-portrait drawn by David Biro in May 1990.
(Photo by Sharon White)

Letter found in David Biro's red notebook, which reads in conclusion: "My name is Cain and I kill people."

(Photo by Sharon White)

Winnetka slaying seen as a 'professional hit'

By Gary Wisby and Jim Casey

The baffling murder of a young couple in a Winnetka town house has "the earmarks of a professional hit," police said Monday.

"It appears the offenders went there to do what they did," said Winnetka Police Lt. Joseph Sumner. But police said they did not know of a possible motive in the first double slaying ever in the affluent North Shore suburb.

Richard Langert, 30, and his pregnant wife, Nancy, 25, were shot to death Saturday night, apparently just after returning home from dinner at a Chicago restaurant. But police said they doubt the couple died as the result of interrupting a burglar or burglars at work.

Sumner said he was forming a task force made up of other investigators from suburban police departments including Glenview, Northbrook, Deerfield and Wilmette and may seek assistance from the Evanston Police Department.

If it is determined that professional gunmen were involved, Sumner said, he will seek assistance from the FBI and the Bureau of Alcohol, Tobacco and Firearms.

The parents of both victims declined to talk to reporters about the murders and referred all questions to the Winnetka Police Department.

Neighbors of the families also were reluctant to talk. One neighbor of Richard Langert's parents in southwest suburban Oak Lawn said, "I don't know why anybody would want to kill him. . . . He was a fine boy."

Police all but ruled out burglary

Monday. Nothing was believed to have been taken. That included several hundred dollars in $20 bills and $50 bills torn from an envelope in Nancy Langert's purse.

Also, the home invaders, who entered by smashing through a double pane rear patio door, could see from outdoors that the living room contained nothing but a television, VCR and a chair, Sumner said. The couple was living there temporarily and had not hung any drapes. The lieutenant also noted that burglars seldom carry guns or kill their victims.

Police searched the Langerts' town house, at 722 Oak St., with a police dog trained to sniff out narcotics but found nothing.

The Cook County medical examiner's office said Richard Langert was

Turn to Page 10

Slaying

Continued from Page 1

shot once in the head and Nancy Langert was shot twice in the torso and once in the arm. An autopsy also revealed she was two months pregnant.

The woman was found lying on her coat, indicating the couple had just returned home. The bodies were in the basement. Police said the Langerts may have been led there to cover the sound of shots.

One Oak Street neighbor reported hearing something large fall, along with loud voices, but assumed it was noise from a television. Sumner said a shelving unit was knocked over, possibly by one of the victims after being shot.

Another neighbor said he thought he heard two firecrackers go off, the other said. But police Saturday took several complaints about youngsters playing with fireworks.

The bodies were found Sunday by Nancy Langert's parents, M. Lee Bishop, 60, a Winnetka lawyer, and Joyce Bishop. The two couples had dined together Saturday on the North Side.

The Bishops, who live on exclusive Indian Hill Road, recently bought the town house with the

idea of moving. The Langerts had lived there less than a month, using it as a base while looking for a house to buy or rent in Mount Prospect or Arlington Heights, police said.

Many of the couple's belongings were still in boxes.

Both worked at the Arlington Heights headquarters of Gloria Jean's Coffee Bean Inc., a chain store operation. Nancy, employed for a year, worked in the franchise sales office. Richard, who began working there six months ago, was in charge of manufacturing at one of the company's two warehouses.

Owners Ed and Gloria Jean Kvetko offered a $10,000 reward for information leading to the arrest and conviction of those responsible. "Both [Langerts] were excellent workers, plus they were very, very good friends," said a company spokesman.

Richard Langert had worked for 10 years for Saratoga Specialties Co., a chemical and spice manufacturer. Don Knaus, general manager of the chemical division, said Langert "stopped in a week ago" to pick up some material and "everything was looking good. He was positive and upbeat."

Police asked anyone with information to call the investigators' hotline at (708) 446-0136.

Contributing: Art Petacque, Lou Ortiz and Lynn Sweet.

Police have not found a motive for the double murder of Richard Langert, 30, and his pregnant wife, Nancy, 25, in their Winnetka home Saturday night.

The slaying has baffled police, and also friends and co-workers of the Langerts, who said the couple appeared to have everything going for them.

American dream

Page from David Biro's red notebook with newspaper clips claiming the Langert murders a "professional hit."

(Photo by Sharon White)

Joyce and Jeanne Bishop walk in front of Malcolm Jones and his wife Jennifer at the Chicago courthouse during a break in the trial.   *(Photo by Sharon White)*

Lee Bishop, Nancy's father, entering the courthouse during the trial.   *(Photo by Sharon White)*

Robert and Deloris Langert, Richard's parents, at the courthouse at 26th Street and California in Chicago.

(Photo by Sharon White)

Defense attorney
James Kissel
walks with Joan
Biro as Nicholas
Biro follows them
during a break
in court.
*(Photo by
Sharon White)*

In this courtroom sketch, David Biro watches Phu Huang, his classmate at New Trier High School, testify as the prosecution's key witness at the trial. *(Artist sketch by Marcia Danits)*

Defense attorneys Robert Gevirtz and Dennis Born.

(Photo by Sharon White)

Cook County Assistant State's Attorneys Anthony Calabrese and Patrick O'Brien after the Suppression Hearings.

(Photo by Sharon White)

Attorney John Corbett *(left)* and Victoria Vhrel *(right)* of Corbett & Matthews in Chicago are joined by Jeanne Bishop in announcing a $10 million lawsuit brought by the Bishops against the Biro family and their attorney John Lewis.

(Photo by Sharon White)

The tombstone marking Nancy and Richard Langert's grave at Kenilworth Union Church. *(Photo by Sharon White)*

husband. Lee led his family into the station, hoping for some kind of news from the police. Lee had been in the marine reserve in the 1950s, and his friends knew that something had died within him when he realized he couldn't protect his family. "There's some part missing when you talk to him," one of them said.

As he took a seat in the office, Lee fumbled for a pen and told Gene and Lieutenant Sumner, "I want you to issue a press statement saying that no one was involved in any illegal activity, and Nancy and Richard were just victims of a senseless crime. I want you to clear their name."

"Well, we can't really make that kind of guarantee," Sumner said.

"You're the ones who said it could be the Mafia, the IRA, and drugs. You have to say so everybody knows it's not true."

"But we don't know, Mr. Bishop," Sumner replied. "We have no idea what's going on yet."

"Miss Bishop," Kalvaitis said to Jeanne, "if you can give us just a little more information about your activities. Look at it from my perspective. Don't you find it ironic that you get this threat not to go back to Ireland, then you go there and come back, and it's only a matter of forty-eight hours and this happens?"

"I don't feel any of that is relevant at this point," Jeanne answered.

"We're only a police department. We can't go into your activities outside this country."

"But you will turn over names that I might give you."

"Yes, there are certain agencies I go to, to check up on the names. It's not because I want to, it's a matter of investigation procedures."

Jeanne returned his glance with a glare, and her mother sat with that odd expression of hers, listening carefully and yet seeming to block out everything being said. Seeing that her daughter would not comment, Joyce told the officers, "No, we won't do it."

As the family was leaving, Jeanne told the officers that "maybe six, seven months down the road, you'll find out it was some drug addict or a kid that got scared and killed them."

Sergeant Kalvaitis, still angry over Jeanne's refusal to answer questions, remained certain that the murders had their roots in Northern Ireland. In late May he and Lieutenant Sumner drove to the modern courthouse in north suburban Skokie for a meeting with Larry Lykowski of the state's attorney's office. Kalvaitis had a list of ten people he wanted called before a grand jury, including the Bishop family, acquaintances of Jeanne, and business associates of Lee. Some of the questions he wanted asked involved certain killings in Ireland by the IRA.

"None of these are suspects?" Lykowski asked, just to make sure he understood.

"No, we don't have any suspects."

The prosecutor with bushy brown hair sat back and gave the list a little thought. Then he sat up straight, and Gene sensed what the answer would be.

"A grand jury—you want all the Bishops to give names in front of a grand jury? Gene, think it over. We call Jeanne to the stand. What is she going to say? She's going to take the Fifth Amendment, and where would you be then? Don't you see the press would have a field day? Look what happened when that IRA rumor broke."

"I never leaked anything to the media, so don't blame that on me," Kalvaitis said. "Well, can we do it?"

"You're the one who knows the status of the case. All I can say is that we can't just subpoena people without probable cause."

"Look, I have two people murdered and an unborn

infant. I've personally spent hundreds of hours on this case, and nothing's come up. Are you telling me we have to drop everything?"

Lieutenant Sumner jumped up and took Kalvaitis's arm before Gene could say anything more. The Kalvaitis temper was known to shift from park into high gear. "Okay, Larry," Sumner said. "We're going now. And Larry, please see what you can do about our request."

Sumner knew very well what Lykowski would do with it, but he needed a way to keep Kalvaitis quiet until they were out of the office.

In the hallway, Gene's face reddened and he flung out his hands. "Politics!" he yelled. "Cover your ass, that's the name of the game. The hell with solving a triple murder." Sumner quickly led him to the escalator.

May 30

Chief Herbert Timm's seventeen-year-old daughter was getting ready for her morning workout. As head of the cross-country track team, Beth ran a mile or more with other New Trier High School students from seven to eight every morning. While getting dressed, arranging her hair, and having breakfast, she would tell her father about problems at school and whatever else crossed her mind.

"We took a shortcut from Cherry to Oak yesterday and we ran past that house," the girl said. "I felt so creepy! Dad? Kids on the team are asking me if you'll ever solve the murder."

Timm wished she hadn't mentioned that, but he had already made up his mind about what to do with the case. Or maybe he had made the decision some time ago, and it was lying around his brain waiting for a pretext.

What other police department in the country would go to such great lengths as his men had? The much-publicized hotline on the case had received only six calls. The task-force phone bill alone looked like a departmental budget, including calls to Scotland Yard in hopes that the British police had something on Jeanne, and to the Taiwan National Police in a futile request about tracing the handcuffs.

The police chief kept thinking of the newlywed photo Joyce Bishop had thrust in front of him a few weeks before. He wasn't ready to concede that the killer had outsmarted the police, but the time had come to close the books. He drove to the station that clear morning, hung up his suit coat, and called Kalvaitis into his office.

"Gene, you did a hell of a great job on the Langert murders," he began. "I couldn't ask for anything better than the way you organized everything and kept it running. But there's no point keeping everyone tied up with this, is there? Let's send most of the outside detectives back to their departments. And now that it's summer, I'll need you back in uniform."

"On the beat," Kalvaitis said, discouraged.

"We'll bring in Patty, let her work on anything that might come in. After all, she's head of investigations. I'm not taking you off the case, you can work on it at any time; I'm just shifting your priorities. Nobody knows more than I do all the hours you put into this case. You've put off your fishing trip, why not take a vacation now? Just before you go off somewhere, meet with Patty and bring her up to date."

Kalvaitis walked by Patty McConnell's office almost in a daze. He looked in and was glad she wasn't there. He wanted to be the one to tell his men that they were closing up shop. Timm had told Gene not to take the decision personally, but he couldn't help it. Probably never again would he get to head another investigation as complex as this.

By 3 P.M., members of the task force started coming in from their sparse follow-ups. Fay knew something was wrong when he saw Gene shaking his head slightly up and down and from side to side in front of the chief.

"Well, today's the day," Gene told the men. Three of the officers who were typing reports looked up to make sure they had heard correctly. Some of the outside officers had "It's about time" expressions, and the rest looked crushed.

"I want to say thank all of you for everything," Kalvaitis continued. "I feel that we really are a family, and we could tackle anything. In this case, unfortunately, the killer might have come from anywhere and we did not receive all the cooperation we would like. We all feel like we know Nancy and Richard, and I don't want you to forget about them. When you go back to Northbrook and Glencoe and wherever you're from, when you work on a burglary or a shooting or anything with handcuffs, I want your minds thinking back to them, and I want you to keep asking yourself: is there a connection here? And if we get a break in Winnetka, believe me, I will call you guys back to help."

Timm held up his hands for attention and told the officers, "This case is not as difficult as we're making it out to be, I'm sure of it. These were average, honest people just trying to get a start in life. There's something more simple, more up-front that we're missing. But we'll solve it. The case is too big for someone not to talk about it."

A few hours after announcing the end of the task force, Timm had the duty of informing Robert and Delores Langert about the decision. Unlike the Bishops, the Langerts had called frequently over the last month to beg that the case be kept alive. "We lost our son, our daughter-in-law, and our grandchild," the white-haired accountant had said. "If there's ever any way we can help, just tell us."

That Saturday, Gene and Pam Kalvaitis threw a party for all the members of the disbanded task force. Just backyard burgers, hot dogs, and a lot of beer to say thanks and ease the drained feeling the officers had. When hail clattered against the house, everyone went downstairs to the bar the couple had just installed with Gene's overtime money. The officers and their wives sat on throw pillows and laughed over gag gifts. Their laughter was hollow.

Two weeks later, the Bishops did something that friends and even hardened police officers thought was incredible. Rather than selling the townhouse, Lee and Joyce completed the sale of their home on Indian Hill Road for $650,000 and moved into the scene of the murders. To them it didn't seem right to have a stranger live there.

Although a professional crew had just cleaned the house, Lee put on old clothes, filled a bucket with soap and hot water, and began mopping up the blood stains showing faintly through the gray basement floor. The trails of blood could still be seen.

III

"I Am Cain"

"A strange idea was pecking at his brain like a chicken in an egg, and very, very much absorbed him."

DOSTOYEVSKI, *CRIME AND PUNISHMENT*

13

Acting Out

JUST A FEW hundred feet from the other side of the railroad bridge was the home of Nick and Joan Biro. The
Biros and the Bishops were casual friends from the
days when Nick and Lee had worked at the same meat-
packing company. The Biros had three children. The eldest two, Michael and Nancy, were known around the
community and well liked. But their son David was one
of the town troublemakers.

The tall, lean teenager had found a job working at a
local ice-cream shop and became a friend of the owner,
*Kim Chee. The young Asian man liked the company
of teenage boys, and it was said he played long games
of Dungeons and Dragons with them.

Sometimes Chee took the teens to local restaurants,
and occasionally to Belmont and Sheffield avenues in
Chicago, where there was a subculture of punk rock
and the occult. David was intrigued enough to read
books like Crowley's *Magick in Theory & Practice* and
the *Necronomicon*.

In the summer of 1987, Officer Eddie Benoit received information that Chee might be selling alcohol
to minors, so he parked in an unmarked car near the
shop and watched Chee close for the night and climb
into a car that had three young men inside. David Biro

was among them. Benoit followed the car down Green Bay Road and called for the nearest marked unit to pull it over.

"What's wrong?" Chee asked. Officer Billy Caldwell looked in, noticed the three teens in the backseat, and saw what appeared to be opened wine coolers.

The ice-cream-shop owner climbed out of the auto and showed Caldwell his driver's license, but David said, "Hey, Kim, just get back in and let's get out of here. He's got no probable cause, he can't do anything. Come on."

Caldwell turned the flashlight beam into the back of the car. David was just another punk in a black coat thrown over a T-shirt and blue jeans. "You, shut up," the officer said.

"Shut up yourself," David replied.

"Okay, all of you out, out, and show me your IDs."

Watching from a distance as just two teens alighted, Benoit sensed trouble and called for backup.

"I said out," Caldwell told David.

"I know my rights," David said.

Benoit pulled up behind the squad car, and so did uniformed officer Glenn Florkow, one of the younger men in the department. Florkow opened the rear door and made a grab for David's shoulder. "I'm not getting out," the boy insisted. "You touch me and I'll sue."

Caldwell grabbed David anyway and pulled him through the door as Benoit had the two other boys place their hands flat against the car. David tried to wriggle free, but Florkow stopped him. In a moment, the two of them were struggling on the ground. The young officer put a knee against David's back and handcuffed his wrists behind him. Pulling him to his feet, Florkow routinely went through his coat pockets. "I got something," the officer said as he pulled out an eight-inch throwing knife.

"So?" asked David.

"Resisting arrest and now a concealed weapon."

The officers drove him to the station and brought him into an interrogation room. David, amused, sat in silence as the officers wrote out the arrest papers.

"How old are you?" Caldwell asked.

"Twenty-one."

"What's your name?"

"Billy Bonney," David said flatly.

"How do you spell that?" Florkow asked from behind the typewriter, not knowing that the real William Bonney was Billy the Kid and the gunfighter was killed when he was 21.

Sergeant Bill Gallagher came in and saw a familiar face. "What do we have here?" he asked.

"Mr. Bonney didn't want to get out of a car, and he had this." Florkow held up the knife.

"This kid is David Biro, and he's fourteen years old," Gallagher said. "Yes, fourteen. We got delinquency cards on him for two shootings with a BB gun."

Florkow pulled the Bonney report out of the typewriter and tore it up.

Coincidences put young David Biro and the Bishops together even though they never actually met. David was born in Oklahoma City at the time Nancy was in school there. Both his father and Lee worked at the Oklahoma office of the Chicago-based Wilson Food Company and were later transferred to the Dallas office. Lee was a corporate official, and Nick Biro reported to him as head of public relations.

Lee Bishop left Wilson in 1977 and set himself up as a private attorney in the Chicago area. Nick left Wilson to work first at the R.J. Reynolds tobacco company in Richmond, Virginia, and then with Holiday Inns in Memphis. But Nick, who was born in Chicago, wanted to settle down in the Midwest. He bought a home in Winnetka, the same suburb in which the Bishops were living.

That had been in 1981, when David was eight years

old. The Biros had a modest home on Cherry Street, at the east end of town. Nick was earning less now that he had left corporate work, and he was starting on the middle rung of a major Chicago public relations firm, Ruder and Finn. Still, he knew that he had the drive to advance.

Soon after moving to the North Shore, Nick Biro asked for Lee's help in handling some difficulties at his job. The next year, Joan Biro set up her own computer-leasing company in nearby Deerfield after being a housewife for more than thirteen years. For awhile, the Biros and the Bishops exchanged Christmas cards, and the Bishops asked Nick and Joan over to their parties. But that was the extent of their relationship. They had no friends in common and never saw each other at church since the Bishops were Protestants and the Biros were Catholic. David never met Nancy Bishop or her sisters.

The boy spent many late afternoons riding up and down the streets on his bike. He and another boy formed a pact to create a secret clubhouse where kids could get away from their families, and no one would find them. They decided to build it right under every-one's nose, at the Cherry Street bridge. But not being mining engineers, they didn't think of shoring up the walls with scantling, and the tunnel kept caving in.

David hadn't been a troublemaker when he was younger, but all that moving and the loss of his parents to their work was having an effect on him. Everyone was telling the Biros how smart and clean-cut Michael was, and about how levelheaded and pleasant Nancy Biro was. But David started acting up at school, be-came rebellious at home, and let his grades drop below what teachers felt was his potential. Joan had the boy go to the school counselor for two months, but not much changed. He continued having good periods and bad ones.

At Greeley Elementary School, most of David's fifth

grade classmates thought he was a "jerk all 'round." He didn't care for sports but decided to try football. Once, he was running after another player when an older student tripped him on the grass. As David stumbled, the other boys forgot the game and jumped on him, laughing at how easily he fell. David screamed in pain but they taunted him. "Crybaby, fall down," they said. "Quit faking, David. Get up!"

More than a year later, the family moved across the bridge to a white-gray stucco house. It was a bit larger and more comfortable.

With the change in schools, David resolved not to be victimized again. The twelve-year-old put a fake cast on his arm before he was picked up by the school bus. For a few hours instead of being pushed around and humiliated because he was the new boy at Washburne Junior High, he was the center of attention. By afternoon the other children ignored him, just as he had wanted.

When his mother found the homemade cast in his room, she threw it out. Some of the boys guessed the truth the next day, and David was ridiculed all over again. He became even more afraid to make friends. "I don't really know how to really get to know other kids my age," he said a couple of years later, "because I don't know what they'll think of me."

Uprooted and withdrawn, David masked his loneliness by making jokes at school about the common enemy—teachers—and became a regular visitor to the principal's office. His friends loved the way he would sneak out at any opportunity. They also found that they could set him up to do pranks they didn't have the courage to pull off themselves.

David liked being the center of attention in small groups, and occasionally he made a friend, usually someone who was considered a "nerd." One was Sofia, who was often picked on for being overweight. On a few summer evenings, David took her on his bike to the Tower Road Beach at the northeast end of town. There the sand is barely more than a curving ribbon at the foot of the bluff, and trees rise fifty feet along the steep slope. But David and Sofia were changing and, like all his friends, she eventually went her own way.

David had long ago stopped communicating with his family. His older brother was planning to go to Purdue and never involved himself much with David, his sister had her own friends, and his parents were always busy or unwinding from work.

Nick Biro was an outgoing man with snow-white hair and an often eager expression. He had a restless nature and considered himself a perfectionist. But whether from the permissive influence of the 1960s or some personal reasons, he adopted a hands-off approach to David. A school friend of David's said that this attitude is common among North Shore parents. She called it "shoving problems under the two-thousand-dollar carpet."

David's features clearly came from his mother, Joan. The trim, attractive woman was unconcerned that her hair was turning gray. She dressed in conservative clothes and tried to keep her home a structured environment despite David's attempts at unraveling it. She even drove home for lunch every day to make sure everything was all right.

Joan had a sharp, practical mind and disliked being the disciplinarian of the family, but her husband was never good at establishing limits. Each of them had been an only child, and they were not accustomed to the tactics children use for attention or getting their way.

If her younger son resented her absences, he never showed it. But he and his mother sometimes were seen in screaming matches outside their home, even though he seemed to love her.

When David was in seventh grade his fifteen-year-old brother suggested that David join him working backstage at the Children's Theater at the Winnetka Community House. David—still with braces and weighing just one hundred pounds—was in charge of the props until he was dismissed for smoking during a rehearsal. With David, nothing lasted long. His life was a series of hobbies picked up and soon forgotten.

In Washburne Junior High, David found math was a way to show his intelligence without relying on anyone else. David was also fascinated by the newly installed computers. He and another boy—Phu Huang—would master one program and immediately pester teachers about others.

Phu was one of the most serious students in the school. He had come to America at age two, and his father headed an international trade venture between companies in the United States and Japan.

Just the opposite was Burke Abrams, whom David was drawn to but didn't particularly like. Burke was two years older and more daring. While the Biro boy just gaped, Burke would chortle as he tore through traffic on his skateboard. David admired the way Burke laughed at danger.

Once, Burke bought a power slingshot and said it had more accuracy than David's air rifle. The husky older boy showed how it worked and aimed at a bird, then dared David to try. David clumsily put the shot in the rubber band, brought back the tension, and let go. A squirrel flipped out of a tree and struggled in the grass. David wanted to stop, but Burke kept chanting, "Kill it, kill it!" David picked up the slingshot and fired BB after BB at the squirrel, blinding the animal as it tried to crawl away.

When David was fourteen, he began having run-ins with a female teacher. In one fight, he called her a bitch. She later began receiving hang-up calls. The next afternoon, as she was getting into her car in the school lot, she saw David standing a few yards away, just watching her. He stood there, almost shaking in concentration and feeding on her fear.

Sometimes just for fun, David would set fires in the weeds growing along the railroad tracks. A neighbor told Mr. Biro not to worry, "He's just going through a phase."

The real problems began in the spring of 1987.

David hurled eggs at his house as if he hated it. Sometimes he filled balloons with urine and threw them down at kids to watch them scatter. One night his parents were awakened by a phone call from the reservation desk at O'Hare Airport. David had just been caught trying to use their credit card in hopes of booking a flight to Florida. The five-foot-six-inch boy had dreams of running away, but he still looked too young to pass himself off as an adult. The Biros took no action against him.

David didn't talk to his family about what he was feeling, but that spring and early summer he was forever lying about his sister and brother, and denying anything he did wrong. When a motorscooter suddenly appeared in the basement, David said it must have been put there by a family friend who had been visiting from New York. When his father went to a store where the boy had been caught stealing a bike lock, David demanded to be released because he had not been identified in "a legal police lineup."

The boy told lies as if testing his family, and he became angry when his word was not accepted. David had gone from feeling he was the least favored to finding ways of becoming the center of the family. Nick tried believing all of his son's stories, but he wore himself out checking the stories with other people only to learn they were lies.

To some neighbors it appeared that an iciness settled upon the family in their comfortable stucco home. Under the mansard roof, a large enclosed porch gave the building a boxlike appearance. The house had five bedrooms, five washrooms, and five television sets.

David's room was on the third floor, and by general agreement he could do anything he wanted there. He had rock posters, a set of drums, and a fish tank. His personality was spread out in all its fragments. Under his bed were stuffed toys including a Winnie the Pooh he had won at a carnival, his two BB guns, and a loaded revolver that had belonged to his grandfather, a Chicago policeman. David had taken the gun from his father.

On nice days, David could open his window and look out at the driveway and sidewalk. Sometimes he would grab his air rifle, put a chair next to the window to steady his elbow sniper-style, and take a shot at a squirrel.

In May of his fourteenth year, his target was a seven-year-old boy walking home from school. The schoolboy stiffened as a pellet bit into his shoulder. When the crying second-grader looked up, he saw David taking aim again. The boy sought cover behind a stop sign, and David screamed, "You coward, don't hide from me! Come on, come on!"

Sergeant Bill Gallagher arrived less than twenty minutes later. David handed over the gun and calmly claimed he had been shooting at the sign, not knowing a boy was behind it. He and his father were taken in for a discussion at the station.

"If you were an adult, David, you would be handcuffed, fingerprinted, and charged with aggravated battery," the stout, tall Gallagher said. "You would probably get fined one thousand dollars or placed in jail for one year. If you continue as a juvenile to commit crimes, a social worker will be ordered to examine your family, and you will be put in a detention center or a foster home. Now, you don't want that, do you, David?"

This was Sergeant Gallagher's basic speech for

fledglings. Some kids laughed it off, some got scared. But the officer looked into David's face and couldn't find anything there. The boy gave him a half-grin and slumped defiantly in the chair.

"David," Gallagher said, "would you please step outside so I can say a few words to your father?"

After the boy left, the sergeant told Mr. Biro, "I'm going to release your son to you, but you better do something about him. I've been an officer eighteen years. Sir, I have never seen a kid react like that. I don't know what the problem is, but you are going to have trouble with him."

After the family left, Gallagher brought David's yellow juvenile case card into Chief Timm's office and said, "So help me, Herb, one day that kid is going to kill someone."

Nick was more concerned about the boy who was shot. The public relations man asked the child's name so he could give the family some money. Nothing more was said at home.

That July, half a dozen motorists complained to police that their car windows were shattered as they drove by Willow and Linden streets. No one knew who the sniper was until one woman went the wrong way down Willow. She put her car into reverse to make a turn from the Biros' driveway just as a pellet came through her side window. The woman looked up and saw David pumping shot after shot at her from an air rifle. She had to crawl to the passenger's side to open the door as safety glass cracked around her.

"Get out of my driveway," David yelled to the woman, who ran screaming across his lawn.

Squad cars soon surrounded the house, which was only a few hundred feet from the station. David already had his door open and handed Sergeant Gallagher the gun. "She had no business being in my driveway," the boy said.

"No warning this time, she's pressing charges."

"I'm getting a lawyer."

"We'll be glad to see him. Now come along with us."

Unlike in Chicago, police on the North Shore are used to seeing teenagers appear in court with high-priced lawyers, even for routine violations. Often the counselor would be a corporate attorney from their father's firm.

In a corridor outside the Skokie courtroom, Sergeant Gallagher said to David's lawyer, John Lewis, "Strange kid you're representing."

"He's got a power complex," Lewis shrugged. "He probably wants to be Patton or Napoleon. But I think he can channel that into something. You wouldn't know it, but he's a bright kid."

The matter was settled without a trial, but the Biros were offended when Gallagher had the police social worker examine the family as he said he would. To the social worker, there was a pattern of directing hostility toward strangers, as if David were detouring any feelings he couldn't handle. She recommended immediate psychiatric counseling.

Nicholas and Joan could not bring themselves to admit that David might be disturbed. The social worker talked to them about family tensions as if no other family had them. David was a little wild, but so were a lot of teens.

This looking the other way ended abruptly on August 20, 1987. At around noon, Nancy Biro was having lunch in the kitchen. She was a likable girl, but she was not as academically inclined as her older brother, Michael. Nancy noticed a discoloration on the surface of her glass of milk. She poured the milk down the sink and opened the other gallon. But that one was spoiled as well.

Joan came home for lunch as usual and she, too, smelled the milk. It wasn't just rotten, she realized, it was tainted. She took the gallon to the police station and asked that it be analyzed. All that afternoon, David behaved as he always did. Then a call came in from police. Someone had mixed wood alcohol into the milk.

Nick couldn't understand how such a thing could happen, but his seventeen-year-old son, Michael, went up to his brother's room and came down with a bottle half-full of wood alcohol Nick had kept in the basement for paint thinner. All eyes turned on David, and the boy shouted with a gasp of innocence that Michael was trying to frame him. But no matter what David said, even his father knew that his son had crossed the line.

14

---◆◆◆---

Punk Nights

August 21, 1987

ONLY A FEW hours later, at four in the morning of August 21, the Biros drove their youngest son down Sheridan Road to the North Side of Chicago. In the dark, Lake Michigan was only a moonlight glitter. They pulled into the driveway of Charter Barclay Hospital, a private psychiatric facility specializing in treating teenagers with problems such as suicidal depression, eating disorders, and drug addiction. The family walked under the security lights, and Nick rang the night bell. Joan waited with her arms folded as her son stood beside her.

A staff member led them inside, and a nurse asked the parents to fill out a questionnaire and sign a release form. The Biros were shown part of the five-story building, and they saw that David would be comfortable in the dormitory-style setting of salmon-pink walls and floral prints. The staff kept a disciplined schedule for the children: up at six o'clock, therapy sessions privately or in groups, and classes in math, history, English, science, art, and physical exercise.

While his parents continued answering questions about the family, David was taken to a unit where he was searched for weapons and tested for drugs, then led to a side room for an admitting psychiatric evaluation.

"Why are you here?" asked the psychiatrist.

"My parents think I was trying to kill them."

"But you didn't?"

"No, my brother did."

"Do you ever feel that you might lose control and hurt someone?" No answer. "How would you do it, David?"

"No," the boy said blankly.

"Have you ever been violent or shown intimidating behavior toward others?"

"Maybe with a BB gun, that's about it."

"Have you ever thought about killing someone?"

"No." But the psychiatrist noticed anger under that calm expression.

"What do you see as your strengths and weaknesses, David?"

"I have no idea."

"What do you see for yourself in the future?"

"I can't see in the future," David answered.

Some time past dawn, David was introduced to his roommate. Later that day, David attended an informal meeting of the patients, "the community," and was asked why he was in the hospital. "I poisoned my parents," he replied. A staff member wrote down that the boy had a smile on his face.

Although David was sure he would be out in a few days, the staff felt the minimum time would be thirty to forty-five days. In early interviews, psychiatrist Judith Stoewe saw David's antics at home as a power play he would likely repeat with staff members. She believed that his misbehavior—getting out of hand only in the last six months—was a possible sign of major depression. More troubling, it seemed to Stoewe that Nick and Joan Biro had been turning their heads away from the problem for years, and they did not seem capable of providing the limits David needed. That meant any progress he made at Charter Barclay could be lost once he returned home.

Stoewe—a plump, middle-aged woman with her hair pulled back—visited David in his room and asked about his life in general. He answered flippantly that he didn't care about others and did exactly what he pleased.

"Where do you think that kind of attitude will take you?" Stoewe asked.

"I'll probably wind up in jail," David said.

Dr. Stoewe finished her rounds, then wrote in her report that this was probably the way David had behaved in school, putting on a "tough guy" act because he was afraid of relating to people his own age any other way. For example, he and his roommate pulled a prank by slipping a pen in their door to keep it from opening and then claiming they had been locked out. But when David was alone, he sometimes let his guard down. He told Stoewe he had been abused by other children when he was younger. The memory of being tripped during an informal game of football was so painful he couldn't talk about it.

Stoewe knew that this vulnerability could provide a way of reaching him, but there was still a danger in his smoldering hostility. "It is my belief that the safety of this family as well as David's potential safety are at risk," she wrote.

The staff felt that David's essential problem was an inability to develop friendships and trust.

Only recently have psychiatrists understood the dynamics of peer-group rejection. Children in the fifth and sixth grades might taunt other kids for being skinny, fat, tall, short, sickly, or clumsy, but the underlying reason is that they attack children who are lacking in accepted social skills, kids who have not learned how to handle themselves in the complex world of "playground politics."

New studies show that children commonly lack skills

for interacting with others when they have not experienced a warm and positive home life, and each year makes it more difficult for a child to overcome his awkwardness. A boy rejected in the fifth grade might expect rejection in the sixth, seventh, and eighth grades. Some children retreat entirely, but others act cool and tough to win friends. Maybe not the best friends, but friends.

David was expected to benefit from positive members of the Charter Barclay community, but he gravitated toward the troublesome ones. Three of them were members of the Simon City Royals, the largest white street gang in Chicago. The Royals were less violent than many of the black and Hispanic gangs, but membership was regarded as an honor for many boys growing up in North and Northwest side neighborhoods, where life usually consisted of watching television until bedtime.

Despite his dubious new friends, David told skeptical staff members that he was making progress. Dr. Stoewe recognized this as part of his "transparent magical thinking." David was trying to make things happen by talking about them. Nevertheless, she and the other experts thought David was ready for a session with his parents. But David didn't.

As soon as the meeting was suggested, his behavior suddenly regressed and he had to be placed in a "quiet room." The next day, his thirteenth, he lay on his bed and refused to look Dr. Stoewe in the face or say anything that wasn't sarcastic. When David went to the recreation room, he unscrewed one of the net supports from the ping-pong table and slipped it into his pocket, then added six packets of sugar. Not even Stoewe knew why.

A little later, David started a fight with another boy and lied to make himself look innocent. At other times that week he bumped into boys in the hall and walked on without an apology. Staff psychologist David Kenis found him to be "a rather cold-blooded young man who has very little compunction about hurting others to get his own way."

When Nick and Joan sat down for the family therapy session, David came in angrily and shouted, "What are you doing here? You don't care a damn about me, you never believe anything I say! It's always Michael or Nancy." The Biros were startled at the change in their son and assured him that they cared. Afterward, Dr. Stoewe wrote in her report that "It is quite clear that David has thrown down the gauntlet and has been engaging in a power struggle."

Kenis wrote in his own report that the Biros were still refusing to recognize that David was capable of "malicious, destructive behavior toward them." The psychologist also spoke to the family about applying for an Illinois Department of Mental Health grant to pay for extended treatment. Nick nodded sadly and replied, "Anything you say."

David's acting up continued for days after his parents left. When a staff member asked him to step into the hall, the boy snapped, "Fuck you, I'm not doing anything." Later a teacher took David's watch away after the boy repeatedly looked at it in group therapy. But David persuaded an attendant to get it back for him, then caused a brief commotion by hiding the watch and accusing his roommate of stealing it.

The boy might have been trying to act like a rebellious loner, but Dr. Stoewe saw that he was easily manipulated by his "peers." He became what they wanted him to be, as if his only identity were a reflection of the darker thoughts of those around him. One psychiatrist called the problem ego-syntonic, but Stoewe and Kenis used the simpler term "scapegoat." David himself had some awareness of this. He told the staff social worker, Barbara Lapin, that "I lie and steal to keep up with my reputation . . . because if I don't, I'll feel like dirt."

David was transferred to the intensified treatment

unit to keep him away from the temptation to misbe-
have in order to gain admiration. After that, the storm
within him passed. The boy became quiet in his room
and was able to talk to Dr. Stoewe for the first time
about his strange behavior. "I guess I've been pretty
rotten to my roommates," he said.

"You don't get along with them very well, do you?"

"I think I pick fights with them sometimes just to let
out a little steam. It's *their* fault."

"Your parents?"

"The way I can pull any shit and they never say anything about it. They're teaching me that doing bad
things is okay. Don't you think so?"

"I think that is an interesting thing to say," Dr.
Stoewe remarked. "You might be getting to understand
yourself a little better."

In fact, David was responding to therapy so well that
he stood in as the chairman of a "community meeting"
and came out of the session all smiles. He began doing
his homework, and Stoewe wrote in her latest report
that "Rather amazingly, David is continuing to do very
well." He even spoke of running for chairman of the
community. Stoewe was afraid he might not be mature
enough at this point to handle losing, but he didn't have
to. The other teens elected him.

His progress ended on October 7, his forty-seventh
day at the hospital. That was when his sister, Nancy,
and brother, Michael, joined the family session for the
first time. David once more shouted at his family and
flung out his arms. The academic Michael cringed in
fear. *"You're* the one who did this," David told his
brother. "You poisoned the milk and you blame it all on
me!"

"Please," Michael said to the staff members, wiping
away tears, "I don't want him back with us!"

Their father was deeply hurt but said little. Joan
stood up to her children, telling Michael to sit back
down and David to stop screaming. Instead of returning

to his chair, Michael ran out of the room. Mrs. Biro apologized to Stoewe and Kenis, saying her two older children might be upset because the family had recently been in a car accident.

As the staff led David away, he kept telling other teens at the hospital that he was innocent of the poisoning and that it was his brother who had tried to kill the family. No one believed him.

Later, David was found making gang signs of upside-down pitchforks in his notebook. As Lapin noted, David had run full circle back to the way he was and now had to be put in the quiet room again. Although he had been elected community chairman, it took just days for the other teens to lose their trust in him. He was abusive to the staff and called their technical talk "B.S.-ing." This was followed by a sad period, and Kenis knew he was still upset by the family session with his brother and sister. The psychologist added in a report that "David appears to have a rather grandiose outlook about his activities. He believes that he is much smarter and sneakier than he really is."

The Biros were also upset by David's latest tirade, and they blamed it on the staff. Hoping that the boy still might re-enter the mainstream, the therapists arranged for David to meet a psychiatrist who worked with the local school district. The therapist told the Biros on October 17, a Saturday, that the meeting would be for just an hour or so, and that they should not take David out to eat, since this was not an earned outing.

But the family never brought him back. Six hours after signing David out, his father called the hospital to say he had brought his son home but that somehow the boy slipped out. The therapists advised Nick and Joan to contact police because David could be a danger to himself or others. David's roommate then found a note from the boy informing the hospital staff that he was leaving.

At 10 A.M. the following day, Nick called Charter

Barclay to report that David had decided to come back home and that he was all right.

"Mr. Biro," the therapist said, "don't you think you should take your son back here?"

"No," he replied, "that won't be necessary."

After David's abrupt departure, psychiatrist Robert Muskinatow of the Associates in Adolescent Psychiatry issued a summary of the more than two hundred pages of documents written by the staff. He found that David's relationship to both parents "appears to be angry and conflictional in nature. In relationship with his mother, the anger rather than being directed toward her is directed out into the world."

In an accompanying final discharge report, social worker Barbara Lapin said David used his intelligence—with a full-scale IQ at the superior level of 122—to reduce in his own mind the impact of his "destructive acting out." She added, "It appears that the Biros are extremely protective of their own. They appear to have some difficulty expressing emotions openly . . . The family dynamics are such that there appears to be little connection between David and his father."

She added, "We do have serious concerns about David's future welfare although he does not pose a risk to society at the present time."

On the day David returned home after his twenty-four-hour attempt to run away, his grades from the school at Charter Barclay were transferred to the prestigious New Trier High in Winnetka. In some ways, this school is the heart of the village. Twenty-two percent of all tax money spent by the town goes to the "Mercedes of American education." Its graduation rate is ninety-eight percent, and eighty-eight percent of the graduates go on to college.

David stayed out of trouble his entire freshman year, although he liked to pester the driver of the school bus every morning by harassing some boy or drumming out the "Lone Ranger" theme on a seat near her. In that year, he grew half a foot, and classmates called him "Beanpole."

When the boy was a junior, he joined the Peace Alliance and in the spring of 1989 volunteered to become a math tutor. That was how he met *Helen Berson. The lively, pretty girl was a creative student but she needed help in raising her math scores. David spent lunch breaks with her in the park outside school. She told her friends David was a "sweet guy" but that she wasn't really interested in him.

With his height and deep voice, David took her a couple of times to a restaurant-bar that had a reputation for not carding teenagers. Soon after David's sixteenth birthday in May, his father bought him a used car. Using a fake ID, David took Helen to a nicer restaurant and ordered wine with the meal.

"How did you get the card?" Helen asked.

"I got friends in Chicago," David boasted.

One Saturday in the final weeks of the semester, Helen was working in school for a theater project when she was surprised to see David during a break. Without a word, he handed her two red roses tied with a red ribbon. Helen didn't know how to respond, so the lanky boy ended the awkward pause by stating the obvious: "I bought these for you."

"David . . ." How could she put it? "David, I'm not dating you. I like you, but not this way. This is going too far. You helped me in math, and I appreciate that, but now we're done. Do you understand?"

David stared at her, then plunged his hands into his pockets and walked off. He never went out of his way for a girl again.

On spring and summer nights in 1988, David would drive forty minutes from the orderliness of Winnetka to the punker district of Chicago, bisected by rattling elevated trains at the Belmont Avenue station. On Saturday evenings, boys and girls as young as nine went to the juice bars and dropped in at the fad shops. In places like The Alley, they browsed among displays of black jackets, black hooded shirts, biker necklaces, earrings, throwing stars, dragon sculptures, and skull ornaments. The customers just seemed interested in annoying their parents and school principals. In other stores, they bought records of heavy metal and punk music filled with lyrics about violence and death.

In the Chicago Tattoo Parlor, young men stripped to their waists and leaned over to have their skin decorated in any of dozens of designs. David, who was now letting his hair grow fairly long, went in only to be told he was too young. Instead, he had some friends ink in a cross on his right arm and, on the left, a design that included the Simon City Royals' pitchfork. Although his head was rather small for his long body, David was nearly handsome now. But he would rather look tough. He wanted to be like Burke Abrams, the street gang members he met, and the cold-blooded villains he saw in movies.

At Madusa's juice bar, he would walk up the long, narrow stairway with a crowd of other punkers, pass a couple of muscular bouncers, and be searched for drugs or liquor. From there he would enter a large windowless room of black walls and illuminated by strobe lights. The pounding music was so loud the floor vibrated through his shoes. Kids, most of them girls, stood on platforms at opposite ends of the bare room. They danced en masse as a movie set in a junior high school played against them as if their faces and rocking torsos were the screen. "Do it, do it, do it," chanted one song, "be yourself, do it, do it."

David had found a place where he felt he belonged.

15

The Most Cunning Animal

TEACHERS AT NEW Trier considered David bright but a little immature, the sort of student who might do well if given a little encouragement. He had the unusual gift of both abstraction and imagination, and when he was late turning in his assignments he shrugged it off as part of being a "creative genius."

Without hesitation, the faculty in the early spring of 1990 approved David's request to run for senior class president. The boy felt he could be elected again on the basis of his eccentricities, as he had been at Charter Barclay. He told the editor of the school paper that "chicks dig me," and he made posters facetiously identifying himself as the only "Non-Communist" candidate. No one took David seriously.

When it came his turn to make a campaign speech before an assembly of students from the school that had produced Charlton Heston and Ann-Margret, his energy shot over the top. In his disconnected speech, he said into the microphone on stage, "Who do I got to blow around here to get elected?" David was led away as hundreds of students sat either shocked or giggling.

David continued to hang around a sandwich shop in Northbrook because it was owned by a friend of Kim

Chee, and it was just down the street from his father's public relations business. Teens gathered at the shop for tough talk, trying to outrage each other with spiked hairdos and accounts of pranks they had pulled.

There were undercurrents in student life on the North Shore that not many parents understood. Coming from Chicago, Sergeant Patty McConnell considered Winnetka a teenage wasteland, with high rates of suicide and substance abuse by students under twenty. It was as if youngsters saw their parents' success as a dead end. As Sergeant Caldwell put it, "There's no real idea where they want to go." Lieutenant Sumner said ninety percent of Winnetka crime "is kids."

In late January, the Biros contacted attorney John Lewis about getting David out of minor trouble again. The compact, balding man had a thin mustache that helped give him a comfortable, almost British look. Lewis held a black belt in karate and was honored for hand-to-hand combat as a Green Beret in Vietnam.

Lewis had met David about two years before, when the boy was charged with stealing a bicycle lock, and never quite knew what to expect from him. But as far as troubled kids went, David wasn't as bad as some Lewis had known.

The family explained to the lawyer that David had tried to open an account at the First Chicago Bank of Winnetka by forging the name of a stranger from Glencoe on a three-hundred-dollar check stolen from a locker room at a North Shore country club. Tellers recalled that the person was a tall, thin young man. Detective Robert Kerner showed them mug shots of several people, and all of them picked David's. But Lewis persuaded the bank to accept full restitution from the Biros rather than press charges.

Nick Biro didn't say much about having to pay three hundred dollars and lawyer fees to avoid forgery charges for his son, just as Nick and Joan never asked where David had been when he came home at four in the morning. They never waited up for him. He had his own life to live.

David no longer counted Burke Abrams among his friends; they had become superficially so much alike that there was a clash of egos whenever they met. Officer Caldwell said it seemed as if the boys were competing for the honor of being "the bad guy of the village."

But sometimes David and Burke had to be together because they had mutual friends, such as the time a New Trier student drove David and some other teens to the Abrams home on their way to a party. Burke, dressed in black and wearing his long hair in a ponytail, showed off his collection of knives and Oriental throwing stars. Then he passed around a gun he claimed he was selling on the black market for several hundred dollars.

David would not admit the influence of his one-time friend. But not long after the party, he took a girlfriend with him to a gun shop in another suburb to look over the automatic pistols and revolvers. But he was told he needed to have a state Firearms Owner Identification (FOI) card, certifying that he was twenty-one and not a criminal or recent inmate at a mental institution.

Having no intention of waiting five years, David filled out an application with information from the Swiss passport of Ron Matzig, a young Evanston man who had been introduced to him by their mutual friend, Kim Chee.

On Friday, February 2, Joan Biro picked up the mail when she came home for lunch and found something addressed to Matzig at the Willow Street address. Joan opened the envelope and found an FOI card with Matzig's name and social security number, but with David's photo.

Furious that her son was forging again, Joan called

Lewis's office in Skokie and asked what to do. "Bring the card in or send it to me," the lawyer said. "And, Joan, you better search his room for any guns. Who knows what he needs the card for."

She broke open the lock on David's room and searched through his mess but couldn't find any firearms. She did find several more checks that didn't belong to him.

When Nick came home that evening, Joan showed him the FOI card and told him to have a talk with his son.

"What's this, David?" Nick Biro asked in his soft voice.

"It got sent here by mistake," David said.

"David, that's you," Nick said of the picture, "that's not Ron Matzig."

"Can I have it? I'll give it to him."

"We're keeping it." That was all the father said.

That night, the house had the stillness of a family that could say something but does not.

Two days later, Joan turned the firearms card over to Lewis, who put it in a file jacket. A little afterward her son called the lawyer and demanded the card back.

"David, do you know how serious what you've done is? If you use this card you could be sent to prison for a minimum of five years."

"There's a lot more involved than just me," the boy said.

"What are you talking about?"

"Give me that card or I'll take it."

"David, just cool down, all right? You've got good parents, now stay out of trouble."

Enraged, the boy said in his penetrating, deep voice, "You will never represent me again."

Something in David's tone said: If you don't give it to me, I'll come in and get it. Lewis, a former prosecutor whose wife was an FBI agent, was naturally on guard when anyone made a veiled threat. He asked an off-duty policeman for help in finding ways of making sure the sixteen-year-old thief and forger couldn't take the card back.

As one precaution, the policeman taped the windows to make it harder for David to come in. He decided to put the card behind the furnace in his office. While they were at it, Lewis added his wife's Smith and Wesson .357 Magnum revolver, which he had brought to the office so he could clean it and change the grips.

A few days later, after it seemed there would be no trouble from David, Lewis began to feel a little foolish over his concern. He put the gun case back in the bottom of the drawer and the card in a folder.

By now David had an air of sophistication, but he was still very much an adolescent. The trappings of evil and death were seductive for him. His fantasies sometimes merged with films he saw. In 1986 it was *River's Edge,* in which several teenagers visit the body of a strangled friend and, in fascination, vow not to tell authorities. The young murderer cries out at one point, "I wanted to show the world who's boss!"

David also enjoyed *Heathers*, which was released around the time he was entering New Trier. In the film, a teenager in a long black coat teaches two "assholes" a lesson by hauling out a large revolver in school and shooting them with blanks. Later on, the games turn deadly as he helps a girl eliminate people they don't like. At last she tells him, "Do you actually think you're a rebel? I say you're psychotic."

The boy, glib and soft-spoken, never shows emotion. His philosophy is that "society nods its head at any horror a teenager can bring upon himself." The girl soon finds that he is trying to blow up the school, and he admits an underlying reason for his behavior: "Maybe I am killing because nobody loves me." The boy changes his mind about the school and uses the dynamite to blow himself up.

After seeing the movie *Best Seller*, David couldn't stop talking about the character of a hitman described as an "amoral mistake of nature." His friend Phu Huang thought that David was "obsessed" with the film. David even repeated some of the tag lines, such as, "Anybody can kill anybody. Even a president."

In one scene the corporate hitman played by James Woods borrows a burning cigarette and tells a writer, "Willpower is what distinguishes the amateur from the professional. Pain doesn't bother me, I don't let it." The hitman then presses the cigarette into his own palm. "That's what I mean by willpower. Do you have it?"

David loved that sneering grin of James Woods so much he adopted it as his own. Then, to impress other students even more, he would put a lit cigarette against his hand and watch their faces.

For several years David had been keeping a red notebook of drawings and his thoughts. The first sketches were too formal to be promising, but they showed a sense of form. By his early teens he was drawing a Japanese-inspired avenger in black. The enemy is to be imagined. As he grew older, David drew the stern face of a handsome teenager with his hair held back by a warrior headband.

Sometimes David wrote about Cain, the first killer of the world, the young man who slew his brother out of jealousy. In his notebook, he wrote a cryptic proclamation as if giving a Biblical warning to the world:

Remember,
Remember that I am the Advocate, the Chief
  Cornerstone
Remember that I am the Adversary, the Interloper
Remember that I hold all seven seals, and hold the
  power

to open them
Remember that I am war, strife, famine, pestilence,
*   martyrs, great signs and silence*
Remember that I am the Lord of the tribe, king of the
*   jungle and hunter of great beasts*
Remember that I am Jaws, the great white shark,
*   terror of*
the seas, lord of the water
Remember that I am the Viper of the pit, the most
*   cunning*
animal whose poison is the deadliest known
Remember that I am the hawk, hunter of the night,
*   master*
of the sky above
Remember that I am the second son of Adam and Eve
Remember that I rose up in front of god and
*   slew my brother Abel out of greed*
Remember it all, but if you should somehow forget
*   some of*
it, just remember this
My Name is Cain
and I kill people

The spring of 1990 was just a long, cold shadow of
winter. Students were thinking about vacation and discussing midterm reports. David had several female
friends who could not quite be called girlfriends. One
of them was sixteen-year-old Megan O'Callaghan. She
was drawn to David because she thought his glibness
and biting humor showed how smart he was.

Megan, her hair in a pageboy and wearing preppy
clothes, was talking to David and other friends about
a report for her sophomore year at the Academy of
Sacred Heart. She was basing it on the 1924 "thrill
kill" murder of young Bobby Franks by Nathan
Leopold and Richard Loeb, two extremely bright
Chicago teenagers from wealthy families. They had
agreed to commit a murder just to see the trouble

they could stir up among the police, and to prove themselves above the law.

The main feature of their plan was that the victim would be picked virtually at random. Their theory was that if there was no motive, police would never be able to find the killers. But the arrogance of their intellect made them careless.

On the first night of spring vacation—Monday, April 2—David put on his usual black clothes and drove to his attorney's office in Skokie. Determined to find that firearms card, he cautiously removed the door hinges and went to his lawyer's desk.

Rummaging through the lower drawer, he found a foot-long bluish-gray plastic case. He opened it and discovered a chrome .357 Magnum with a four-inch barrel and black grips. Also in the drawer were four full speedloaders, three with .38-caliber special ammunition and one with .357 hollow point cartridges with copper coating on their jackets.

Still playing the game of stealth, David put everything back except the gun and speedloaders. He slid the door back and pushed the hinges in so that when Lewis returned to work, he wouldn't notice that anyone had been there.

Over the first couple of days of spring break, David and Matzig—a marketing employee who still lived with his mother—talked over ways they could go to Chicago bars together. That Wednesday, April 4, the two of them went to the Illinois Secretary of State's office in Niles, a north suburb close to the city. After waiting in line, Matzig said he had lost his state photo identification and needed a replacement. But it was David who went in for the picture. Within an hour he had an ID card with Matzig's name and his age as twenty-three.

But going to bars seemed trivial now. He was as well-armed as the hitman in *Best Seller*. But whom would he choose? His thoughts on those long days when he was off from school and his parents were at work must have been like a spin of a roulette wheel, the ivory ball moving in several directions at once until settling upon a number.

Thinking of the double-paned patio door at the townhouse where the Langerts were staying, David went to his basement and found a broken piece of glass. Using a glass cutter to add drama, he practiced scoring it in his room. But it was still just the fantasy of a teenage boy who had written, "My name is Cain and I kill people."

16

Execution Style

Saturday, April 7, 1990

ON SATURDAY MORNING, Nick Biro and his wife went to a seminar at Northwestern University in Evanston. Afterward, they had Cokes and coffee with friends before returning at around 5 P.M. David spent the evening watching television downstairs until Nick went to bed around 9:40 P.M. and Joan followed him a few minutes later.

Their youngest child put on a T-shirt that bore a portrait of Jesus with a crown of thorns. Then he slipped on a black hooded sweatshirt and a pair of black gloves. Since he didn't have any large pockets, his handcuffs, a glass cutter, and Lewis's .357 Magnum were hidden in the fold of his sweatshirt.

David didn't have far to go. He rounded the block, walked a few hundred feet down Green Bay Road, passed the police station, and crossed the Cherry Street bridge. Officer Billy Caldwell, who had scuffled with David a couple of years before, made a mental note of him while driving by.

The boy went to the first house past the dry ravine and walked down the path of wood chips. He opened the gate of the six-foot-tall stockade fence and closed it

162

behind him. Safe from the eyes of passersby, he peered inside the townhouse and began to score the glass of the patio door just as he had practiced at home. In time, he had an opening large enough to reach through and unlock the door.

David soundlessly walked around the house, gun in hand, to make sure no one was there and to enjoy the sense of control. He returned to the front room and looked over some of the belongings in the boxes. To while away his time, he read Nancy's and Richard's marriage contract, then tossed it onto the metal table. Sometime during his wait, he turned on a side light and pulled up a folding chair to sit in the shadows, so the illumination would be in front of his victims, obscuring him. When he became bored waiting in the eerie glow, he considered opening a gift-wrapped box on the table, but he decided that wouldn't be professional.

David heard voices outside and tensed. He pulled the hood farther down his face and listened for the key turning in the lock. The door opened and Nancy and Richard appeared at the threshold. At first they didn't see David, but they sensed that something was wrong. Then they saw a dark figure and the glint of the revolver.

In his deep voice, David ordered them to keep quiet and close the door behind them. When they recovered from their shock, they thought they might be able to talk the intruder out of whatever he had in mind. Assuming he was a burglar, Nancy held out her purse and said they had no money. David ordered her to throw the purse to him. Keeping the gun trained on them, he picked it up and found the pay envelope with more than five hundred dollars in it.

"You held out on me," he said.

"Look," Richard said, "we have a portable compact disc player, you can take that—and our television set and VCR."

David was annoyed that they were mistaking him for

a punk. He reached for the handcuffs, but he discovered that he had brought only one pair. In his anger, the boy tossed them to Nancy from his chair and told her to cuff her husband, then he had them back up against the wall and lie on the carpet. Richard stayed quiet to avoid antagonizing the hooded figure, but Nancy talked back to him and kept asking what he wanted.

Instead of replying, David—sitting so his face would be in shadow—said, "Tell me something about your-selves."

The request was incredible, and they could see that he was drawing power from their fear. As they tried to reason with him, he fidgeted with the gun, not knowing he could fire the double-action weapon without cocking it. Two fingers remained on the trigger as he listened to their pleading.

"Please leave us alone," Richard said. "My wife is pregnant. You can take whatever we have, just go. We can't identify you."

"I am pregnant," Nancy said. "I don't show yet, but the baby is due in October."

As David paused to think this over, something made the cocker spaniel bark upstairs, and the boy was so startled he pulled back the trigger as he sat in the chair. The .357 Magnum recoiled, and the bullet slammed against the baseboard. Richard and Nancy jerked reflex-ively in terror as they lay on the floor.

David damned his jumpiness. Now everything was ruined; he had to run out of the house or kill them quickly.

"You better get out of here, because the police will be coming any minute," Nancy screamed. "The sta-tion's just over the bridge!"

David's heart was racing, and his hands sweated in his leather gloves. He had to gamble. Maybe the police weren't on their way. There had been fireworks near the house a few hours earlier and no one reported them.

He rose and told the Langerts he was going to lock

them up in the basement so they couldn't call for help, then he would leave. "Come on, hurry up," he said as Nancy and Richard climbed to their feet.

As David followed them down the steps, Nancy turned and saw his features in the basement light. Now he had an excuse to kill them. "Kneel," he commanded from the bottom of the stairs.

By then, Richard knew the police weren't coming. That meant he had only a few seconds to stop this crazy teenager. With all his strength, the powerfully built man twisted the handcuff out of its lock. He tried jumping to his feet, and his head hit David's face. Taut with fear and anger, David fired a copper-jacketed bullet into the base of the man's skull and into his brain. Richard sank to his knees and fell dead to the floor, his glasses shattering as he struck a metal shelf.

As Nancy huddled in the corner, too shocked to move, she saw the gun turn to her. There was another explosion, and she felt a burning through her elbow and side. She clutched at the spot under her coat while the hooded teenager took aim at her once more.

"No," she shouted. "Not again!"

The boy reconsidered. He had killed. He had done what he had set out to do.

"No!" Nancy screamed again.

David knew he had to leave the house. A neighbor might not report one shot, but two shots were bound to bring in calls. The boy started running up the stairs and Nancy, hoping her ordeal had ended, moved toward her husband. David paused on the steps, turned, and fired a final time before running out. Nancy convulsed as the bullet ripped into her back.

An elderly woman next door was in her bathroom when she had heard Nancy shout "Not again." But when there was a shot, she told herself it was just the television set next door.

Nancy lay on the gray concrete floor, feeling herself grow weaker from hemorrhaging. Her body swelling from internal bleeding, she struggled to pull off her blue coat. She rolled onto her side to lift her arm out of the sleeve, but she no longer had the strength. She tried to close the wound at the upper left side of her abdomen. It was just a third of an inch across, but blood was filling her hands.

Grabbing the bottom step, she started pulling herself up by her hands and elbows. Richard's killer had left the basement door open. All she had to do was go up those few stairs and reach the phone. Nancy clawed at the second step and managed to lift herself a few inches, but her strength was gone. One of her arms shook and her hold gave way, sending her sliding onto the floor on her back.

Her breath was labored. The stairway might as well be a mile long. Slowly she turned to her side so that she could crawl again. She looked at Richard, his face distorted and discolored as blood poured from his ears, nose and mouth. She cried, but her voice was too weak to draw anyone down there.

Nancy saw a hatchet lying on the top of the opened toolbox. She took the handle in a faint grasp and tried pounding on the metal shelf Richard had struck as he fell. The loudest sounds she could make were just hollow thuds.

Her body felt on fire, and damage from the two slugs was twitching her in spasms. She lowered the hatchet and thought of using the handle to pull herself forward, but it did no good.

Nancy lay still for a moment. She dipped her finger into her own blood and formed a mark on the lower shelf. Then she made another, but the third blurred with her pain.

Some strength came back, and for a moment her thinking was clearer. She thought she might raise herself by putting all her energy into one hand and pulling at the upper shelf. Then perhaps if she could slide off her coat, now becoming heavy with blood, she might be able to climb the stairs. But her weight made the shelf clatter against the bottom one, and she fell with it.

Nancy inched back toward the stairs, moving farther away from her husband. She neared the bottom step, but then there was only pain. Her unborn baby soon died with her.

When David rushed outside through the open patio door, his gloves were so heavy with sweat he pulled them off. One of them dropped onto a bush. He shoved his foot onto the chain-link fence, then clambered over and dropped to the slope of the ravine. As he scurried down he could feel blood dripping from his nose, where Richard's head had struck him. Suppose the police were responding to that second or third shot? They would be sure to stop him and ask why he was bleeding.

He held both nostrils together to stanch the flow while he hid in the underbrush and shadows. For the time he had the victims trapped in his web, there had been a rush of power. He felt he could do anything. But now he was trembling and confused.

In a few minutes, when David realized that no squad cars were speeding to the scene, he left the ravine and walked quickly to his house. Trying not to wake anyone, he went to his upstairs closet and grabbed his gym bag. To his close friends he had referred to this as his "getaway bag," because it held everything he might need to escape from trouble, from money to Matzig's passport.

He stepped downstairs and took his mother's car keys from the kitchen table, then drove to the sandwich shop in Northbrook, just ten minutes away. If he had arrived just a few minutes earlier, half a dozen teens would have been there, most of them dressed in black, and some of the boys with tattoos and earrings. But it was five minutes after midnight and the night man, John Mercer, was closing up. David tapped on the glass of the locked door. Mercer, in his mid-thirties, let David in and noticed that not only was the boy's nose bloody, he was shivering as if in a fever.

"What happened, David?"

"I need to talk to someone," the boy said.

Mercer gave him a soft drink and asked, "Were you in a fight or something?"

"Yes," was all David would say.

But that didn't seem like him. The few times Mercer had seen him, the boy had fought back only with sarcasm. "I'll fix you something for your nose, how's that?"

David kept his head back and didn't answer.

Mercer's girlfriend, Brenda, was at one of the tables waiting to give John a ride home. While Mercer was putting ice into a plastic bag, she asked the boy, "Did you get the guy back?"

"Huh?"

"You said you were in a fight."

"Yeah, I got him very good," David answered, his hands still quivering. He pressed the ice pack against his nose for a few minutes.

"Do you need anything else?" Mercer asked.

"No, I'll be all right."

Around twelve-thirty, David handed the ice bag back, thanked John, and left the shop. He could not go home with so many feelings churning in him, so he drove down Chicago's North Clark Street. He found a parking place reasonably close to Neo's, a night spot that served occultists, misfits, graduates of the punker district, and middle-class young people looking for a weird experience to tell their friends about.

He walked down an alleyway alongside a wall painted with huge fluorescent bones and a full-sized red devil. A three-hundred-pound bouncer gestured with a wiggle of his fingers for an ID. The sixteen-year-old boy flashed the fake card with his photo and Matzig's name. He walked by and entered a dim room that looked like a cavern in decay. Neo's was packed with its after-midnight patrons, and for David there was no greater place to be alone. In a raised corner booth, a disc jockey with a baseball cap was playing music so loud that the odd sorts at the bar had to shout to be heard.

David entered the black washroom and, under the dim light, tossed cold water on his face to wipe off the blood. In the mirror he could see that his nose was still red and puffy. When he came out, he ordered a drink and watched the paradise and tiger fish darting at each other in a tank along the wall. He was hoping to lose his sense of self, to erase what had happened in the last few hours.

He watched couples and strangers move to the blasting music on the sunken dance floor. Amid the throb, specks of light from a revolving globe swirled like stardust on faces and arms as if to reassure everyone that nothing was real.

17

After-Games

Sunday, April 8

NICK BIRO KEPT in shape by riding a bicycle. That Sunday evening, he was biking on the east side of town when he saw a number of squad cars by the townhouse at Cherry and Oak streets. A crowd was forming along yellow police ribbons. That was strange—he wasn't aware that anyone was living in the house yet. The public relations executive thought Lee and Joyce should know about this, so he turned around and rode straight home.

David was in the kitchen with his mother when Nick came in and told them what he had seen. The man dialed the Bishop home on Indian Hill Road, but he couldn't get an answer. His younger son pretended to be mildly curious and started walking across the bridge to join all the people staring at the police cars pulling in and driving out. Before reaching the end of the bridge, he saw the front door opening and men bringing out two bodies.

The boy did not stay long, he had seen what he wanted to see. His expression as he mingled with the crowd must have given no hint of what he felt. Friends had said that with David, "you can never tell what is going on behind those eyes." When the boy told his family what he saw, his shocked parents turned on the news to learn what had happened.

Over the next few days, David began creating in his mind a slightly fictionalized version of himself—celebrating the cool professionalism of the executions, and glossing over the fear and panic which had gripped him that night.

For one thing, David cut out articles about the murders from the Chicago papers and put them in his notebook. On Thursday, David read and re-read the front-page story on the murders in the Winnetka weekly. He wanted to have handcuffs again, so that he might relive the moment when Nancy and Richard were in his control.

Dressing again all in black, the boy drove to Bess Hardware in Northfield. He went down aisle nine and asked the assistant manager about handcuffs. Kevin Karr, a tall man with an athletic build, demonstrated their strength with a display model. David said he wanted a pair, but none of the keys Karr had unlocked the cabinet. He had to pry the door open before handing the boy one of the yellow boxes. David paid at the front counter and left.

There was nothing unusual about the sale, but Karr noticed that for some time the young man stayed inside his car just playing with his new handcuffs in the front seat.

The second weekend after the murders, David drove to Purdue University in East Lafayette, Indiana, to see a friend who had graduated from New Trier the year before. They went to dinner near the campus, and all David talked about was the murders—especially the possibility of a paid assassin. "What do you think about the glass cutter?" David asked. "What do you think about the money being left behind?"

The friend wondered why David was being a bore. David even continued jabbering about the murders when they returned to the student's apartment. "Look," David said and pulled out his red notebook of articles on the killing. The college student went through the pages just to be polite.

Once David returned to Winnetka, he could no longer adjust to his ordinary life. When Matzig dropped by, David showed him the gun he had stolen but kept all the other secrets to himself. Yet the boy wanted admiration for more than just breaking into a lawyer's office. One day when he was talking to Kim Chee in the sandwich shop and the topic turned to Richard Langert, the boy said flippantly, "*I* did it. Sure, I killed him."

"Oh, David, cut it out," Chee told him.

But the teenager was not always trifling about the killings, for something was troubling him. It had been on his mind ever since Richard told him that his wife was pregnant, and the shame stayed with him into the next few weeks. During the small talk in and around New Trier High, he asked a few friends a couple of times about when a fetus might be considered a baby. He didn't say why he wanted to know.

Whenever David was feeling low, he would seek a rush of adrenaline. Now, although he already had two computer systems in his room, he started thinking about ways of getting more.

School was open late on Friday, May 11. Dressed once more in black, David parked in a side driveway and went down the halls. After entering an empty classroom on the second floor, he climbed out a window and looked around to make sure no one could see him. He walked across the roof to the architectural laboratory, where a light was on and a window was open. He slid inside the empty room feet first, then checked to make sure no one was walking down the corridor before disconnecting the components. David had to make a couple of trips across the roof, but he managed to carry the equipment out without suspicion.

The thrill of getting away with the theft was enough

to make David want to do it again. Ten days later, on a Monday night, he returned in his black clothes. Since the school was closed, he fired his air rifle at the window of the sculpture room, but it wouldn't break. Frustrated, he used the butt of the gun to smash the glass. Then he knocked out the jagged pieces remaining and eased himself through the frame. So that he might not be seen carrying the components in the glow of the school lights, he hid them in the bushes until he could return with his car.

The school thefts were just tweaking the nose of authority. David wanted something to stir his imagination again. Nothing immediately came to mind, but he kept alert for opportunities. Although school was letting out for the summer, David joined the cross-country track team to build up his credits. He was usually quiet during the runs. But a few times as he and about seven other boys passed the townhouse as they ran beside the railroad tracks, David said police would never catch the murderer. Other times he said, "Who do you think killed them, I did!"—and laughed.

Most of David's friends liked him for his unpredictable sense of humor, but he had a special relationship with Phu Huang. There was a bond between them because they were both bright and yet complete opposites in their personalities. Phu, tall and slender like David, took everything literally and seriously. He found in David's companionship something to make up for the imagination and sense of daring he had lost in growing up, and David enjoyed Phu's aura of stability. Phu was only sixteen, but he already had his lifetime mapped out step by step. Sometimes David enjoyed saying wild things just to see Phu gulp it all in.

In the last weeks of their junior year, David decided to test Phu's loyalty. They didn't have any classes together, so David came into his friend's sculpture lesson and asked him to come over and help him with a computer program. The next day Phu went to David's room and saw the new computers in a closet. As the Asian student was trying to work the program, David asked if he had heard about the break-ins at New Trier.

"What about it?"

"Look," David said and turned the keyboard over to show him the blue stenciled school initials, N.T. "I did it," he boasted.

"You?" said the other boy, not sure how to respond.

When Phu didn't seem concerned that the equipment was stolen, David nudged their conversation in another direction. He reached under his pillow and handed Phu the .357 Magnum, saying he had stolen it from "an office building." David wasn't specific. The revolver was empty but there were some bullets in the speedloaders.

David didn't have to tell his friend to keep quiet about the computers and the gun. Though Phu had a strong sense of what was right and wrong, he still found this delinquent side of his friend intriguing.

David was still testing the waters of how daring he could be without getting caught. In July he took the gun for target practicing at the Skokie golf course with a friend, Mark Chapin. Mark was perhaps the most outlandish of David's student friends, with earrings and a shaved head. They didn't need paper targets when there were so many trees. Birds scattered as the boys took turns firing.

That same month, David toyed with his computer. Using the Old English script on his printer, he typed out a long, apocalyptic message for the world that also was a justification for his closest friends to read. He wrote that "people will look at me and scoff and think I am crazy. Oh but we will have fun won't we. I feel that there is a beast in all of us that is waiting to come out. Let it be free or it will come out when you least expect it. People must throw away these silly social institutions that really only hinder us . . ."

David could clown around with Mark and most of

his other friends, but he kept thinking about Phu. How can there be true friendship if one of them holds back a secret? So on the last Saturday in July, more than three months after the murders, David dropped by at the Walgreen's where Phu worked on weekends.

Phu was wearing a company smock, and David came in wearing his *Rebel Without a Cause* garb of a white T-shirt with its sleeves rolled up to display his tattoos of an upside down cross and a serpent. He was jittery as he walked to the camera section near the front of the store.

"What's the matter, David?" Phu asked.

"I wanted to see you to say good-bye. I'm leaving town for awhile."

"Where are you going?" Phu asked.

David didn't answer right away. Instead he said, "I'm working on a project and have just dropped off some letters to a friend. In the next few days, one of three things will happen. I could be (a) in the morgue, (b) in jail and on the ten o'clock news, or (c) going into hiding some place. Maybe Los Angeles."

Before Phu could say anything, David asked, "Can we go somewhere?"

"I'm working—"

"Take a break."

Phu received permission to leave, and David was uncharacteristically silent as they drove through that warm, humid evening to David's special place, Tower Road Beach near the north end of Winnetka. Parked on the rim of the bluff, they couldn't see the narrow beach through the trees but they could look out at the vast lake.

"Now, what are you talking about, David?" Phu asked.

"It's connected to something I did in the past."

"Can't you tell me?" Phu asked.

"What's the worst thing I could have done?"

The tall, thin student hated to be in a position like

this, not sure whether David was serious or not. "You could have killed someone," Phu said uncertainly.

"Who is it I could have killed?"

Since David was making this a game of twenty questions, Phu could think only of replying in the same way. "Is this person on the local or national level?"

"Local."

Hesitantly, Phu asked, "Is it the Winnetka murders?" David chuckled.

"Is that laugh a yes or a no?" Phu asked.

"It's a yes."

There, it was out. With nothing in David's expression to show that he was joking or remorseful or proud, all Phu could do was act as if his friend hadn't said anything. Their conversation trailed off until there wasn't a conversation anymore. David dropped his friend off at the Walgreen's, and Phu completed his shift, less shocked by what he had heard than disturbed by the weight David was placing on him.

On Sunday afternoon, when Phu's parents were out, he called David from the kitchen of his family's one-story red brick home. "David—What you said yesterday, I want to hear more about it."

"Why?"

"You're not joking with me, are you?" David assured him he wasn't. "Then I want you to tell me everything."

Phu listened for nearly an hour and a half, barely saying a word. There could be no doubt that David was the killer; he gave Phu the slightest details of the shadows and sounds and feelings of that night. All this was too much for Phu to think about. If he fully accepted what David said, he had lost a friend forever and he would have to tell. But then Phu realized a way out. He told himself that turning David over to police wouldn't bring Richard or Nancy back. What was done was done.

There was nothing for David to do but wait out Phu's

reaction. The police could come knocking on his door at any time, and the suspense was wearing him down. A few days later he went to the Winnetka Youth Organization in the Community House, where Nancy Bishop often performed. Friends saw that he was upset about something and tried to talk to him, but David said only, "Leave me alone." He remained silent in a chair for two hours and left.

Before telling Phu about the murders, David had given a friend named *John a sealed envelope containing three copies of the apocalyptic message, to be mailed if he didn't return in about a week. "You'll know when to mail them," David said. "It'll be on the news." Once the week was over, and he was sure that Phu was keeping the secret, David went back and told John to do anything he wanted to with the letters. John gave the envelope back without looking inside. David erased the file from his computer.

None of David's concerns stopped him from getting up before 6 A.M. every day that summer to report for practice with the boys' varsity track team. David invariably would prop his long legs on a desk as Coach Doug Chase told the twenty-five boys what course they would take that day. David was one of the students who went on the longer runs with Chase while boys who were less gung-ho ran with the assistant coach. By 8 A.M. the two sets would meet up, towel off, joke around, and return to their bus.

Chief Timm's daughter, Beth, had mentioned to her father a couple of times that the former troublemaker was on the team. Although Beth seldom saw David because the girls ran on a different schedule, she told her father, "I think he's turned himself around."

"Well, God Almighty," Timm replied. "God bless him. I hope you're right."

At the end of the running season in August, the boys' and girls' teams went into competition with other schools. Dozens of parents drove to the field. David preferred running alone or in his own pack. Now, with everyone watching him, he was holding himself back. That was his old, self-sabotaging problem of fearing comparisons with anyone else. But as David neared the finish line—sweat sliding down to the elastic of his running shorts—he started pushing himself.

"Way to go!" Timm shouted. "That's the way to finish, son!" The New Trier students and parents screamed as David neared the finish line. "Great job, David!" Timm cheered when the boy was just a few yards from the line.

But David stopped two seconds from the end of the race. He turned to the police chief with a strange, hard glance, as if trying to cut him down. Timm got the feeling that David was looking right through him, but he couldn't understand why. Then the boy turned and finished the race.

School resumed not long after that, and David was back to his attention-grabbing habits of boasting and pulling pranks. He doused a cigarette in his hand as he stood with some kids under the rotunda of the school. The freedom of knowing that Phu had not told police about the murders allowed him to dream up other schemes.

By then he was dating *Karen Lyons, a short, pretty blonde whose father worked at the First National Bank of Winnetka. She would come to track meets to be with David, and they would go to movies and restaurants. Karen mentioned in a casual conversation that her father had beaten her around Christmastime.

David offered to kill her father, but she didn't want that. Even so, he began plotting revenge.

In mid-September, David reached Phu Huang outside the New Trier auditorium. "I've got a plan for something big," he said. Phu didn't want to hear it, but he listened. "I'm going to go up on the roof of the bank some night and take out the ceiling. Then I'm going to use an acetylene torch on the vault and grab the money, but I'll stay there until the morning."

"Why don't you just leave with the money?" Phu asked.

"Listen, I said. I'm going to wait until the morning crew comes in, and then I'm going to kill them all and leave a note saying I killed them just to spite the police."

Phu told himself not to believe a word of it, that David was joking, but David took him to his room and showed him a large bag with ropes, chisels, spikes, drills, a hammer, wire cutter, flashlight, and police scanner. Phu could believe the murders of Richard and Nancy, but not this crazy scheme.

In a few days, police showed up at the Biro house and reported that David was beginning to open up accounts under assumed names. Phu suspected that David might be planning to use the accounts to hide thousands of dollars from the bank vault. If that much was true, then his plans to murder the morning crew could be as well.

Officials at the small bank soon filed a report with the police, stating that someone had broken off the brackets for a vent over the skylight of the A-frame roof. The vent had tumbled to the street, and repairmen had to be called to put in new brackets. A slender thief quite possibly had lowered himself through the vent but discovered that there was a flat ceiling underneath and gave up.

Sergeant Patty McConnell and the other police went over the report on the off chance that the thief might try again.

18

━━◈◆◈━━

"It's All Falling Into Place"

Thursday, October 4

SERGEANT GENE KALVAITIS was back in uniform and working the midnight shift. Anytime his work took him to the east beat or the Cherry Street bridge in the slow hours before dawn, he would pause a moment to look at the row of townhouses. It was as if some force were drawing him there. What drove a cold-blooded killer to murder two fine, loving people?

The investigation had cost approximately one million dollars, including the salaries paid by other suburbs for their own members of the task force, yet they had virtually nothing to show for it except for binders with a foot and a half of paper. Gene knew that if the police had spent two million dollars, they still wouldn't be any closer to an answer.

The *Wall Street Journal* had said that "Suspicions abound that the Langerts were linked to an eerie substrata of intrigue and violence," comparing the murder and its aftermath to the television series "Twin Peaks," which premiered the day Lee Bishop found the bodies. In August, *Chicago* magazine had published an article entitled "Made for TV Murder," dragging out every old theory from a terrorist plot to attorney Jerome Boyle's

180

claim that "if they ever do catch the culprit it will turn out to be some local teenager."

Chief Herbert Timm was taking advantage of the long Columbus Day weekend to drive his daughter to colleges in the East. Before he left, he told Lieutenant Sumner, Patty, and Kalvaitis that "It's not like we're Chicago or New York, this case is solvable. Somebody knows."

Patty McConnell was working her usual 3 to 11 P.M. shift. She had just left on her lunch break at 7 P.M. when Phu Huang and his girlfriend entered the station. Phu, wearing a sweatshirt and jeans, nervously approached the glass-enclosed dispatch desk and said quietly, "I want to speak to a detective."

"That is Sergeant Patricia McConnell," the dispatcher told the youth. "She will be back in half an hour. Can someone else help you?"

"No," he said, "we'll come back."

Phu and Kate Ostrowski—a petite, curly-haired blonde—walked down Green Bay Road and turned west to David's house. David seemed happy to see them and took the two teens to his third-floor room, where everything was in disarray and the stolen computers sat shrouded with a white cloth. He had shot a crossbow bolt into the wall and let the point stay there. When he was bored, he strapped on a shoulder holster he had bought and practiced drawing the .357 Magnum.

"I want to show Kate that gun," Phu said. "Is that okay?"

With a grin, David pulled the silvery revolver from under his bed and showed it to her. Phu found himself looking at David in a new way, almost studying his features in this hour of betrayal. Why hadn't he realized such arrogance before? The Asian boy kept looking at his watch until saying, "We have to go, David. I'll see you around."

As they walked down the back stairs and headed for

the station, Phu told his girlfriend with a sigh that "I wanted to see him one last time."

When the teens returned to the station, the dispatcher paged McConnell over the intercom. Patty, dressed in a bright red silk top and black pants, walked up to the front desk and asked, "Yes, can I help you?"

"Please," said Phu, who had been expecting someone who looked more like a movie detective, "we need to talk to you about information for the police."

Patty smiled reassuringly and led them to her office. She closed the door and pulled up chairs so the three of them could speak in a circle rather than from across a desk.

"We can't tell you our names," Phu began, "just that we live here in Winnetka. I want to ask you some questions about the federal witness protection program. If we tell you our names, we may get killed."

McConnell lost her smile of greeting and pressed her hands together. She respected the concern of the two apparently average teenagers, but she wondered how they could possibly think their lives were in danger. "All right," she said, "tell me what your information is."

"We can tell you about something that was used in a crime and we can tell you where it is. Can you search the house—I mean, is it hard to get a search warrant?"

"Just because you tell me a house has something, that's not enough. That's a basic right of the American people, to be free from unreasonable searches of their homes. It may be hard for you, but you'll have to tell me something more."

"Oh God," Phu said, sitting back deeply in his chair and taking a deep breath. "I am a senior at New Trier. I also went to Washburne Junior High—" Then he stopped, as if hoping this would be enough for the detective to ask questions.

"You're going to have to make a decision whether you trust me or not," McConnell said. "We can't talk in this vague language. You're going to have to let me know what you're talking about. I don't know how to help you if you don't."

Phu turned to Kate for a moment and asked McConnell, "Can she and I talk alone for a minute?"

"Sure, right in the hallway. I'll close this door."

The teens left the room, and McConnell tried to think over what might be so disturbing for them. A moment later there was a knock. The two teenagers sat down again, and Phu said, "I'll tell you everything I know. It's about the Winnetka murders."

"You mean Nancy and Richard Langert?" McConnell asked, a chill racing through her.

"Yes."

Phu looked at the floor as the detective sergeant hit a button. "Hold my calls," McConnell said. She turned again to the tall, lean young man. "Go ahead. What do you know?"

Slowly, Phu explained how his friend David Biro broke into the townhouse, then sat with the gun and handcuffs waiting for the Langerts to arrive. Phu also spoke of a gift that David had played with as he waited in their home, one of the details that were never made public.

The words were coming out without emotion, as if Phu had already wrestled with his feelings. Kate gave little nods as the student told of seeing the gun in David's room. There was so much that McConnell could barely grasp it all. Everything made sense by itself, but there was no motive.

"What made you come to us now?" McConnell asked.

"He told me something else. He told me he would break into the roof of a bank and kill the morning crew just to embarrass the police. He said he was going to leave a note saying he broke in and killed the people just for fun. I . . . I thought he had to be stopped."

Patty asked Kate, "What do you know?"

The girl glanced at her boyfriend and said, "Just what he told me. David just showed me the gun."

"You still don't want to give me your name?" McConnell asked Phu. He answered by shaking his head.

"All right, that's fine. You're doing great. I know this is hard for you, being a friend."

"I want to leave now," Phu said. "Can we leave?"

McConnell rose, gave Phu her card, and said, "If there's anything more you want to tell us, any time, just ask for me. They'll get me wherever I am."

The young man and his girlfriend left the station at 8:30 P.M.

The detective intentionally hadn't made it clear how little police could do with anonymous information; she didn't want to discourage Phu into holding anything back. She now went to the New Trier yearbook the station kept on file and opened it to the 1989 junior class photos. She had just started when the front door opened and Phu and Kate were there again.

"Yes?" McConnell asked.

"We forgot something more," Phu said.

McConnell led them back to her office and Phu recounted the time David told him about the burglary at New Trier. "He said he broke into a window, and that's how he got the computers."

What did computers have to do with the murders, McConnell wondered. "You saw them?" she asked.

Phu nodded. "They're in his room. He's got a sheet over them now. I knew that what he told me about using the BB gun to get in was true because I saw a janitor replacing the broken window. That's all I can tell you."

"Please, before you go," the officer said. "Maybe this boy, David, didn't tell you but can you think of any reason why he might have wanted to kill the Langerts?"

"Well, he's talked about wanting to be a hitman ever since seeing the movie *Best Seller,*" Phu answered matter-of-factly. "He told me over the phone that 'It was my destiny to do the killing, there is no room for morals in this world.' "

Incredible, she thought.

McConnell thanked the teens again, and once they were gone everything started coming back to her, from all the crime-scene photos to the hundreds of pages of reports. But the case would go nowhere as long as the information remained anonymous.

Patty returned to the yearbook. With the young man's height and Oriental features, it was easy to scan the faces and find him. The name given was "Hung." She went to the lobby desk and asked the dispatcher to go through the listings for vehicle stickers. Nothing was under "Hung," but the dispatcher found a "Huang," and the address was near Washburne Junior High. That had to be it, McConnell thought.

"What's this about?" the dispatcher asked.

"Keep quiet about this until I get back."

She called the Kalvaitis home and told his wife to wake Gene up even though he normally would be at work in a couple of hours. When he came on the line, McConnell said excitedly, "Gene, we've got a break in the case!"

McConnell also phoned the homes of Lieutenant Sumner and Larry Lykowski from the state's attorney's office, then she had the dispatcher set up a twenty-four-hour watch on the Willow Street home. "I want to know if David Biro leaves the house," she said.

But by then, he had already gone. Phu could not bring himself to feel that he had become David's enemy. From the station, he and Kate had returned to the house and suggested that they all have pizza together. For those two hours, David was as animated as usual, but Phu hardly said anything.

Most of the officers knew David. If he wasn't in trouble, he was giving them a sarcastic wave as he walked past the station on his way to or from home. When Caldwell heard of the tip, a forgotten detail from six months ago clicked in his mind. "I spotted him!" he said. He hadn't notified anyone the Saturday night he saw David near the townhouse, but he had called the information in that Monday morning. He had never connected David to the killings because all the detectives were thinking that outsiders must have been involved.

Kalvaitis and McConnell pulled all the reports covering the New Trier burglaries and the murders. The officers thought they had all they needed to move on an arrest, but Lykowski came in and advised that they be patient. "What we got is hearsay," he told them. "We need the kid you talked to to get on the stand, or we don't have a case."

"You didn't see him, he's too scared," McConnell said. "He wouldn't give me his name, and I said that was all right."

"I don't care what you promised him. We've got to get him to testify."

Sumner, McConnell, and Kalvaitis drove across town to Phu's house near Ridge and Sherman. Along the way, Patty pointed out the Biro home while Sumner dialed the dispatcher from his portable phone. "Call the Huang residence," he said, "and tell them to meet the police at the front door." It was now 1:40 A.M.

Phu's short, slender mother answered the door, and a moment later her son came down the stairs, still wearing his sweatshirt and jeans. Necessary as this visit was, Patty felt ashamed that she had let him down. Phu understood. As he and his mother rode with the officers, the boy said with a sad resignation that "I knew you would find me."

Inside the station, Lykowski asked the student to repeat everything he knew and to take his time. The assistant prosecutor, Sumner, and Kalvaitis were convinced that this young man was telling the truth. Many of the things he mentioned had never made the news, including the paycheck envelope, the gift, the Discman, and the fact that Nancy was shot only twice.

After relating for a second and a third time everything that David had told him, Phu looked at the early morning darkness outside the window. He was tired and agitated and relieved.

Lykowski and the three police officials excused themselves and held a conference about what to do. They hadn't even called Chief Timm yet, because they were afraid the case might fall apart. The assistant prosecutor said they weren't ready for a warrant.

"Larry," Gene said, "I want a search warrant for that kid's bedroom. I've been working on this case for six months, and we got nothing. Now we've got everything. If you wait a few days maybe Biro'll get rid of the evidence."

"Apart from what Biro may have told Huang, all Huang knows is that there's a gun up there," Lykowski said.

"The computers," Kalvaitis reminded him. "Phu told us he saw 'N.T.' on them. That proves they're stolen from New Trier. We got enough to get a warrant on them. David told Phu and the girl he stole the gun. Let's treat it like a burglary and work from there."

"All right, we can go with that," Lykowski said.

"And we can tell Timm it's solid," Gene added with enthusiasm. It was 4 A.M.

At that time, the police chief and his daughter were sleeping in a Syracuse, New York, motel. They had looked over a college in Schenectady and were planning on driving to others in Maine. When the phone rang, Timm was so disoriented that his first thought was, "What's that?" He picked up the receiver and heard Lieutenant Sumner say, "Herb, this is Joe. I'm sorry to wake you."

Just hearing Sumner's voice made Timm sit straight up. "Oh, Jesus, what happened?"

"We cracked the Langert homicide."

"What!"

Sumner repeated the words Timm had thought he might never hear. "We cracked the Langert murders."

"Thank God," the police chief said. "What happened? Wait, let me get my glasses." As his teenage daughter sat up in her bed, Timm grabbed a pen and some paper from the bedstand. "Who was it?"

"David ..." Timm started writing down the name. ". . . Biro."

The pen stopped and the police chief said, "I don't believe it." He turned to Beth and told her the name, and she stared at him. David was a classmate, he had run for class president, he was on the track team with her. Everyone thought he had turned his life around.

As Sumner started giving what information they had, Timm mumbled, "Jesus, it's all falling into place." Occasionally people had said the killer might be some neighborhood kid, but the possibility had seemed so farfetched no one in the department had given it any real credence. Now it seemed logical, even obvious.

"Is he in custody yet?"

"He's at home," Sumner said. "Huang's still here in the station."

"Okay, I'm heading back now. I'll be in by mid-afternoon."

"What?" Sumner couldn't imagine anyone driving that fast.

"I'll leave the car here and I'll get a plane. Somebody can meet me at O'Hare. Keep a lid on things until I arrive. That doesn't mean don't do anything. Just that I'll be there."

Timm hung up, exhilarated. He started to tell Beth about what Sumner had told him, but she turned away and said, "I don't want to know any more."

There was such a heavy stillness in the motel room

that the police chief stood up and suggested to Beth, "Let's take a run."

Timm and his daughter jogged for three miles through the chilly dawn.

19

Cat And Mouse

Friday, October 5

PHU HUANG NEVER got to go home. So many people wanted him to repeat his story that he never knew when he would be needed, so he slept a little on the floor of Chief Timm's empty office.

The overnight dispatcher had called Benoit at home to ask him to come in a few hours early. When he showed up at 6 A.M. and Kalvaitis told him who the killer was, Eddie replied, "Naw, I can't believe it. I know this guy is an asshole but he's, what, sixteen?"

"He turned seventeen in May," Kalvaitis said.

Benoit didn't say anything else, but he kept wondering: How could everybody have been so wrong?

Sergeant McConnell was spending the early morning at her cluttered desk. In her fourteen years as an officer, she had never written up a search warrant and so she went over it again and again to make sure the document covered everything without being too broad. The two IBM PSII 230–286 computer systems, the two DXY Plotter machines, the color monitor, the "mouse," the glass cutter, the gun. The affidavit for the warrant made no mention of the murders, and it listed the source of information as "John Doe."

Although school was closed that day, David awoke around seven-thirty so he could drive his mother to her office in Deerfield. After he returned, Nick came home from work early, feeling a little sick. He parked his red Toyota Corolla behind Joan's car in the driveway.

At 8:30 A.M., a judge in the Skokie courthouse put his signature on the warrant, and McConnell thought they were ready to roll. But when she returned to the station, one of the four assistant prosecutors sent over by State's Attorney Cecil Partee, Anthony Calabrese, wasn't satisfied. "This is too limiting," he told her. "It says third-floor bedroom. Suppose we see something major elsewhere in the house. Then what?"

Lieutenant Sumner had another kind of worry. "I don't think we should just show up at his door and announce ourselves," he said to Kalvaitis. "This kid is a cold-blooded killer. I think we should call Deerfield and bring in their SWAT team just in case."

Sumner's phone buzzed, and the dispatcher said WBBM-TV reporter Jay Levine was in the lobby to see him. The officers stared at one another as if to ask, who leaked the news? Then Sumner said, "I forgot! Levine is doing a six-month anniversary on the murders. Don't worry, I'll handle him."

The lieutenant closed all the doors so the TV crew wouldn't notice the activity, then met Levine in his office. "Anything new on the case?" the tall, square-jawed reporter asked as his cameraman positioned a lavaliere microphone on Sumner's collar.

Like Timm, Sumner had a close way of speaking and was able to keep his excitement from showing. "Well, Jay, we are working on a lot of leads and something may develop. There's nothing to say that some phone call or some conversations along the line won't open up one of those areas and put us back on that track instead."

Levine thanked Sumner, they shook hands, and the WBBM van drove off.

Just minutes later, the communications and weapons van of the Northern Illinois Police Alarm System Emergency Service arrived from Deerfield. A fire truck was driven out of the rear garage so the gray vehicle could pull in without notice. The team commander, Gary Stryker, jumped out in his black uniform and bulletproof vest, then he and his men settled in the police station as at least three plainclothes teams kept watch on the Biro house.

McConnell woke up Phu and took him to a room where Kalvaitis and assistant prosecutor Timothy Joyce were waiting to hear his story. Gene gave him pen and paper and asked him to draw David's room. Phu was able to show the location of the glass cutter and the bed the gun had been under, but he still didn't want his name on the warrant.

Assistant prosecutor Joyce said, "Look, Phu, we understand your feelings, but there's a problem I don't expect you to understand because it's about the way the courts work. We have a warrant from Judge Dunn, but the Biros are bound to ask that the evidence we find be thrown out. That's routine. The trouble is that it won't be Judge Dunn who'll hear the motion. So without the name of our source, you, the new judge might throw out everything we find. That means we could never use it, and we'd be worse off than if you never had the courage to come forward."

"But then everyone will know my name."

"You want to stop the killings, don't you?"

"Please, Phu," McConnell said softly beside him. "We will protect your name until the trial. I know it isn't an easy decision to make, but trust me. I will be there with you all the way."

Phu lowered his head and sighed, "Okay."

McConnell was so relieved that only then did she begin to realize how tired she was. She drove Phu to the Skokie courthouse.

At 2:20 P.M., David came down the stairs of his home

and asked his father if he could move the Toyota out so he could get his mother's car ready for picking her up in a few hours. Nick gave him the keys, and David went outside. He was wearing khaki pants, a shirt with the top unbuttoned as usual, and a white rag around his head like the headband of his avenger sketch in the red notebook.

The crosstalk on the police radio went like this:

—"We have spotted our subject. He is walking out of the house. Now he's on the driveway."

—"This is Kerner. We see him. If he goes around the corner, we will pick him up."

—"He has just backed up a red Toyota in the driveway and is now entering another car."

A few hundred feet away, the SWAT members scrambled into their van. Officers Bobby Caldwell and Glenn Florkow left their stake-out car and approached David as he was getting back into the Toyota to bring it back to the driveway. The boy didn't seem to remember the officers from fighting with them at the traffic stop more than two years before. "David Biro," Caldwell said formally, "we are placing you under arrest and taking you to the Winnetka police station. Put your hands on the car."

David leaned against the trunk as they searched him. "Why am I arrested?" he asked. "Hey, what's happening?"

"You are wanted for questioning about a major investigation."

Benoit arrived to slap the handcuffs on him and put him in the backseat of one of the squad cars. David smiled faintly. In less than a minute they were at the station. The SWAT team left, glad they had not been needed.

Not long after that, Nick Biro—feeling better after resting at home—went to his car and drove back to work without knowing that his son was being questioned.

At 3:30 P.M. McConnell had a second warrant signed, this time by Judge Joan Corboy. With this in hand, Kalvaitis rang the front bell of the Biro home. When no one answered, he lit a cigarette to calm his nerves. He went around to the back and was surprised to find a door unlocked. The officers walked through the immaculate house and went up to David's room. They opened the door and saw shattered glass on the floor, an arrow point in the wall, and pellet holes in the wallpaper. The bed was unmade and clothes were tossed about. "This is a pigsty," Gene said.

On the large television set was a plaster sculpture of a skull with a green cobra winding through its mouth and one eye socket. On the floor was David's long-barrelled BB pistol. Kalvaitis looked around and thought, God, it's all here. Nearly everything listed on the warrant was visible, from the glass cutter to the hooded sweatshirt and the black bag with enough tools to break into a bank. The only item not in view was the murder weapon.

"Pick up the mattress," Gene said.

The men rolled back the mattress, and a jolt went through Kalvaitis as he glimpsed the .357 Magnum.

"Okay," he said, "let's not touch anything. Let's take pictures of where everything is. We also have to make a list of everything that's not on the warrant, so we can come back here and get it."

On his mobile phone, Kalvaitis asked property officer Liz Ford to pick up the .357 and bring it to the crime lab. Then he told the dispatcher to put the lab staff on notice that something hot would be coming their way in less than half an hour, and he called in the serial number of the revolver to start an ownership check.

When Nick Biro drove into the driveway from work, he saw two squad cars in front. "What's happening?" he asked the officers.

"Are you Mr. Biro?" one of the policemen asked.

"You can't go inside, they are conducting an investigation into a burglary. Here's a copy of the warrant."

"Has my son been arrested?"

"I can't say," replied the officer. "We're just securing the premises."

Kalvaitis came out and found Nick sitting on the back stairs. "We're executing a search warrant," Gene said. "When we're completed, we will give you a copy of the items we seized."

"A search warrant for what?" Nick asked in disgust, but Kalvaitis didn't answer. Instead, he allowed the father inside but told Officer Joe Pellus to keep him in the kitchen.

A prisoner in his own home as officers moved in and out speaking in low tones among themselves, Nick was even more on edge than when he was waiting outside. Since no one would tell him anything, he decided to go to the station but was told he would have to wait before he could speak to his son. Nick received the impression that it might be hours before this was possible, so he returned home.

From there he tried calling his wife at work, but she had left her office. Nick drove to Deerfield and found Joan standing impatiently outside. She had been waiting for an hour and a half, not knowing why David had failed to show up as promised. As Nick drove his wife home, he dialed the number for attorney John Lewis on his car phone.

The lawyer had been watching television after dinner when the call came in. Nick was frantic because he couldn't speak to his son. Lewis told Nick not to worry, he had dealt with Winnetka police a number of times before, and he always found them reasonable. It was now 6:45 P.M.

All this time, David was talking to Patty McConnell and Assistant State's Attorney Sally Bray in the fifteen-foot-square interview room. There were a few chairs, a couple of desks, and a bench with a permanent set of handcuffs on each end. With light fading from the window, police brought in some McDonald's hamburgers for the prisoner.

When assistant prosecutor Timothy Joyce entered the room and pulled up a chair next to him, David asked, "What's happening?"

"David, you do understand your rights?" The boy just stared at him. "We are looking into certain matters including homicides for which you can be prosecuted and sentenced as an adult. Now, do you own a gun?"

"Look, I don't want to talk to you," David said.

"Do you own a gun?"

"No."

"David, do you know anything about some burglaries in which computers were taken at your school last May?"

"No."

The assistant prosecutor smiled back and said, "That's strange, David. We just found computers stolen from New Trier in your room. How did they get there? Tell us what happened, David. It will be easier if you tell us the truth."

David shrugged and gave them all the details. But whenever the questioning strayed from thefts to the murders, he avoided all their traps. Timothy Joyce took a deep breath, exchanged professional glances with Bray, and left the room.

Bray knew that if she were ever to get the boy to admit the killings, it would be by tapping his pride. She began by asking David how well he did at school. He told her and McConnell that his IQ was 144, the genius level (and twenty-two points higher than he actually scored). He said he regarded himself as "superior" to other people, even though he had just a B-plus average.

The two women could see that David enjoyed intellectual exercises of his own devising. Part of the game was to deny even the obvious. He didn't have any gun, he said; then he claimed that maybe he did but he didn't remember. Maybe some friends hid it under his bed, he suggested, straight-faced. As to his clippings about the murder, David said he had kept them because the murders were interesting, and because his parents knew the Bishops.

"Who do you think killed them?" Sally Bray asked. "I mean, do you think there was an assassin?"

"He must have been a powerful person," David said with those no-tell eyes.

"Why do you say that?"

"Just from what I read. I mean, he had handcuffs and cut his way through the glass. You can tell he was no small-timer."

"Ordinary burglars could do that," the assistant prosecutor suggested.

"But he didn't touch all the money that was on the floor," David reminded her. "There was a pay envelope right on the floor, he didn't bother to pick it up. He was strong enough to walk away from it."

Bray continued as if they were speaking of abstractions. "A hired killer would have picked up the money as he left, wouldn't he? If that was all it was about, money."

"Then he made a mistake," David remarked. "Maybe he was in a hurry to get away."

"Why do you know so much about the murders?"

"I read everything on it."

"I'm not so sure the killer was a hired assassin," Bray said. "Police say he might have been insane. Don't you think so?"

"I don't believe in insanity."

"Never?"

"No," David answered. "Insane, that means they don't know the difference between right and wrong, doesn't it?"

Bray nodded.

"Well everyone knows that."

"Do you?"

"Of course."

"Then why would someone kill them if he wasn't paid to do it?"

"Maybe the Langerts heckled him."

"Heckled? In what way?"

"I don't know."

During the conversational questioning, assistant prosecutor Timothy Joyce had come back into the room, and now he picked up Bray's line of thinking. "David, I think you killed the Langerts," he said. There wasn't much reaction in the boy's face. "I think you killed them because you're insane."

"Do you think I'm crazy and would tell you?" David asked calmly, playing his mind game again.

And so it went for hours, with the prosecutors trying to lead David into an incriminating statement, and David dancing on the rim. After a while, Sergeant McConnell left the interview room for a soda. She didn't know whether she felt more like screaming in frustration or flopping down somewhere for a long sleep.

Kalvaitis and Benoit saw her at the soft-drink machine and asked what David was like under questioning. "That guy is really scary," she told them. "He just makes your skin crawl."

"Did he say why he did it?" Benoit wondered.

Patty shook her head.

Nick Biro looked down at the kitchen floor as police swarmed about his home, but his wife could not stand by so passively. She insisted that she and her husband be allowed to go in any room they wished. When Officer Pellus attempted to make her understand, she took a swing at him.

Pellus didn't even flinch. "Mrs. Biro," he said, "you're upset and I'll give you that one, but the next time you're going to have to go down to the station with me."

After some haggling, police agreed to let the couple have free use of the lower floor. Although the Biros now had more room, they didn't say much to one another. They couldn't imagine why police were treating them this way just for some burglary.

When the officers left a little before 8 P.M., Joan turned on the television in hopes of catching something on a news break. A WBBM reporter announced that a juvenile was being held in the "Winnetka murders" and that he was making statements.

David's parents were stunned.

When property officer Liz Ford rushed up the stairs of the Highland Park police station with the .357 Magnum, Bob Wilson of the Northern Illinois Police Crime Laboratory couldn't have been more excited. He had been hoping for this moment for six months, but he had to handle the gun like the hundreds of others he had tested in his career.

The balding former Du Page County police detective worked in a cramped room barely larger than a pantry, crammed with weapons ranging from derringers to broken Saturday-night specials and a tommy-gun that had belonged to the Capone gang. An odd-looking, tilted concrete tank of water was at the other side of his little room.

Wilson put a round in the chamber of the revolver and went up a step to the crude platform of the tank. The walkway was so narrow he had to go sideways. Bob, a lively man in his sixties, put on headphones to muffle the sound and fired into a small opening. Next he went "fishing," using a string pulley to lift the slug out on a horizontal screen at the lower end of the eight-foot tank.

Next, Wilson needed to compare that slug with the bullets from the Langert murders. There was no "Ah-ha!" involved. Lands and grooves are never as precise as fingerprints. It took a long study under the dual lenses of the comparison microscope before he could establish a match. Wilson's eyes were bleary after working for fourteen hours. But Winnetka police were waiting for an answer, and he personally had to know whether the evidence was strong enough to file charges.

After arriving from O'Hare Airport, Chief Timm kept quiet as he passed reporters and camera crews at the station. As soon as he was alone with Lieutenant Sumner, he demanded, "How in the hell did they find out about this?"

"It wasn't us. It's an election year."

"Is the Biro kid talking?"

"He's said things, but nothing we can charge him on except burglary."

"What about an attorney?"

"He hasn't been asking for one."

Actually David's lawyer, John Lewis, was still trying to get information from police. After an uneasy couple of hours, he drove up to the station at 9:25 P.M., pulling up in back because of all the news vans on Green Bay Road. Lewis tried to be inconspicuous as he told the woman at the reception/dispatch desk that he was there to represent a client. Lieutenant Gallagher, one of the officers in the dispatch office, told him to stay in the lobby for a few minutes. The officers and Assistant State's Attorney Tony Calabrese were still preparing a third warrant.

A couple of the reporters began to suspect who Lewis was, but he ignored them. When Gallagher didn't get back to him, he called his partner, Lou Bruno, and left this message on the answering machine: "I am at the Winnetka police station and I can't see David. I want you down here, I need a witness."

An officer walked into the glass-enclosed dispatch room with a printout from the serial number of the revolver. The gun belonged to none other than attorney John Lewis. But Calabrese and Sumner showed no surprise at all.

"Don't you know who this guy is?" Gene asked, taking a cigarette from his mouth and chuckling at the irony. "The John Lewis who owns the gun and that man standing out in our lobby waiting to represent David Biro are one and the same."

"You're kidding," Calabrese said.

"No, I'm not kidding, I've dealt with him for years. No wonder for once David's not eager to see his attorney!"

"Well, this changes the whole picture," Calabrese said. He loosened his tie for what was shaping up to be a long night.

At 10:10 P.M., Judge Corboy in her north suburban home signed the third warrant for the day, this time letting police seize items they saw in David's room but which had not been listed earlier, including the handcuffs and practice glass, the T-shirt with a Jesus design, and the red notebook.

When the officers returned to the home, they went through the notebook and saw articles, drawings, and the strange notations of a mind drifting on its own. One line stood by itself at the top of a page. Apparently it had originally read: "I am one of the original devils that was damned to hell, and I will use all my cunning for evil." But sometime after writing that, perhaps after the killings, David crossed out the word "will." He did not cross it out as if he had made a mistake or changed his mind. He covered the word over neatly with overlapping pen strokes.

The message was now more chilling: *I am one of the original devils that was damned to hell, and I use all my cunning for evil.*

Attorney Lou Bruno arrived at the police station, and Lewis had time to brief him on what little he knew before Lieutenant Gallagher returned. By then Lewis was fuming. He was taking notes on everything and demanding to speak to an assistant state's attorney. His client had been in custody for eight hours, and he insisted it was time to talk about charges or release him.

Calabrese asked Bruno to wait in the lobby, then he and Kalvaitis took Lewis to an empty room and closed the door. Gene sat at the desk, Lewis took a chair, and the assistant prosecutor sat on the edge of the desk. By now it was nearly midnight.

Lewis was taut with indignation, but the two officials couldn't be open with him because of the remote possibility that he had been involved in the killings. They started with roundabout questions about the gun that disappeared. The attorney was so concerned about representing his client that he failed to make the connection. He kept wondering what the assistant prosecutor was getting at until Calabrese told him, "We found that gun in David Biro's room this afternoon."

"Oh my God," Lewis replied and almost sank through the chair. "Do you have the serial number?"

Calabrese held out the inventory list and read off: "124—"

"That's it," Lewis said quietly.

"You understand, Mr. Lewis, this means you are now a witness against David. You can't represent him anymore because we'll have to interview you."

For a moment, Lewis didn't say anything. His gun had killed those people—it was as if he had taken part in the murders himself. At last he said, "Excuse me, I have to call the family and tell them I'll get another lawyer for them."

Police were still questioning Phu Huang off and on, hoping to find something more to use against David. Finally, sometime before dawn, they told Phu he wouldn't be needed anymore. The young man walked out of the station exhausted and emotionally drained from a day and a half with authorities.

In the interview room, David was becoming weary of games with police and prosecutors. When told that the revolver found under his bed had checked out as belonging to his lawyer, he admitted stealing the gun, but he claimed he had given it to a friend, whom he declined to identify. The friend committed the murders and gave it back later, he said.

"What did your friend tell you?" Sally Bray asked.

David described the murder detail by detail, just as Phu had related. It was disturbing to hear such deadly calculation spoken without a trace of emotion. But David assured them the killer had some humanitarian feelings. His unnamed friend had said he decided not to kill Nancy when Richard told him she was pregnant. Unfortunately, he had no choice after she saw his face.

"Where was Richard shot?" Bray asked.

David lowered his chin and pointed to the back of his head, where his neck joined the skull. "Here, he shot him right here. Very close."

There was one difference between what the suspect was saying now and what they had heard from Phu earlier. David assured Bray and McConnell that his mysterious friend had shot Nancy three times, just as the news had said. Why would he lie about that? Then Bray realized he was covering himself in case no one believed the story about his friend.

"Did your friend make any mistakes?" she asked.

"A few," David answered in a tired voice. "He left the handcuffs on Richard and the money on the floor. And that first shot, that was a mistake."

From then on, there was hour after hour of questioning in which Bray, Calabrese, and David simply repeated themselves. The assistant state's attorneys agreed among themselves at 4 A.M. that they had reached a stalemate for now. David was led in handcuffs to the lockup. Bray took a nap on the floor of one of the side rooms. Chief Timm put on his trenchcoat and went home for a little rest. Officer McConnell caught some sleep on an empty cot at the firehouse in the back of the station. Gene Kalvaitis called home for a change of clothes and his shaving gear.

IV

"Evil Does Not Have The Last Word"

20

"Ask Yourself,
What Happened Here?"

Saturday, October 6

AT SEVEN O'CLOCK that morning, police began inviting
David's friends to the station. The officers assured the
acquaintances that they weren't in any trouble and tried
to keep the conversations casual. Then a lawyer came
in, saying, "I'm representing all these kids, and you're
not going to question them."

Out the kids went, leaving Kalvaitis and Timm open-
mouthed. "Well, Gene," the police chief said, "that's
what we've got grand juries for." Anywhere else, they
thought, parents would be telling their children to cooperate completely. But this was the North Shore.

David spent a couple of hours that morning lying on
a bed in the lockup before he was taken out for more
questioning.

By 10 A.M., Timm was becoming impatient. The
crime lab still had nothing to report from ballistics
tests. In a meeting with prosecutors, he urged them to
charge David before they violated his rights. "It's getting close to twenty-four hours."

"State law does not specify twenty-four hours," Calabrese reminded him.

"If you're waiting for a confession, forget it. He's playing games with us."

"Since you want something now, we could charge him with burglary," Calabrese suggested.

"Burglary my ass!" Timm exploded. "Sorry. I apologize if I'm being a hot-headed German. With burglary, he can bond out. I don't want this kid back on the streets again."

Having made that clear, Timm picked up the phone and called the crime lab once more. "Andy," he said to the director, "what the hell is going on?"

"We're getting close, Chief," Andy Principe answered.

"Is it the gun or isn't it?"

"Yeah, it's the gun, but we just can't prove it yet."

Timm set the phone down and told Calabrese he felt as if he were in a hospital waiting room before a delivery.

For Nick Biro, the day was a blur. A little before noon, he called the station again and asked Lieutenant Sumner if he and his wife could visit their son.

"Prisoners are not allowed to see visitors."

"He hasn't seen anybody since yesterday."

"Oh, he's seen a lot of people," Sumner replied on edge, "we're going in and out all the time."

"David's just seventeen, maybe he doesn't know he is allowed to see his family or an attorney."

"We told him his rights, Mr. Biro, and they're all over the wall."

Four hours later, Bob Wilson put the .38-caliber slug he had just fired from the .357 under the twin-lens microscope and compared it with the bullet taken from Nancy's abdomen. He took off his glasses and studied the marks until he was sure they were identical. He turned the bullets over and snapped one Polaroid shot after another. He enlarged the photos and held them to the light. With a smile, he called the station and announced, "Chief, we've got a match."

Timm was so tired he could reply only with a weak "That's good." But as he sat back in his chair he thought, "Oh, God, thank you!"

It was hand-clasping time as Timm gathered his top officers and the prosecutors in the conference room and informed them of the match. Winnetka's only unsolved murder of the century was cracked at last.

With the investigation no longer depending on David's statements, he was led back down the pale green hall to the lockup. But the police could not book him on their own. Felony charges had to be approved by prosecutors, and State's Attorney Cecil Partee was still making weekend appearances in his election campaign. Cook County's first black top law-enforcement official was a political appointee, and he needed all the publicity he could get. He decided to announce charges personally at a news conference at 8 P.M., nearly thirty hours after David's arrest.

Joan Biro had been listening to the news throughout the day, learning about the allegations and her son's situation only in fragments. When she heard about the press conference, she called the police station and asked that she be given the charges before hearing them on the air. Kalvaitis told her burglary, theft, and the murders of Richard, Nancy, and their unborn child. Mrs. Biro, always so self-reliant, was crushed.

David was awakened in his cell and taken to the booking room, where Officer Bobby Caldwell told him the charges. David didn't show a reaction, not even to the count of intentionally killing a fetus, which had been imposed only a few times since becoming a state law four years before. The boy maintained a fixed smile as Caldwell took his mug shot and Benoit fingerprinted him. Benoit knew it was impossible, but the kid looked as if he didn't have a care in the world.

The prisoner asked to use the phone and dialed his house. "Dad, this is David, do you know where I am?" His parents said they had been trying to see him since learning of his arrest, and that an attorney would be meeting him soon.

But at the time, the family didn't know who that lawyer would be. Lewis had been attempting all day to contact a good lawyer who was free to take the case. That evening he reached Robert Gevirtz, a slender dark-haired man who lived only a few miles from the murder scene. Lewis—a former prosecutor—respected Gevirtz from a few criminal cases in which they had been on opposing sides.

Gevirtz pulled an old leather jacket over his loose sweater and drove to the Biro home to introduce himself. He found the parents distraught not only because the allegations were incomprehensible but because they were still being prohibited from seeing their son.

Partee's news conference was set up in the firehouse. Sergeant McConnell didn't have the time or energy to return home for a change of clothes, so she wore shorts and a blouse borrowed from Chief Timm's teenage daughter. The Bishops and the Langerts were waiting in the former task-force room in the basement, where they wouldn't be bothered by reporters.

State's Attorney Partee, a kind-looking man, arrived in a dark suit and went downstairs with Chief Timm. "We are at the end of a long journey here," Timm told the families. "We are charging a young seventeen-year-old boy from Winnetka. His name is David Biro."

Joyce closed her eyes and lowered her head. "Oh God," she said in a muffled tone, "we know his family." Lee was dazed—the Biros were such nice people. Jeanne sat back and released six months of tension and uncertainty. She lightly touched Timm's arm and said, "I'm sorry for the trouble I caused you."

The police chief couldn't tell the families how sorry he felt that the case had taken so long, and that so many wild-goose chases had been publicized.

Partee returned upstairs and announced the charges. Immediately the news media stopped caring about the supposed drug connection, the mob connection, and the IRA connection. The Bishop and Langert families at last had become old news, leaving them to recover from their wounds.

McConnell went home to her sleeping daughter, Kristen, and picked up Frances, the black-and-white stuffed rabbit that had fallen to the floor. She placed the worn-out toy back in the arms of the three-year-old and touched her face. Dear God, McConnell prayed silently as she thought about Joyce and her daughter, please don't let anything happen to my baby.

At the Biro home, a harsh white light poured through the windows from a television van parked outside.

Now that the urgency of filing charges was over, police talked over how to make sense of the crime so that the charges would stand up in court. The officers were convinced they had enough physical evidence to convict David, but the absence of a demonstratable motive opened the way for a defense attorney to tell a jury the murders must have been committed by someone else.

Police questioning teenagers in hangouts near New Trier over the following week heard rumors of a "black book" David had been keeping. But not even a search of his three lockers at school turned up anything.

Kalvaitis heard a rumor that David had returned to the townhouse a few days after Lee found the victims and brought a friend from Kenilworth. David supposedly broke in and showed the other teenager where the bodies had been, as if reliving the film *River's Edge*. The rumor made sense. Police had noticed that the seal over the lock on the back gate was broken some time after all the evidence was removed, but Kalvaitis assumed until now that some reporter was responsible.

Detective Fay studied a bare-chested photo of David, taken by the Winnetka *Talk* sports department a few weeks before, and thought the amateur tattoos might be satanic symbols.

Fay knew from a course he had taken that many teens used devil-worship buzzwords and symbols. He went outside the school during lunch periods and informally talked to teens as they sat on the long steps or played hacky-sack with a beanbag. He began by asking about students known to participate in role-playing games. He found out that David had played Dungeons and Dragons, and that he had a couple of books on witchcraft. But David lost interest in all that about a year before, when he stepped up his thefts. Even so, the detective was left wondering whether David might have imagined himself rising to one of the most intriguing roles a Dungeons and Dragons player can adopt, the assassin.

Fay also went over drawings in the red notebook, especially one showing a thorned finger touching a flower. That surely must be satanic. Strangely, the upper half of the illustration, showing a sun between clouds and framed by four small crosses, resembled an altar-cloth design.

As news of David's arrest spread, Sergeant McConnell began getting calls about him from other departments. Police in Kenilworth said that while visiting a friend two weeks earlier, David had threatened two schoolboys with a toy rifle. "You better leave or I'll shoot your heads off!" he shouted as his teenage friends stood by. The incident had occurred just a block away from the Kenilworth Union Church, where the Langerts were married and where their ashes now lay in the memorial garden.

A neighbor called police, and David was placed handcuffed into a squad car. At the Kenilworth station, one of the officers noticed that David's Illinois Secretary of State's photo identification card had been issued to Ron Matzig. "This is a phony ID," the officer said.

"I'm just holding it for a friend. He forgot it."

"But this is your picture."

"He just looks like me."

Yeah, sure. Identical twin friends.

David paid his twenty-five-dollar fine, then politely asked for the card. "Oh, no," the officer told him, "have Mr. Matzig come down and talk to me if he wants it back." David replied with a sarcastic smile like James Woods in *Best Seller* and rolled up his sleeve to expose his gang-signal tattoo. David's message was clear: "Fuck you, Officer!"

Hearing from New Trier students how much David liked *Best Seller*, Patty McConnell rented a copy and handed it to Kalvaitis the next day. "It's incredible," she said. Kalvaitis watched the movie on his VCR at home. The similarities sent chills up his back.

Police, searching for a motive, heard a rumor that some time before the murders, Richard had told some friends of David that if he saw them selling drugs again he would call the police. Could that seemingly minor incident have been the reason David had singled out the couple? The story was plausible, but none of the officers could verify it from another source.

The officers heard something else unsettling. David's girlfriend, Karen, was upset over his arrest and told Benoit about how she went several times with David to fire a rifle with a telescopic lens. When she had mentioned having trouble with her parents, David asked if she wanted him to kill them for her. He didn't mention the Langerts, but he said he had once tried to poison his own family. Karen didn't take him seriously at the time, but Benoit wanted to bet that David's fantasies of killing had not stopped after he murdered Richard and Nancy.

That same Monday, Coach Chase called members of the track team together to talk over their feelings. "David ran with us, trained with us; David is one of us," Chase said as he walked between the desks. Some of the boys' eyes were red from crying. "There are going to be rumors everywhere," Chase continued, "so I want all of us to promise that we will not talk about David to anyone except the police until he has his day in court."

As the students trotted outside in their T-shirts and shorts, they chanted into the eye of a TV camera, "We're not talking!"

New Trier Principal Diana Lindsey felt violated by television crews trying to get into the hallways of her school. Some students felt disgusted that a killer had walked down these corridors, sat near them, and eaten in their lunchroom. Others were excited that they had sat so close to evil.

There was little shock among David's friends. Detectives had never seen a case like this. How many people had David talked to about the murders—half a dozen? Ten? Maybe twenty. Kalvaitis wanted to follow up the rumor that David had taken the son of an influential man into the townhouse after the gate was sealed. Gene was sure he could convince the father that his son should tell what he knew about the murders. But the state's attorney's office said bringing the boy before a grand jury would only confuse the issue. Police blamed the decision on the election year.

On Tuesday, October 26, police executed a fourth search warrant for the Biro home, this one seeking a black leather jacket and seventy-eight floppy disks. The officers fed the disks one by one into a computer still hooked up in the former talk-force room. One of David's files was an Illinois Secretary of State form. There was no doubt he had planned to sell phony identifications, because he also had eighteen plastic card holders in his room.

Most of the computer files were routine, but police were startled when they retrieved passages that David wrote in July, three months after the murders. Although the words had been erased from the disk, they were retained in the computer memory. Lieutenant Sumner rushed upstairs and told the police chief, "Herb, you got to see this."

Timm followed him back and read the message, which began with huge block letters: IMPORTANT READ THOROUGHLY!

"Many people like to think of themselves as good people," began the passage in its archaic script, "whether or not they are religious doesn't matter; these are strong law-abiding citizens or so they would like us to think this. I ask all of you to take a moment and look inside yourselves, and he who hath not sinned may cast the first stone; be honest now. Did Christ condemn only external acts of murder? . . . But I say to you that everyone who is angry with his brother shall be liable to judgement . . . Who is a murderer? Everyone who hates his brother is a murderer."

Timm read with horrified fascination as he advanced the statement line by line on the computer screen.

"Ask yourself, what happened here? What quirk of nature, what genetic defect could bring about this vicious ammoral [sic] killer. The morals of the people today are terrible, everybody is out for themself [sic]. Nobody cares about their fellow man as long as they can get over on somebody else. The secret is revealed; no cosmic potion was stirred up and out he came, it was you. I am merely a seed, if you should be angry at anyone, you can only blame yourself. I am merely a seed, a product of my environment, of my society. I am merely a seed, a chemical reaction waiting to take place. If proper love and care were added at the right times maybe things would have been different, but luckily hate, greed, racism, and violence were added in just the right place to spawn the whirlwind."

Timm could feel the fantasies of power behind the words.

"Blame yourselves," the message continued, "for I may fail, but my predecesors [sic] won't. There will come along a smarter seed, a faster seed, a finer seed than mine that will complete the task at hand. People think that they are invincible, but they aren't, people have come close; Christ, Alexander the Great, Ghengis [sic] Khan and Subutai [his general, Sabutai], Mussolini, Hitler and many others. But it isn't too late, you must change your way, you must, or perish! People will look at me and scoff and think that I am crazy. Oh but we will have fun won't we. I feel that there is a beast in all of us that is waiting to come out. Let it, let it be free or it will come out when you least expect it."

"See, what did I tell you?" Sumner asked. But Timm was not yet finished.

"People must throw away these silly social institutions that really only hinder us rather than help us," the message continued. "At this point you need not wonder why the Langerts were killed. They were an unlovely, cantankerous, vengeful couple that were never loathe to evil to serve their own preconceived ends. But I must say in parting that they were, what is the word, toothsome, yes; yes, toothsome to me. Pretty Boys and Pretty Girls, this is only the beginning."

Timm slowly shook his head and muttered, "Jesus Christ."

David signed the message with a large cryptic symbol—apparently satanic or gang code—followed by computerized hieroglyphics.

By coincidence, Assistant State's Attorney Pat O'Brien was in the station. O'Brien, who was to be the principal prosecutor in David's trial, was a deceptively mousey-looking man who could be brilliant in the courtroom. He scrolled through the message and told Timm, "We're not going to use it in the trial. Who's to say David wrote that?—a friend could have been playing around on his computer."

"You know damn well who wrote it."

"Besides," O'Brien continued, "all of this is open to various interpretations. Gevirtz and his partner are pretty sharp. We don't want to introduce anything the defense can use against us." That included a computer message that a jury might accept as a hint of insanity.

O'Brien pushed his thick glasses up his nose and asked, "Do we understand each other?"

Timm and Sumner didn't like it, but they realized that O'Brien might be right.

A day later, a student told police about a small hiding place next to David's tank of piranha fish. The boy even drew a map.

On the evening of Thursday, October 11, officers returned to the Biro house for the final time. They were hoping the baseboard would hide a single black glove, perhaps even a souvenir from the crime. Detective Kerner pulled back the floor tank as Gene removed a section of molding. He reached into the hole David had made in the wall and discovered—not much.

Inside was a camouflage pouch with a key ring, four generic handcuff keys, a vial containing white powder, a bullet, and a photo of David in white slacks under the neon sign for Neo's, the Chicago night spot where he had gone after the murders. Whatever the objects meant to David, they wouldn't mean anything in court.

21

A Number, Not A Name

Sunday, October 7

BECAUSE THE DAY following David's arrest was a Sunday, he needed to appear at a preliminary hearing in Holiday Court in Chicago's Criminal Court Building. Newspaper photographers rushed in for a quick shot as the Winnetka car pulled up at the brooding gray courthouse. David, wearing a striped shirt, his wrists handcuffed behind him, stuck his tongue out at them.

David's father was driven to the courthouse by Robert Gevirtz's law partner, Dennis Born. There could be no mistaking the lawyers for one another. Gevirtz had dark hair, usually wore black, and moved somberly. At thirty-eight, Born still had a blond, boyish look and animated gestures.

In a hearing that hardly lasted three minutes, the judge denied bond because David was charged with multiple counts of murder. As the young defendant was led away, Nick noticed that the police had given his son paper slippers rather than shoes. David's sneakers had been impounded for comparing with the footprints found on the ravine near the Langert home. "He should have shoes, shouldn't he?" Nick asked Born. "The other men have shoes, why can't my son have shoes?"

Born drove Nick to an aging downtown department store. There, Nick studied brand after brand, as if postponing the reality of his son's arrest. "Just find something that fits," Born said.

Before the shoes could reach David, the boy was led to a social worker in one of the courthouse offices. "What are you here for, a boy like you from New Trier?" she asked.

"Murder," David answered calmly. "They said I killed three people."

"You, a seventeen-year-old boy?"

"They say I shot them. A husband and his pregnant wife."

"Well, I am putting you with younger people, more like your age." She looked into his blue eyes. "Seventeen, you got your whole life ahead of you."

"I didn't do it."

"Officer, take him to Division Six."

David kept silent as the tall black guard took him through an underground tunnel. Puddles of water seeped into his paper slippers. He had no idea what was about to happen in the next few minutes, let alone the months between now and his trial.

Twenty-foot-high gates of brown steel clinked shut behind David. As if on an assembly line, he was checked in, his handcuffs were removed, a number was written in black ink on his right forearm, a white ID band was attached to his wrist, and two photos were taken.

Next he and the guard were buzzed into Division Six, the juvenile section. David was stripped, and a guard wearing plastic gloves searched his body cavities for weapons or drugs. The correctional officer who had been escorting David handed him a white T-shirt and a yellow-tan uniform with the initials of the Department of Corrections stenciled in black.

"Now listen," the guard said, addressing David by his number as they walked into an elevator. "Every time you enter an elevator from now on you never face the door, you face the back and look at the back wall and place your hands behind your back, where we can see them at all times. You understand me?"

"Yes."

"You ain't in the real world anymore. You in jail and you do what we tell you, when to talk, when to eat, where to walk, even when to shit. You hear me? And if you listen and if you cause no problems, then things go right for you. But if you don't, we have to take care of you. You understand me?"

David, as tall as the guard, returned his glare with a "Yes, sir."

"Good, then we get along fine."

The boy was led to a dayroom where sixty inmates were housed because there were no beds for them in a jail complex teeming with eighteen thousand inmates. Lunch tables stood between worn-out mattresses, and a color television set droned over the steady murmur. A few of the teenagers were eating potato chips purchased from the commissary.

When the 10 P.M. news came on, David saw himself on the screen and boasted, "Hey, that's me!" He was so used to attention grabbing, he didn't notice that the hardened inmates around him didn't share his enthusiasm. As the newscast continued with snippets of reactions from New Trier students, David called out, "Look at all those people who say they know me, and I never met them!"

"Hey," *Leo Garcia said, "you killed a pregnant woman. What's the matter with you?"

A glacial quiet settled on the room.

"Okay," a guard's voice came over the speakers, "lockdown lights in five minutes."

Not understanding what to do, David followed the others as they settled down on their mattresses. The room was dark except for lights coming from the guard room. David watched the black-on-black movement of one of the large cockroaches scuttering across the floor. He pulled a blanket over his head as if to hide from the world.

But he could hear the whispers.

There were always whispers. Tonight, they were about how David shouldn't have bragged about killing a pregnant woman. One youth let it be known that if he could get Biro to talk, he could make a deal with the state's attorney's office.

Breakfast was a carton of milk, an apple, and a small cereal box in a plastic tray. When the morning news rehashed David's arrest, the room became strained once more. This time, he kept quiet.

A short time later, a guard took David to Violence Court for a routine hearing affirming the no-bond order. One of the young inmates motioned to the officer and said he wanted to speak to Guard Captain Tensor. "Tell him *Johnny O wants to see him." Another guard accompanied Johnny to Tensor's office. The boy claimed that at the change of shifts, some of the teens were planning to beat David, and one of the Latinos was going to shove a fist into his mouth.

When David returned to Division Six, he was led directly to the captain's office. "People here don't take to people too much who are accused of killing a pregnant woman," Tensor told him. "Killing a man, that's okay, but killing a woman is a sign of weakness."

David, who had been sitting with his legs apart, tossed his hand over the back of the chair and said with a bored rolling of his eyes, "I didn't brag about anything."

"You said something. The word is they want to beat you real good."

"I can take care of myself."

"Where you live?"

"Winnetka."

"This ain't Winnetka anymore, this is a jungle here. The inmates make their own rules. We can stop fights, but we can't stop them before someone gets hurt. Maybe you shouldn't say anything about the case to anybody here, all right? You're seventeen and I'm fifty-three, and I know a hell of a lot more than you. You better stay out where a guard can see you at all times."

David pretended not to be scared, but he started shaking when he was led back to the dayroom and Garcia called out, "Hey, David." It wasn't what he said, but the way he said it.

The Winnetka boy turned to the guard and asked, "Can I make a call on that phone?"

"Collect only."

David phoned Gevirtz and told him about the threat. The lawyer had friends among the guard officials, and by evening he was able to have the boy transferred to another dayroom. Within two days, David was taken to a cell in the isolation area of Division Four. The area was eight by five feet. In that space were a bunk, a metal sink, a polished metal mirror, and a stopped-up toilet. A five-by-three-inch slot in the door for receiving his meal dish gave him bleak glimpses of the corridor. His grimy window, covered by chicken wire, gave him a third-floor view of barbed wire and the rear of the courthouse. Here David was kept for twenty-three hours a day, for his own safety. He roamed the cellblock and watched a television set mounted out of reach in the wall for that one hour of freedom while all other inmates were exercising outside.

David's only chance to get away from the cells came when his lawyers visited him. David was quivering when they first interviewed him, but in a few days he had adjusted to confinement. Gevirtz and Born never asked him if he was innocent, just for his version of what happened. It was upon this that they would build a defense.

The lawyers took turns visiting David to gain his confidence in each. When it was Gevirtz's turn, he advised the boy not to speak to anybody in the jail.

"Don't make friends. Because if you start talking to somebody, that person might try to get some easy time by saying he's willing to testify you confessed even if you didn't."

"Yeah," David said. He was learning.

Gevirtz and Born concentrated on ways of turning the state's evidence upside down. As part of Gevirtz's routine, he sat at his computer at home and put everything into an eight-page outline, then he just stared at the screen until his ideas formed a plan of action. Born and a third partner, Jim Kissel, had another way of preparing a case. They went to the library of the Kent College of Law in Chicago and looked up similar trials late into the night.

The partners had found long ago that Sundays were the best time for strategy meetings, because then they weren't distracted by all the other cases they were handling. The more the lawyers studied the state's evidence, the more they were disturbed by it. For one thing, they were skeptical about Officer Bobby Caldwell's assertion that he had seen David near the townhouse on the Saturday night of the murders. The officer claimed he had called it in that Monday morning, the day after the bodies were found. If there really was a "lead card," why was David never questioned during the six-month investigation?

The attorneys also held a round-table discussion with David's parents in their living room, the eighteen-year-old Nancy Biro quietly sitting in. The lawyers told the family to expect hell from the news media for a few days. Nick and Joan understood, they had already bought an answering machine to screen their calls.

After an indictment was returned, the defense attorneys asked the Biros to meet them at their office in Northbrook. Gevirtz, Born, and Kissel told the parents the fact that the police had kept David isolated during questioning might be grounds for having the evidence dismissed.

Jim Kissel, with his white hair and bald spot, was the eldest of the law partners and had the advantage of looking least like a lawyer. That let him approach a client or a family more as a friend. At this meeting, he pointed out that he and his partners were asking for a court order to preserve the tapes of phone calls the Biros and John Lewis had made to the station during David's questioning. But Nick wasn't grasping any of this. He looked at the three lawyers and asked, "What is our defense?"

"I don't know yet," Gevirtz admitted.

Joan Biro stopped taking notes in her shorthand and looked up from the marble table. "I can't believe how quickly the police have turned on us," she said. "All the time David was in trouble before, they treated us with respect. It's as if they are blaming us for everything."

"I'm afraid that's often how it is when a juvenile is accused," Gevirtz said. He knew that, in effect, the whole family would be put on trial.

Now came the hardest part of the meeting. Although the lawyers had said there was a chance David might be freed, they needed to prepare the Biros for the possible sentence. David would not be facing execution if he were convicted, because he had been a minor when the crime was committed, but a state law called for mandatory life imprisonment. Life in prison for a teenager—to the parents, it sounded as if the state were trying to bury their son alive.

As the lawyers mentioned the various possible tactics, Nick cut in by asking Gevirtz, "Did you discuss this with David? What did he say?"

"We can't tell you," Gevirtz answered. "David is our client. We can't break our bond of confidence."

Nick's inner pain was obvious by the look in his eyes. He ran his fingers through his full white hair and said, "It's my son."

"I'm sorry," Gevirtz replied, "it has to be that way."

* * *

The defense attorneys were beginning to feel what they regarded as political pressure. The state's attorney's office petitioned to have the case moved for greater security from Skokie to the Criminal Courts Building, across from the jail. Gevirtz and Born wondered whether the real reason might be that the prosecutors wanted to do some judge-shopping.

The case was assigned to Judge Shelvin Singer. One plus in the defense's favor was that Singer was considered fairer than some other jurists at "Twenty-sixth and Cal" (Twenty-sixth Street and California Avenue). But just to be sure, Gevirtz used a preliminary hearing to offer several motions testing him. When the stocky, balding jurist gave considered responses, the attorneys dropped their efforts to transfer the trial back to the suburban court.

One day, while Kissel was speaking to David in an anteroom, a special deputy sheriff stood listening to them. "Excuse me," Kissel said, "I'm talking to my client."

"I have orders from my chief that I'm never to let David Biro out of my sight."

"We'll see about that," Kissel said.

The attorney had to have Judge Singer order that the lawyers be allowed to speak to the boy alone.

The lawyers by then had received the thousands of pages of police reports to start formulating their attack. Gevirtz would read approximately a hundred pages and pass them to Born. He would read them and pass them on to Kissel. "There's nothing in here that ties David to the scene," Gevirtz said. "No physical evidence. The boy never met the Langerts. It's like his name was pulled out of a hat."

"Can we go behind the search warrant?" Kissel asked with a lilt of excitement.

"They kept going back to David's house," Born put in. "To me, that's fishing."

Gevirtz stood with his hands on his hips and looked

out at the night from the sixth-floor window. "We have an argument as to the issue of probable cause which will be used in a motion to quash the warrant. Right?"

"Right," Born and Kissel answered. At least they had a starting point.

Grasping at another straw, the defense team asked a California ballistics expert, Charles Morton, to test the revolver seized from David's home. Chief Timm assigned Sergeant Connell to accompany the .357 Magnum on the plane, making sure it never left her sight. Morton, who had worked on the Kennedy assassination investigation, spent five hours firing bullets from the weapon and studying the slugs under microscopes in his private lab. Then he called Gevirtz two thousand miles away and said, "They match."

David turned eighteen in the Cook County Jail. On August 4, 1991, Judge Singer conducted a hearing to consider defense motions to throw out the evidence. Virtually every officer and assistant state's attorney ever involved in the case was called to testify. David sat at the defense table and gave a "What do you make of this?" wink to a young woman sitting with a few other reporters in the otherwise empty jury box.

John Lewis took the stand and discussed the odd experience of going from defense attorney to state's witness when the murder weapon turned out to be his wife's gun. Under questioning by prosecutor Pat O'Brien, Lewis admitted he believed that "David thought he was smarter than the police."

As Nick and Joan Biro testified about how police wouldn't let them speak to their son, David twiddled his thumbs. Next David took the stand, still in a yellow-tan jail uniform, his hair in a ponytail. The boy insisted he was never notified of his Miranda rights to an attorney and that he had asked to see his parents more than fifty times. He added that Timothy Joyce of the prosecutor's office had told him in the station, "I talked to your parents, and they don't want to talk to you. I guess you are going to get a public defender. Isn't that funny, a Winnetka kid having to get a public defender."

The boy added that throughout his interrogation late that Friday and early Saturday, he had nothing to eat and "I couldn't keep my eyes open." He added that assistant prosecutor Sally Bray had to keep nudging him. " 'David, you need to wake up,' " he quoted her as saying. " 'You need to talk to us. Don't sleep.' "

Judge Singer was unimpressed. He wryly remarked that the way David had made statements only after being left alone with Patty McConnell and Sally Bray was "coercion by charm." The judge also noted that the way Winnetka police couldn't encourage Lewis to contact his client even when Lewis was in the station presented a possibly unique legal situation, and that he could see why David had no representation for some time.

Singer acknowledged that David might have been tired, "even dog-tired," but as to the youth's testimony that he couldn't stay awake—"I am sorry, that's unbelievable." He added that "the defendant is a cocky young man, and I believe he thought that he could handle it himself."

David kept up his contemptuous nonchalance as a deputy sheriff led him out of the courtroom. He still didn't seem to realize that although the prosecution had 107 pieces of evidence against him, the most damning exhibit would be David Biro himself.

The defense team decided they would have to turn that image upside down if they were going to put David on the stand. His height and deep voice would work in his favor. He would have to wear a suit, have his hair cut, and avoid any appearance of arrogance. But they couldn't base their case just on David's appearance. They needed some way to tie everything together for the jurors.

"Why let the prosecution have all the police witnesses," Gevirtz suggested at one of the long tactical discussions with his partners.

"Since juries automatically believe everything a cop says," Gevirtz continued, sitting with his feet on the desk, "why not call one for ourselves—Sergeant Gene Kalvaitis."

Kissel was amused, and Born didn't know whether he was serious. Calling the head of the task force to testify for the defense?

"We don't have to ask him about what the police did once they heard about David," Gevirtz explained. "The issue is whether they needed an arrest to look good. Nobody knows better than Kalvaitis all the money that was spent on the investigation. All those wild motives they were looking at, and the state's attorney running for election. There must have been incredible pressure to nail someone, and who else to nail but the town troublemaker? Kalvaitis thinks David is guilty as hell, and that's all the more reason to call him. He will get the jury to thinking."

"It's worth a shot," Kissel said.

22

"He Knew He Had To Kill Them"

Monday, November 4, 1991

BUILT IN NEARLY the exact center of Chicago, the stark gray Criminal Courts Building acts as a sewage drain bringing the affluent and poor together unwillingly. At any time of day, a sheriff's deputy in a black uniform might be seen herding a jury from one part of the building to another. No one may speak to anyone wearing a red "juror" sticker, and the jurors may not even discuss their case with one another until a judge gives them permission.

Jury selection for David Biro began on Monday, November 4, a brilliantly sunny but bitterly cold day. Because of all the spectators, reporters, attorneys, and law students interested in the case, the proceedings were moved from Singer's second-floor court to one of the larger rooms on the fifth floor. Singer, a fairly short man with a wisp of white hair over his scalp, looked ordinary until he put on his robe and stepped up to the bench. Despite the dignity of his office, the judge maintained a lively, avuncular style of friendly discipline.

One element important to this trial was geography,

since the killings had occurred in a place where murders weren't supposed to happen. Judge Singer asked each prospective juror whether the fact that the crime occurred in Winnetka would affect his or her opinion. Then the lawyers for each side were invited to begin the winnowing, asking seemingly innocuous questions in an attempt to get a panel that would be responsive to their respective cases.

Assistant State's Attorneys Patrick O'Brien and Scott Nelson asked the veniremen if they were "against holding the defendant responsible despite his age." The prosecutors had another concern, the absence of a clear motive. Without explanation, they questioned each potential juror that "if you found the defendant guilty of the various elements, would you be reluctant to sign a guilty verdict if you had lingering questions about the other elements?" Each man and woman answered "no" without even asking the prosecutors what they meant.

On the second day, a panel of seven women and five men was sworn in. There were six blacks, seven whites, and one Hispanic. The panel included a fire-fighter, an accounts manager, a registered nurse, a computer expert, a claims adjuster from Atlanta, an elementary school teacher, a high school biology teacher, a social worker, and a policeman's widow.

On Wednesday, more than one hundred spectators filled the ten benches and the aisles to observe the opening arguments. At David's arraignment more than a year before, two of his black-jacketed friends had giggled when he was brought in. Now they either stayed away or had been advised to blend in with the crowd to avoid alienating the jurors.

David could have passed for a law student when he walked to the defense table, dressed in a conservative black suit and his ponytail replaced by a traditional haircut. But a television reporter sitting in the line of chairs set up for the news media whispered that "he looks like a young Norman Bates."

The defendant and all the attorneys rose when the jurors entered through the side door and filled the jury box. After the lawyers sat down, Born handed David a stick of gum to help him relax. Throughout the trial, that would be their daily ritual. A good-luck stick of gum.

Jeanne Bishop sat with her burly brother-in-law, Malcolm Jones. Her parents and her sister, Jennifer, could not be with them on this first day because they were on the witness list.

State's Attorney O'Brien began opening arguments by outlining the final night of Nancy and Richard Langert. "When they opened the door to the peace and security they thought they had, what they found was a nightmare—fear, terror, and, finally, violent death."

As O'Brien continued, Mrs. Biro, sitting in the fourth row, seemed detached as she made brief notes in shorthand and peered at him over the tops of her half-glasses. The jurors waited for the prosecutor to make sense of it all for them. What was the motive, what was the link between the victims and Biro? He didn't tell them.

In contrast to O'Brien's stand-in-place monotone, defense attorney Dennis Born spoke with energy, moving from the jury box to behind his seated client, forcing the jurors to look at this young man in a suit. David was so well dressed, his face so open, that it would seem anyone would be proud to have him for a son.

The boyish-looking member of the defense team stressed that David had been charged only after the police conducted an extensive search for a motive, and that their work involved Ireland, the New York docks, the FBI, Scotland Yard, and even Interpol. "You will learn the orchestration of the isolation of David Biro; the orchestration of the attempt to extract a confession from a seventeen-year-old New Trier High School student."

In other words, Born implied, David was a victim, not a killer.

The first witness was Joyce Bishop, looking spritely in a fuchsia two-piece suit and a gold turtle brooch. She described Nancy as "very healthy, very happy." O'Brien led her to her casual acquaintance with the defendant's family. From the spectators' bench, Joan Biro clucked her tongue when Joyce said "we saw them socially, at least once a year." Joyce added that David never came along.

There was no cross-examination.

After the lunch break, Lee Bishop looked tired as he walked to the stand. He spoke calmly but his body stiffened as he told of finding the bodies of "my children," Nancy and her husband.

During cross-examination, Born had Lee Bishop confirm that a reward totaling twenty thousand dollars had been offered. Then Born sat down, but O'Brien rose. "Mr. Bishop, has anybody claimed that reward?" the prosecutor asked.

"No, sir," Lee answered.

"That's all," the prosecutor said.

Gevirtz began by asking oblique questions. "So you told the police everything," he remarked about the initial family interrogation, hinting that something might come out much later—the supposed IRA connection the family had refused to discuss with detectives. "You were truthful that first night. You answered all their questions."

"The best I could," Lee replied, "in consideration of the condition I was in at the time."

"I rest," Gevirtz said and walked away.

The prosecution then called its star witness, Phu Huang. Wearing a white shirt, but no tie or suit jacket, the computer science student repeated for the jurors what he had told detectives so many times before, David's minute-by-minute account of the killings. "He said he knew he had to kill them."

David stopped taking notes to glare.

The witness said he had spoken to David about the murders at least twice more that summer. Once, in a call from the village hall, "I asked him if he regretted what he had done, and he said 'No.' He said that there was no room for regret in this world. He said that the Langerts deserved to die, anyhow. He said they were annoying, and—"

Here he paused. The courtroom was silent.

"—he said that he wouldn't have been the way he was, or he wouldn't have done what he had done, if people hadn't dicked him around in his life."

The prosecutor brought Phu a white evidence box. As the college student identified the handcuffs, glass cutter, ammunition, and speedloaders he had seen in David's room, a juror eased back and turned his stare to David. The defendant kept up his mask of indifference.

On cross-examination, Gevirtz asked about Phu's state of mind after he gave the police David's name. "Would it be fair to say that you were feeling bad?"

"I wasn't feeling bad," the witness said, "I was feeling sorrow."

"Would it be fair to say that you weren't sure whether or not you were doing the right thing?"

"No."

"When David made this statement to you, you didn't know whether to believe him at the time, did you?" Gevirtz asked.

"I believed him."

"Well, David was the kind of kid who liked to tease and shock people, isn't that fair to say?"

"Yes."

"He would say things to see what kind of reaction he could get out of people, right?"

"Yes."

"It was kind of a teasing way that he told you this, right?"

"Yes."

"He made a game out of it?"

"Yes."

"And he didn't respond. He just smiled, right?"

"He laughed."

"But knowing David, it didn't surprise you that he might say something like this?"

"It did surprise me, yes."

"You spent two hours with him, right? You weren't afraid of him?"

"No, I was not ... I was afraid that he may commit more crimes."

When Gevirtz finished, O'Brien asked for a sidebar conference as the witness remained on the stand. The court reporter carried his tripod over to the bailiff's desk beside the judge's bench. O'Brien said out of earshot of the jurors that the questioning had left the impression that "it was a joke by the defendant, in keeping with his character. We feel that an earlier conversation that the defendant had with Phu would show that there was a sense of trust built in with the defendant."

Judge Singer agreed, and O'Brien went into a re-direct questioning. Over defense objections, he was able to ask Phu about seeing the missing New Trier computers. Phu then told of David's plan to break into a bank and kill the morning crew. "It made me realize that David did not regret what he had done, and he would continue to commit crimes, continue to murder people."

"No further questions," the prosecutor said.

When Phu stepped down, his parents left the courtroom to be with him. The tall young man was taken down a back elevator to the guard area on the first floor. TV crews stepped out of their waiting place behind the lobby console of switches to film him rushing to the back door for a waiting car. Headlines the next day ran:

Biro Laughed About Slayings,
Witness Says.

23

---◆◆◇---

Web Of Evidence

November 7

THE CAVALCADE OF witnesses resumed the next morning. Attorney John Lewis waited tensely in a side room until a guard brought him into court. The lawyer described his suspicion that David might steal the gun and firearms owner's card. He added that he didn't discover that the revolver was missing until June, two months after the theft, because the empty plastic case was still in the desk drawer.

Lewis's expression didn't show the disgust he was feeling about everything that had happened. The issue of the false firearms card had raised so many questions in the legal community that the Illinois agency regulating attorneys was looking into his role, as if he could have prevented the murders by turning David in for forgery. He was also bitter because there had been so many pre-trial rulings on what he could say about his former client that his testimony hardly seemed necessary.

During the lunch break, Lee Bishop arrived from work in his beige trenchcoat and Irish tweed hat. He kissed his wife and daughters in the cafeteria. David's father was still unable to attend the trial because he would be called to testify again after the prosecution rested its case.

Sergeant Patty McConnell was nervous as she took the stand in the afternoon. She glanced around for familiar faces among the spectators. Then she relaxed but wished she could have a cigarette. McConnell testified that Phu Huang had anonymously given her the tip about David, and that she then identified the boy through a vehicle registration and high school yearbook.

Gevirtz sounded skeptical that McConnell had not taken action immediately. "You didn't even ask his name, did you?"

"No."

"This case had been going on for six months but no breaks."

"No."

"You were aware that there may have been an IRA connection?"

"Objection," O'Brien said from the prosecution table.

"Sustained," said Judge Singer. "The statement is outside the scope of the investigation," meaning the indictment.

This was the first blow to the defense's plan for portraying David as a victim of police desperation.

Gevirtz then went on to the warrant that had allowed police to search for items taken in the New Trier burglary. "You didn't put anything in there about requesting information about a homicide?" he asked.

" 'Requesting information?' " O'Brien asked. "I'm going to object to that question."

"Sustained."

"No further questions, thank you," the defense attorney said.

Ron Matzig was called to testify about helping David obtain a false state identification card just three days before the murders. The tone of the questioning changed suddenly when Matzig described the revolver he had seen in David's room as being "dark in color."

This was the first contradiction in the prosecution's case, and O'Brien quickly asked whether he recalled saying on page thirty-three of the grand-jury transcript that he had "observed a silver gun." Matzig then modified his description to "metallic ... I can't say silver."

The prosecutor handed him the weapon and asked, "Does this look familiar?"

"It's like the gun," Matzig replied with growing uneasiness. "It could be the gun that I had in my hand, but I don't remember specifically."

"When is the last time that you spoke to me?"

"This afternoon," Matzig said.

"When was the time before that?"

"Saturday."

"This afternoon or Saturday, did you tell me the gun was dark in color?"

Gevirtz objected, and Judge Singer replied with a "Sustained." But O'Brien had no further questions to ask. He walked away as if sorry for having called Matzig to the stand.

Matzig returned to the witness room and put on his camel-hair coat and white scarf. A reporter chased him down the courthouse stairs and to a boulevard across from the parking lot. "Did you get him false ID to take him to bars?" she asked. "What kind of bars were they?"

Matzig turned sharply to her, gulped instead of responding, and darted across the street.

In the courtroom, Winnetka police officer Bobby Caldwell told of seeing David near the Langert home at approximately nine o'clock the night of the murder and calling Eddie Benoit about it from home that Monday. Joyce looked in alarm at her husband. This was the first time they had heard that police might have solved the case in one day.

"You just call in anytime you see somebody walking down the street?" Gevirtz asked.

"Certain individuals," Caldwell responded.

Gevirtz immediately changed the subject and asked about the message card. With a hardened tone, he inquired, "Did anyone follow that lead over to Biro's house?"

"I have no idea," Caldwell said.

"Are you aware there were over five thousand pages of reports in this case?"

"No, I was not," the officer answered, but the words were almost drowned out by Nelson's objection.

"Sustained," said the judge, and once again he ruled that references to the extent of the investigation were outside the scope of the trial and could be construed as an attempt to distract the jury.

Gevirtz could feel the rug being pulled out from under him. Questions he had planned to ask he now erased from his mind as he went to the next point. Handing a card to Caldwell, he asked, "Is that message card time-stamped anywhere?"

"It doesn't appear to have a stamp," the policeman replied.

Gevirtz left it up to the jury to decide whether police might have manufactured the evidence.

He then called Officer Ronald Schimian to testify about the condition of the townhouse when the bodies were found. Schimian admitted that police did not make a plaster cast of a footprint on the ravine, saying the sole and heel were "very nondescript" and that the cast would not have held in the loose dirt.

The officer also told of finding a tipped-over metal shelf along the east wall of the basement. "I noticed that there were marks apparently on top of the shelf, and the bottom looked like it had been pounded upon, and there was also some type of writing written in blood."

This was the only mention that would be made in

testimony about the riddle that had baffled investigators for a year and a half.

During Schimian's testimony, David occasionally looked up from the defense table and smiled at his mother. But with David, a smile was always enigmatic.

On the third day of testimony, John Mercer of the sandwich shop in Northbrook told how nervous David had seemed when he appeared just after midnight and said he had been in a fight. The testimony was a strong point for the prosecution, but Delores Langert still needed to work off her tensions by going into the corridor and smoking near the No Smoking sign during a break.

Around the corner, Joyce Bishop was adjusting Jeanne's gold necklace so that it hung in the exact center of her bosom. Jeanne could stand up to the police, reporters, and the FBI, but when it came to her mother she was a dutiful child again.

There was no suggestion that the trial was about to enter the cruelest phase for the families in any murder case—the medical report. Before the jurors were led in from the break, attorneys on both sides discussed which autopsy photos should be submitted. Gevirtz objected to all close-ups and one other slide in particular, showing Nancy's abdominal incision, along with her dead fetus. "I have never seen a more inflammatory picture," the defense attorney claimed.

"I agree," said Judge Singer.

During the break, O'Brien angled a slide projector and screen in front of the podium and Singer's bench so that the jury, the judge, and the court reporter could see them. This coincidentally meant that the screen was turned away from the spectators. When the jurors took their seats, Deputy Medical Examiner Mitra Kalelkar—wearing a white pantsuit, her dark face framed by a mass of black curls—used a pointer and a diagram to explain her postmortem findings. When the lights were turned off, Nelson showed autopsy slides on the screen. The first photo was of Richard, his head shaved to clarify the bullet wound.

Dr. Kalelkar testified that she had found handcuff marks on Richard, but that there were no such marks on Nancy. The pathologist also said Nancy "would have remained alive ten to fifteen minutes after she sustained these gunshot wounds."

The lights came back on, and the pathologist left the stand.

Bob Wilson of the Northern Illinois Police Crime Laboratory was called by the prosecution, but his testimony largely helped the defense. He told the jury that he had cut out the "web" of the glove found at the scene and found a trace of blood that was not apparent to the naked eye. Moving his hands around each other, Wilson gave a complex explanation of blood typing. But after O'Brien ended his questioning, Gevirtz drove the point home that police could not positively connect David to the glove.

There was a stir in court, and O'Brien rushed into redirect examination. His body moved quickly but his shoulders hunched slowly into a cobra's cawl. He had Wilson clarify that blood type H at times can be equivalent to type O, and so police could not rule out David as the person who wore the glove.

"You're right," Wilson said.

Relieved that he had sewn up the doubt that must have been in the minds of the jurors, O'Brien turned to Singer and said, "Nothing further, Judge."

24

Tarantula Dance

Tuesday, November 12

EACH DAY OF the trial, the prosecution set up an odd display—a large royal-blue poster board on an easel. On the left half were standard male and female autopsy sketches which, at the defense's request, had been covered by blank paper until the medical testimony. On the right half was a niche cut out to hold the gun. Toward the middle were three tiny shelves awaiting evidence yet to be introduced.

Early in the trial, Gevirtz had complained that the setup made the revolver look like a "trophy," but Singer let the prosecution have its display. The jurors were about to see what the little shelves were for.

Bob Wilson was called back to the stand on Tuesday, November 12, following a Veterans Day recess. Assistant State's Attorney Pat O'Brien handed him a palm-sized manila envelope containing three bullets. Wilson pulled a large magnifying glass from his pocket and looked over the slugs. Two of them, Wilson said, had a coating that made comparing them to ones fired by the murder weapon difficult. But the hollow-point slug fired into Nancy showed clear markings.

During the testimony, David leaned over and took notes with his face almost touching his pen.

O'Brien—a plain-faced, short man with weak eyes and a broad forehead—returned the gun to its niche and placed each bullet on one of the shelves, finishing both the display and his case. There was nothing left but for the jury to examine the evidence that had been introduced over the last week.

The jurors passed vials of the victims' blood among themselves and held the gun used to kill two innocent people and an unborn child. One woman didn't want to touch it.

But what sense was to be made of all this? The state never mentioned a motive or touched upon what the "writing in blood" might be, leaving the jurors to form their own story of what might have happened. There also was no mention of statements David had made during his long interrogation on the day of his arrest. This was a tool that could hurt whichever side tried to use it. The statements would be detrimental to the defense, yet the thirty hours of questioning could be used to attack the prosecution. The interrogation created an invisible presence both sides had to walk around.

For a full hour, the jury examined all of the exhibits. Nothing was heard in the courtroom but the occasional rattle of evidence bags. Behind the plastic barrier, Joyce Bishop looked straight ahead as her hand rested on her husband's back. Lee pressed his small mouth in concentration. Finally, two female sheriff's deputies removed the victims' clothing from a large paper bag and walked slowly with each item along the jury box. With the clothes came the smell of death.

At 3:40 P.M. the defense called for a recess before beginning its case. Gevirtz and Born were less confident than at the beginning. They had wanted to show that the prosecutors might have ulterior motives for going after David, but Singer had not allowed any references to the initial investigation.

Away from the presence of the jurors, the defense brought out Sergeant Kalvaitis, who had been chain-smoking in the side room. He hated the strategy that had him appear for the defense rather than the prosecution, but everything had been upside down in this case almost from the beginning.

Gene had barely stated his qualifications as an officer for more than nineteen years when O'Brien was on his feet, objecting that since the witness was not a field investigator in this case, anything he said would be "double, triple, and quadruple hearsay!"

Judge Singer agreed, telling Gevirtz and Born that he was going to limit the questioning because "One, it is hearsay upon hearsay; two, it is generalization, it is non-communication; three, it is irrelevant."

"I motion for a mistrial," Gevirtz said flatly.

Singer lowered his glasses and said, "Denied."

And so the person who knew most about the investigation in the intensive first three months was reduced to telling the jury that the task force met every day and that, to his knowledge, no one investigated the message card report that David had been seen near the Langert home on the night of the murder.

O'Brien had scored a victory over the defense, but he looked tired. The evening rush hour was under way, and everyone was expecting the judge to adjourn for the day.

But Gevirtz and Born called for a quick break and discussed strategy. They decided to use the lateness of the hour to shore up their case. O'Brien might be worn out, but David was not. Besides, the jurors were probably thinking about their homes and families. That meant they might be less skeptical than in the hard light of morning. The defense attorneys returned to the courtroom and called their client to the stand.

At 4:45 P.M., David Biro left the defense table and took the oath. As on all the other days of the trial, he was dressed in a black suit and kept his movements to a minimum. He looked nothing like a reckless practical joker or a cold-blooded killer.

In a voice deepened by a minor cold, the young man spoke of working at an ice cream shop in 1988 and keeping up friendships with people he met there and at school.

"Ever recall meeting the Bishops?" Gevirtz asked.

"No."

Then under Gevirtz's soft questioning, the slender defendant presented an account of his life that explained every piece of damaging evidence against him. With his elbows on his knees, he testified that he had faked the firearms card because a boy he knew, Burke Abrams, made four hundred dollars selling a gun. When he learned that his parents gave the card to his lawyer, he decided that he was going to steal it back. "I took some tools with me that I had in my room, and I went to his office and I broke in there."

The defendant said that he had asked Burke to sell the gun for him. "He took six bullets and he loaded the gun, and I told him that I would see him at the park some time after school."

The next time he saw the gun, David continued, was at around eleven o'clock on the night of April 7, 1990. He said he was watching television in the first-floor family room after his parents went to bed. "I heard a knocking on the back door," and let Burke inside. "When he came in he was, I don't want to say nervous, I guess agitated, and the first thing that he did when he came in the door, he gave me the gun back and he said 'Hide this.' . . . Well, I asked him why. I said, 'I thought you were going to sell this.' And he said, 'Look, I've just killed two people with this, you need to hide it' . . . I thought he was joking . . . [but] he said, 'No, I'm not kidding.' He was very serious, and he told me quickly that he had broken into these people's house and had handcuffed them and took them downstairs and killed them . . . I asked him why he had done this . . .

he told me that he had his own reasons and he couldn't tell me."

David, sniffing occasionally, further testified that after Burke left he just sat around thinking. "I sort of pictured myself walking into the police station with this gun and telling the police that Burke Abrams had just committed this murder . . ."

His next thought was to get rid of the murder weapon. But in his nervousness he tripped down the back stairs of his home, cutting his arm and bumping his nose. He drove to the sandwich shop, then stayed until two in the morning at Neo's, the night spot in Chicago. He added that it was only when his father reported seeing squad cars outside the Langert home the next day that "I sort of realized what Burke was telling me about."

When Gevirtz asked what he did after learning about the killings, David said he met Burke in the park for the next day or two. " 'Dave, don't worry,' " he quoted Burke as saying, " 'they deserved it.' "

"I said, 'Why?'," David continued, "and he told me that he had his own reasons. He can't tell me."

This was not the David Biro who shook uncontrollably when his attorneys first saw him, or who winked at a young female reporter at the suppression hearing—or even the David Biro who had walked contemptuously into court that morning, refusing to glance at his mother or the jury. His words came out as smoothly and clearly as if, like Phu Huang, he were only a witness. Except for one factor. At least one juror felt that David's words lacked all emotion.

David testified that he had then pressed Burke for details, and thus learned about the glass clutter and what the inside of the townhouse looked like.

"Did he tell you how many times he shot each person?" Gevirtz asked.

"Yes, I remember that specifically, because he made a point of it, because he had also read newspaper articles and in all the newspaper articles they had said that Nancy had been shot three times in the body, and he told me, he said, 'Dave, I don't know what they're talking about because I only shot her twice.' "

David said he then purchased a glass cutter and went to Bess Hardware to buy a pair of handcuffs such as Burke had described. "I wasn't sure whether Burke was telling me the truth or not, and I felt that if I could sort of recreate the murder as he had told me, that it might give me a little better understanding to sort of base my opinions on. The reason I bought two handcuffs is because Burke told me that he had killed them . . ." Here he fumbled for words for the first time. "[And] what I took by that is that he meant he had handcuffed both of them."

"What did you do with those handcuffs?"

"I took them home and I played with them a little bit just to, you know. I looked at everything together, the glass cutter and the [newspaper] articles and the gun." Just a sixteen-year-old boy playing in his room with the artifacts of murder.

Next he told of "joking around" with his friends by saying he was the killer. One person he told was Phu. "Well, Phu was always such a serious guy, and he was kind of naive, and he was sort of fun to play with . . . the manner in which I told him was like a game . . . I did not think at all that he would ever take me seriously."

Gevirtz had no further questions.

Sergeant McConnell, who was monitoring the trial for the Winnetka police, left the courtroom and walked down the corridor to a bank of phones. She called the station and announced that David's cross-examination was about to begin.

"Damn it," Kalvaitis said at the other end of the line, "I'd give a year's salary to be there right now."

During the recess, the Bishops were sharing a disturbing sadness. No one had told them David would name a friend as the killer. His explanations sounded strained but within the realm of what an insecure teenager might do. Suppose the jury believed him?

Assistant State's Attorney O'Brien was equally caught off guard. Until now, Burke Abrams was just one of dozens of people David had known, and the two had not even been close for years. But O'Brien was less worried the jurors would be swayed by the story. He moved the podium to within twelve feet of the witness stand as if to say: All right, David, I'm going to expose you for what you are.

O'Brien began his assault. His shoulders rose slightly under his suit jacket, his voice sharpened, and his sentences became more rapid despite their monotone. But as the prosecutor came closer, David—refusing to be unnerved—casually interlaced his fingers on the evidence table in front of him.

O'Brien asked David to list the possessions in his room, including the items seized as evidence and the stolen computer equipment. When asked if the "N.T." on the keyboard stood for New Trier, David answered, "I assume so, yes."

Referring to the scored glass police found in his home, O'Brien asked, "Is that a piece of glass that you were practicing on by using the glass cutter?"

Gevirtz objected to the loaded word "practicing." He was overruled.

O'Brien next asked about the shoulder holster. David said he bought it "a month or so after the murders."

"So it was your intention to keep that gun, wasn't it?"

"I guess you could say that."

"A gun that you bragged about to your friends, that you say you knew was used in the Langert homicides, is that correct?"

"Yes."

O'Brien handed him a photo that showed the marked glass, with tape at the top. Then he said dismissively, not as a question but as a strong aside, "You weren't using that tape to try to see if you could score the glass, put some tape on it and pull the pieces of the glass out without having to break it . . . you weren't doing that, were you?"

"No," David replied. "The tape was just in my room, it had no connection with the glass."

O'Brien then talked about the neighborhood of the killings. David said he was "pretty familiar" with the area between the ravine and the lake because he had lived around there for three years and had run along the bike path with the school's cross-country team.

"Did you ever take any walks at night around Winnetka?"

"Not unless I had a destination."

When the questioning came to the handcuffs, David said he bought two pairs instead of one because he had assumed from newspapers that both Langerts had been manacled before they were shot.

O'Brien put the subject on hold and handed David the .357 Magnum for verification that it was the gun he stole. The prosecutor even prolonged the seconds that the defendant held the gun by asking, "Black grips, is that right?" and "Silver in color?" Yes, David said in a slowly fading voice. Then the teenager wiped his sweating hands together and put the gun back on the evidence shelf between him and the prosecutor.

The cross-examination next addressed David's testimony that he had wanted Burke to find a buyer for the gun. O'Brien thumped the podium and asked, "Instead of trying to sell it after that [the murder], you kept it, didn't you?"

"Yes."

"And you bought a shoulder holster for it, didn't you?"

"Yes . . . After a couple of days had passed, nobody had questioned Burke and nobody questioned me, and I thought it was relatively safe staying in my house."

O'Brien now returned to the handcuffs police had found in David's room. He asked the defendant to hold up the pair to show that the clasp was bent. "Can you close that in the other ring?" As the jurors watched, David inserted the key and tried to turn it.

"No, you cannot," David said, and placed the handcuffs on the evidence table.

By now, the defendant was sitting closer to the edge of the witness chair. Everyone could see that he was wearing down from the barrage of questions, most of them irrelevant or repetitious. Now that he was more vulnerable, O'Brien became mocking.

"You were going to sell the gun, and yet you kept the ammunition?"

"Well, he [Burke] didn't want the ammunition."

Holding up the gun, O'Brien asked, "What were you going to do, fire this with your fingers?"

"Objection," Gevirtz said from the defense table.

"Now, in your story, Burke Abrams doesn't come back and give you a single glove, does he?" O'Brien asked.

"No."

O'Brien cut to the firearm owner's card and asked about the oath David had made first on the application and then before a notary public. "You just ignored it and said or wrote whatever you felt would get what you wanted, isn't that right?"

"Yes."

With a caustic smile, O'Brien, hunching over, asked, "Would it have made any difference if they said hold up your hand and swear that this is true, would that have made any difference to you?" The prosecutor cocked his head and faced the jury as if to say *Can't you see he's lying?*

"Objection," said Gevirtz. "Argumentative."

"Overruled," replied the judge.

"Would it?" asked O'Brien.

"If they asked me to swear before God, yes, it would make a difference," David answered.

"That would have made all the difference in the world?"

"Yes, it would."

"Which part, that they asked you to swear, or to God?"

"Swearing to nothing really doesn't mean anything, but I'm not going to swear to God and lie on something."

"But did you commit two burglaries at New Trier?"

"Yes."

Now David's eyes were drawn to his private notebook as O'Brien took it from the evidence table and put it on his podium. "You kept a series of newspaper articles about the Langert homicides, is that correct?"

"Yes," David replied.

"They occupied a special place in a red folder of yours, didn't they?"

"Yes."

"In fact," the prosecutor said, "you put them in the center of that red folder, didn't you?"

"Yes."

After a few more questions, O'Brien appeared to forget about the notebook. He asked David if he had told Phu about the plot to break into a bank.

"I might have," David answered. "I mean, I played with Phu a lot . . . I told Phu a lot of crazy stories." But he admitted having a tool bag in his room with ropes, a chisel, a hammer, and drill bits.

O'Brien asked him to repeat word for word, as best he could, what Burke Abrams said to him at eleven o'clock on the night of the murders.

"Well, he walked in the door, the first thing he said was, 'David, hide this gun.' And I asked him why. I said, 'I thought you were supposed to sell it for me.' And he said, 'You better hide it, I had just killed two people with it.' And I said, 'You are kidding,' you know, 'quit playing around,' and he said, 'No. I'm serious, I just broke into two people's house, handcuffed them, brought them downstairs and shot them.' I asked him why, and he said, 'I have my own reasons, don't worry about it.' "

"And I believe you said that when he told you this, he was agitated. Is that correct?"

"Yeah, I'd say that."

"Was he shaking at all?"

"No, he wasn't shaking, just a little excited, I'd say."

"Was he pacing back and forth?"

"No," David said.

"And you heard John Mercer testify about how he described you when you came into the subway shop, didn't you? ... Did you hear him say that you were shaking?"

"Yes."

"You were nervous?"

"I heard him say that."

"Pacing back and forth?"

"I think I heard him say that," David said.

O'Brien then went over David's conversation with the shop employee. "And is it your testimony that the reason you told him you got the bloody nose from getting into a fight is because you didn't want to get into all this?"

"Yeah, I didn't want to explain anything, and he just gave me a suggestion. He said, 'Did you get into a fight?' So I just said, 'Yeah.' "

"And by explaining everything, you mean explain about the murders?"

David agreed, saying he had doubted whether John Mercer would believe he was so upset over having just "bumped into the stairs."

"Because you were more agitated than someone who just bumped into the stairs, weren't you?"

"Objection," said Gevirtz. "Calls for a conclusion."

"Overruled."

O'Brien snapped at David as if the objection had never been raised, "Weren't you!"

"Yes, I was."

"You were as agitated as you say Burke Abrams was, weren't you?"

"I was agitated."

And so it went. The questioning and answering had become a tarantula dance, going back and forth and around and around. The longer David remained on the stand, the more tired his replies became. His tone suggested that he just wanted to get this over with.

O'Brien kept verbally jabbing, jabbing, jabbing, trying to break up the confidence that had worked well for David before the cross-examination began two hours before. The prosecutor's questions alternated between what Burke reportedly had told David, and what David had told Phu. Finally, the teenager said, "It's hard for me to remember exactly what I heard from Burke and what I read in the newspapers or heard on T.V."

"Did you tell Phu that you surprised the Langerts, had told them to get up against the wall, and you had them handcuff each other? Did you tell him that?"

"I possibly did."

"Did you tell Phu Huang that the Langerts were pleading with you not to kill them?"

"I joked like that with a lot of people and everyone took it that way, as a joke."

"Well, what portion of that sentence about the Langerts' pleading with you did you see [as] the joke?"

"Objection," Gevirtz said.

"Overruled," responded the judge.

"Where is the punch line?" O'Brien asked.

"Objection to that," Gevirtz broke in.

Judge Singer ruled, "Sustained as to 'Where is the punch line.'"

Not skipping a beat, O'Brien badgered, "Where is the joke?"

"I guess it is no joke," David said quietly. "It's just that I was trying to shock these people."

Lee Bishop put an arm around his daughter Jennifer, who sat spellbound with her hand resting on her chin.

"Well," said O'Brien, "if you were trying to shock him, you wouldn't have had the same conversation, laugh, and tell him it's a joke, would you?"

"Well, that's how it was. It was meant to be a joke."

"Did you tell Phu that you made a mistake because you had the gun cocked when you were sitting in the chair, did you tell him that?"

"I don't know, I might have."

"Well, you haven't told us anything about Burke Abrams telling you about cocking the gun. Have you said anything like that? . . . It's another detail that you just kind of put in there, is that right?"

"No, when he said that the dog scared him and the gun went off, I assumed that he had already had it cocked."

But O'Brien told David that a .357 Magnum was a double-action revolver and did not need to be cocked. "So you just imagined that he must have cocked the gun, is that right?"

"I assumed the gun must have been cocked."

"Did you tell Phu that Nancy Langert told you she was pregnant?"

"That was all part of the joke," David answered wearily.

"What was so funny about Nancy Langert being pregnant?"

"Right now, I can't think of what I saw funny about it."

"Well, while you were sitting in that chair back in 722 Oak, did you see any humor in it?"

Gevirtz rose from the defense table. "Objection. Assumes a fact not in evidence that he was ever in 722 Oak."

"Overruled," said the judge.

"I have never been in 722 Oak," David answered.

"Did you tell Phu Huang that you walked behind the Langerts as they were walking down the stairs to the basement and then you made the mistake of stepping into the light and your eyes met the eyes of Mrs. Langert, and you knew that you had to kill them. Did you tell them that?"

"I might have."

"Well, Burke Abrams never told you that in your story, did he?"

"He told me that he led them downstairs . . . I don't remember everything specifically."

The judge called for a five-minute break. David licked his dry lips and drank water from a paper cup as he remained on the stand.

When the jury returned, O'Brien attacked the defendant's statement that, from what he had read in the newspapers, he assumed both victims were handcuffed. The prosecutor read into the record a line from the Winnetka community paper stating "there was no indication that his wife's hands had been bound." The paper came out several hours before David went to Bess Hardware.

"Now," O'Brien said, "when you read this article, you then immediately went out and bought two pairs of handcuffs?"

"Well, it's possible that I didn't read this article that day or, like I said, Burke said 'they' and I assumed it to be both of them."

"And you bought two pairs of handcuffs . . . Was that because you had made a mistake when you went into the Langerts', and with two victims you brought only one set of handcuffs?"

"I never went into the Langerts' residence."

"Were the purchase of two sets of handcuffs to re-create the crime as it would have been done if you'd been fully prepared?"

"Absolutely not," David answered quietly.

Referring now to conversations with Megan O'Callaghan, the student doing the report on the Leopold-Loeb murder, O'Brien asked, "Did you ever talk to her about committing the perfect crime?"

"No."

Going into David's relationship with Burke, the prosecutor asked, "He was a good friend of yours, you would have made phone contact, is that right?"

"Well, we saw each other almost every day, so there really wasn't any need to call."

"Did he tell you to dispose of the gun?"

"He told me to hide it."

"And by hiding it, he didn't mean to keep it under your bed, did he? . . . And by hiding it, he didn't mean to tell all your good friends that you committed a homicide, did he?"

Judge Singer sustained an objection in that the question called for knowing what someone else intended.

"This good friend of yours, Burke Abrams, ever since you have been in jail did you try to call his house and tell him, 'Burke, the pressure's building, I'm going to name you at some point.' Did you ever tell him that?"

"No," David replied.

"So, this is as big a surprise to him as it is to everybody else, isn't it?"

The judge sustained another objection.

O'Brien changed the subject to David's relationship with his family. Mentioning Nick Biro, the prosecutor asked, "Did he discipline you at all for obtaining a fake firearms ID card?"

"We talked about it and he asked me why did I have this, and I just denied it and told him that [picture] is my friend, Ron Matzig, and he just looks like me . . . He didn't believe what I was saying but, you know, he had no other choice just to accept it."

"Well, did he discipline you by keeping you in at night for the next month?"

"No," David said.

"Did your mom discipline you by keeping you in at night for the next month?"

"I don't think so, no."

"As a matter of fact, they didn't because on April 7 you were at the Subway shop and out drinking."

"Objection," raised Gevirtz.

"Overruled," said the judge.

"How often would you go out drinking at bars?" asked O'Brien.

"Possibly every weekend."

"Did your parents ever know that you were drinking at bars?"

"No . . . They asked me what I could be doing staying out so late, and I just told them I am out with friends just hanging around."

"And sometimes you came in at four in the morning?"

"Yes."

"Sometimes at two o'clock in the morning?"

"Yes."

"And this would be almost every weekend?"

"Almost, yes."

"And your parents didn't discipline you when you were gone all night long?"

Gevirtz objected, and O'Brien changed the subject to whether David's parents knew about the IBM computers marked for New Trier High School. Although Judge Singer sustained the objection, the impression lingered that here was a young man growing up without the usual give-and-take of family emotions.

O'Brien kept at this, asking David if his parents knew about the hammer, the chisel, the drill bits—all lying in a bag on the floor of his room—and the gun under the bed, the bullets in the dresser, the handcuffs, and the "secret hiding place in the back of the wall."

"Not to my knowledge."

Now, after all this, O'Brien finally returned to the red folder. David told him that the reason he had saved the article on Laurie Dann's rampage was because "It was big news, and I wanted to save big news." The defendant added that he kept a piece on Manuel Noriega's indictment only because "It was the first paper of a new decade, and I thought that was kind of neat, January 1, 1990."

"Well, here's the *Tribune* from October 20 of 1987," O'Brien said sarcastically. "Now, did you save that paper because it was the first paper published on October 20, 1987?"

"No, I saved this because it was about the stock market crashing. Again, that's big news."

David admitted not saving anything about events of global importance, but that he had put in his notebook a *Chicago Sun-Times* article with the headline, "Winnetka Slaying Seen as a Professional Hit." He also kept an article that read, "The slaying has baffled police and also friends and co-workers of the Langerts, who said the couple appeared to have everything going for them." The subheading in bold black print was "The American Dream."

"That's the part of that article that you saved, is that correct?"

"Yes."

"That the Langerts apparently were living the American dream, is that right?"

"Well, whatever interested me about it."

"Were *you* living the American dream?" O'Brien asked accusingly. "Was the American dream going to bars at four o'clock in the morning at the age of sixteen?"

Objection sustained.

Gevirtz then received permission for a sidebar conference. He told Singer quietly that the prosecutor was "trying to implicate that he is a killer as a character reference." But O'Brien explained that the articles in the folder reflected David's frame of mine shortly after the killings. The defense was overruled.

Returning to David, the prosecutor had him admit that in the notebook he had written biblically styled sayings, including "My name is Cain and I kill people."

He also conceded that at the funeral he did not tell the Langerts or Bishops he knew who might have killed their children.

"Nothing further on cross, Judge," O'Brien said.

By now David seemed used up. Not relieved after three hours and five minutes on the stand, not tired. He looked merely as if there weren't much left in him for the day. He had prepared himself well for the ordeal, but O'Brien had kept him off balance with what seemed meandering questions. Now it was over.

David relaxed when slender, curly-haired Robert Gevirtz stepped toward him. "David," the defense attorney asked softly, "why did you go to the funeral?"

"My mom and sister were going there, and they asked me if I wanted to come with them and because Burke had done it, he was a friend of mine. I felt sort of compelled to go because I was very upset that this had all happened."

Under Gevirtz's friendly questioning, David also told his jury that the handcuffs in his room were for playing around with and teasing girls. He repeated that the tape just happened to be on top of the glass in his room, and that he had told Phu the Langerts were handcuffed together but now he knew they had not been.

"Some of the things that Phu Huang says you said couldn't have been true, then, is that true?"

"Right."

"Nothing further," Gevirtz said.

But O'Brien wasn't finished. The jury could see his face reddening as he took longer steps, his head sinking half an inch between his shoulders. "Have you looked at all the police reports and phone records in this case?" he asked.

"Pretty much, for the most part."

"So you know exactly what kind of evidence you had to present, is that correct?"

"Not exactly. I haven't seen every piece, but I have seen most of it, as I said."

"Did it seem to you when you were in that town-house that it was an hour or two?" O'Brien growled.

"Objection," Gevirtz brought up. "Assumes a fact not in evidence."

"Overruled," Judge Singer replied.

"I was never in that townhouse," David said.

"Do you think for the person who was in the town-house as they were taunting the Langerts, the time might have seemed like it went on forever?" O'Brien inquired with rapid-fire delivery.

Again, David calmly denied ever being in the house.

"You applied for that first FOI card in order to get a gun to commit this crime, isn't that right? ... And when you got the gun from John Lewis's office you weren't going to give it up, no matter how many people like the Langerts you killed, is that right?"

"Objection, argumentative," Gevirtz said.

"Sustained."

"At the funeral," O'Brien continued, "you weren't compelled at all to tell the Bishops, 'I know who killed your daughter and son-in-law,' were you? ... You were just compelled enough to go there and watch the Bish-ops suffer, weren't you?"

"I wouldn't say that."

"Well, did they look like they were having a good time?"

Objection sustained.

"Did they look like this was some joke?"

Objection sustained.

"Did you see tears on Mrs. Bishop's face? ... How about tears on Mr. Bishop's face?"

"I don't remember."

"Would it have mattered to you if you did, you—"

This last word was spat out as O'Brien turned away in contempt.

"Possibly," David answered to the prosecutor's back.

Neither O'Brien nor Gevirtz had any further questions. Judge Singer recessed the case to the next morning, and the spectators filed out without a murmur. A reporter placed herself in front of the Bishops in the corridor and asked, "Do you believe David Biro?"

"You have got to be kidding," Lee said as he led his family to the elevators.

The session had lasted to eight o'clock, running longer than any of the other trials that day. In time the stream of people involved in the case headed down the short corridor to the exit. First came the Langerts, always silent, followed by their three good-looking sons and their wives. Then came the Bishops led by Joyce, followed by her daughters, and then Lee, shuffling slowly.

Next came the jurors, accompanied by two deputies to make sure no one spoke to them. Then Gevirtz walked alone down the corridor, passing the empty press room and closed sandwich shop. A few moments later O'Brien came down the hallway with one of the display cards as his assistant, Scott Nelson, accompanied him with a file cart. Six minutes later, Joan and Nick Biro passed by, looking neither proud nor sad. They looked and walked like they were going to work. They went through the revolving doors, and the courthouse closed for the night.

25

Pieces Of A Puzzle

Wednesday, November 13

As THE BAILIFF let the jury in, David's eyes focused on each member from the defense table. It was as if he wanted to know what every man and woman sitting in judgement on him was thinking about his testimony of the night before. Once he made eye contact, he held it until the juror turned away.

Nick, a hearing aid in his right ear, wore a black pin-striped suit as he took the stand. He appeared relaxed and smiled at his son, but David didn't once look up. The father told Born of watching television April 7 and of noticing police at the townhouse while riding his bike the next afternoon.

Under cross-examination from Assistant State's Attorney Scott Nelson, Nick said he couldn't remember details of the night of the murders.

"Even after you knew that the Langerts were killed, April 7 wasn't important to you, was it?"

"No."

Mr. Biro said he also couldn't remember David's going out almost every weekend that spring. Never dropping his pleasant expression, the public relations executive added that he couldn't even remember much about the fraudulent firearms card. When Nelson had him hold the card, Nick wouldn't say the photo over the name of Ron Matzig was that of his son. "It looks like David," he said with cheerful obtuseness, not once but three times as Nelson tried to pin him down.

David busied himself at the defense table as if to avoid looking at his father. There was tension between them, yet Nick seemed unaware of it. He was still smiling as he stepped down from the stand. One reporter whispered to another, "He looks like he's going to walk up to David and say 'Okay, son, I'll see you at home at six for dinner.'"

Nick seemed unaware that he had just portrayed himself as a stranger to his own son, letting the boy create in the silences of the family a private hell of weapons and fantasies.

Next on the stand was Ian Schorvitz, a tall, handsome college student who had met Burke Abrams when they worked at an ice cream shop in Winnetka. He spoke of a conversation in which Burke and David discussed selling a gun. Then the defense rested.

O'Brien took over the cross-examination and asked, "Would you describe David Biro and Burke Abrams as friends?"

"Not really," Schorvitz answered. "They never liked to be with each other. Always kind of separated at times. I was pretty much the mediator between the two."

"No further questions."

As a rebuttal witness, O'Brien called Megan O'Callaghan. The preppy Glencoe teenager wore a black outfit over a red sweater and black knit nylons. Her pageboy blonde hairdo kept falling over one eye as she testified that she had met David at New Trier three years before.

"Did David Biro ever mention to you anything about a perfect crime?"

"Not that I recall."

That surprised O'Brien. Turning sharply to the defense attorneys, he noted page ten of Megan's grand-jury testimony: "David talked about people, like, committing the perfect crime, and how people would get away with it and things like that."

The girl became flustered and tried to say the statement was taken out of context, but O'Brien interrupted her and said to the defense, "Nothing further." Megan then explained to Gevirtz that the "perfect crime" was just "a topic that we had talked about" as she was researching a school paper.

"Did David come up to you and say, hey, I committed the perfect crime?" Gevirtz asked.

"No."

"It's a subject that you brought up, discussing a paper that you were writing, right?"

"Yes."

"And besides David, who else did you talk to this issue of Chicago crime about?"

"Everyone. My friends, all my friends. It was a very big paper."

The last rebuttal witness was Bobbie Adams, a pretty Illinois Bell Telephone liaison employee who was called by the prosecution. She told O'Brien that from August 1982 through March 1990 there were no calls between the Abrams and Biro homes. Then on April 2—the apparent date of the gun theft, and five days before the murders—there were two calls, both from the Biro home. That was all.

Closing arguments had been expected that day, but Judge Singer announced that it was too late. The jurors handed their notes to a deputy, grabbed their coats, and went home.

One of the jurors couldn't fall asleep until one or two in the morning because of all the unanswered questions, then had to get up at six-thirty to be in the courthouse on time. She had been so conscientious about not discussing the case with anyone that it took her husband three days to figure out that she was participating in the Biro trial.

Thursday, November 14

The final morning brought an overflow of spectators to the fifth-floor courtroom as a prison-gray sky virtually camouflaged the jail next door. People like Chief Timm, Lieutenant Sumner, and Sergeant McConnell had lived with this case for more than two years. But also filling the benches and aisles were law students, court buffs, and the curious who made a hobby out of openings and closings in major trials. They pointed out family members to one another and whispered about them as if they were celebrities.

Neither side had made a clear presentation in testimony, leaving statements to lie in the minds of the jurors like scattered pieces of a jigsaw puzzle. Attorneys on both sides were now about to assemble those pieces into completely opposite pictures.

O'Brien concentrated his closing argument on the agony of Nancy Langert. "In the last minutes, she tried to get help for herself, for her child, and no one heard her," he said. "The defendant himself was already home and on the way to the Subway shop and the bars in Chicago—to celebrate."

This double murder, O'Brien added from beside the evidence cart, "has earmarks of David Biro all over it: arrogance, deceit, amateurish."

O'Brien now walked over to David and stood over him. "You know why he will give you Burke Abrams's name? Because they're *not* friends. As all of this evidence mounts, as justice is about to come to David Biro, you know, the last-ditch attempt, boom, he throws a piece of information out to try to divert what is about to and what should happen to him. He gives up something he doesn't even care about, Burke Abrams."

David sat with his head slightly lowered, lettting the

words pass over him. When the statement was finished, the defendant cocked his head and looked into O'Brien's eyes without any show of emotion.

In Gevirtz's closing argument, he said it was ridiculous to think that "for absolutely no reason" a teenager would break randomly into a home and kill two people "cold-bloodedly, execution style." David, Gevirtz implied, was the victim of a practical joke that backfired. If the police believed Phu's story, the defense attorney continued, why didn't they mention the murder in the search warrant for David's room and why did it take them from 2:15 P.M. October 5 to 7 P.M. October 6 to charge him? Never mind that the length of questioning had never been mentioned in testimony.

"Once they decide to charge him, isn't it amazing how all of a sudden their case against David Biro gets better?" Suddenly a message card was found and "memories got more convenient."

With half-lowered lids, Joyce Bishop shifted her glance from juror to juror.

Gevirtz said police didn't make a cast of a footprint found on the railroad ravine because "if it did have any evidentiary value, it's inconsistent with what David told Phu, because the footprints were heading off to the north and David's house is to the south."

Going page by page through the well-thumbed notebook as he spoke, Gevirtz continued, "Here is an article about Laurie Dann, the woman who shot up the school in Winnetka. Does this prove that David was there? . . . Here is an article about Noriega. I guess it was David who was the president and drug dealer down in Panama. Here's the article about the stock market crash, was David responsible for that?"

The only reason David obtained the firearms owner card, he insisted, was to buy and sell a gun. But, he said, "there's one piece of evidence that can convince you far better than I."

Gevirtz lifted the metal shelf from the evidence table.

"We know that Nancy Langert did have physical exertion in those last few minutes. We know that she probably pulled this shelf down and took the hatchet and tried to make noises and get help so that somebody would come and give her attention. But, ladies and gentlemen, she did something else, because Nancy Langert learned or knew the name of the person who killed her."

His voice was light, simple, gentle.

"Either she knew it from before—or the killer was so arrogant and, knowing he was going to kill her, he told her his name, at least the first name. Because in the last moments of her life, Nancy Langert with her own blood tried to write the name of that killer."

The attorney held the shelf up for the jurors to see the message once more. But not as the police and prosecutors had studied the shelf before the trial. By holding the shelf at a different angle, the letters seemed to change. Gevirtz let the jurors study the riddle and told them:

"You can see the B and the U. And if she lived long enough you would have seen the R—K—E." His hushed words were an electric current circulating through the courtroom.

"The Langerts have lost a child, the Bishops have lost a child," Gevirtz continued, "but don't compound this tragedy by convicting the Biros' child. Thank you."

Gevirtz and Born had worked out the strategy with the shelf just a short time before, as they looked at it on the evidence cart, but its effect was brilliant. Judge Singer quickly called for a ten-minute break, giving the prosecuting team time for their own strategy session.

Before the jurors were brought in that morning, Singer had vented a little frustration with himself for a decision early in the trial not to let prosecutors use the possibly inflammatory photos. The judge explained that he had sided with the defense to offset the shocking nature of a teenager being accused of a double murder in an idyllic community, and because of David's long questioning by police. But he came to see that a judge should wait until testimony forms a clear context before deciding whether such evidence is necessary.

This was it, the two prosecutors agreed during the break. This was the way to turn their case around.

O'Brien returned and made an unusual request out of the presence of the jury. He asked that photos comprising People's Exhibits 70 and 84 now be shown to correct the impression Gevirtz had made. Exhibit 70 was a close-up of Nancy's body, and 84 showed the position of the two bodies as police found them.

"You can't change the rules in mid-evidence," Gevirtz complained.

"You can't make an argument on something you knew wouldn't be admitted," O'Brien shot back.

Singer let out the sigh of someone who sees unwanted consequences from something he has done with the best of intentions. Looking first at Gevirtz and then at O'Brien, he said, "In light of your closing argument, I will admit 70 and 84, and will allow you to reopen your argument."

"Objection, Judge, you can't change the rules in the middle of the game," Gevirtz said.

"I *can*," Singer answered.

"But—"

The temper of the easy-going jurist gave way.

"Please!" he shouted, more at himself than at the defense team. "I was advised this had little or no relevancy. When I heard the conclusion of the argument—I see I had made a mistake. You contributed to that mistake because you argued the lack of relevancy ... I'm not suggesting that you framed your final argument with that in mind ... [but] it is considerably more relevant now."

The defense team waived their right to reopen their argument, and the jury was let in. Assistant State's Attorney Scott Nelson, who had taken only a minor part in the trial until now, stepped from his chair for the rebuttal closing argument. O'Brien was best in an attack. But Nelson—with his youthful appearance and animated way of speaking—was more effective in getting emotional responses from juries.

"Burke Adams is the straw man," Nelson said. "That's the target for David Biro. In opening statements last week, you didn't hear that name. You heard it first from David Biro's mouth on the witness stand. That was planned, just like everything else about this defendant is planned . . . wait and then play that card at the end. It's a gutsy move, it's a showoff move, it's a childish, amateurish, arrogant move. It's a David Biro trademark."

In a voice that varied from nearly a whisper to almost a shout, Nelson told the jurors that the defendant had confessed to each one of them, but "he's putting a different name on it."

That a teenage student would kill someone for no apparent motive "sounds a little hard to swallow," Nelson remarked, "and that's why Eddie Benoit said just seeing him on the street wasn't worth following up for a murder, not a kid. It just didn't make sense. That's prejudice. That's a prejudice that you have to leave behind, that a sixteen-year-old boy who lives in a huge home in a nice suburb doesn't do this kind of thing. Guess what. Look at the evidence. He did.

"You know," he added quietly from the far end of the jury box, "doing this crime may have been the thrill of his life, but if you're the only one who knows it, [there is] little self-satisfaction . . . Did he sound like he was sorry that he had burglarized a public school of fifteen thousand dollars worth of computer equipment? He's not. Remorseless, just the way that Phu describes him."

After mentioning the way David admittedly had lied to a notary public about the firearms card, and to his father, and to the people in the sandwich shop, Nelson told the jurors to "look at the evidence. Tell him for the first time, 'David Biro, we know you're lying. We're not fools. We don't have to accept it.' "

The young prosecutor pointed to the metal shelf lying against a table in front of the judge's bench. "It's been suggested that Nancy Langert wrote the name of her killer; in her dying moments, she started to write 'Burke Abrams.' Well, did she write the first name? I don't think so. Nancy Langert, as you've seen, died nowhere near that shelf." He lifted up a blowup. "This photograph, People's Exhibit Number 70, doesn't show the shelf, just her, and that's where she was found."

Nelson lowered the enlargement and showed the jury the other picture that had been suppressed. "People's Exhibit 84 shows part of the shelf some distance away, a photograph you've never seen, and it has some very bloody portions to it. But I ask you to look past the blood and look to the shelf and the area where she wrote on it, the blood. Nancy Langert wrote as she looked at the face of the person she loved most, Richard Langert, and she went over there and probably checked on him and realized he was dead.

"No, the message is not a name," Nelson explained. The dying woman's last thoughts weren't of her unknown killer but of the person she loved most. With the jurors' rapt attention, he stated that what Nancy wrote was her way of saying, "Richard, I love you."

There was not a sound in the courtroom.

"That's an I," Nelson said as he pointed to the first figure. His fingertip moved an inch. "That's a heart." In fact, it was like the heart Nancy's mother used in signing letters. Nelson's finger moved to the third figure, and his voice became stronger. "Look at it. That's a U. And then she crawled out and died."

He turned to the judge and said, "Thank you, Your Honor."

The prosecutor sat down, and the continued silence in the packed rows of spectators was like a shared gasp. David and his mother showed no reaction. His father sat with folded arms and lowered his head. David's friends Megan O'Callaghan and Karen Lynch went outside the courtroom to cry.

The jury left to deliberate at 12:42 P.M. In the hall, as if by mitosis, spectators formed three clusters: the Bishops and friends, the Langerts and friends, and the Biros and friends.

When the jurors walked into the deliberation room, they were so numb it took a few minutes before anyone could speak. They listened for seven days, and yet they felt depleted. A few went to the evidence cart, but most didn't want to look at any of it again. Reporters in the press room had a pool over how long it would take to reach a verdict, with bets ranging from three to eight hours.

The jury foreman was a suburban woman who had a friend in the Chicago Crime Commission. The print production worker asked her fellow jurors if they were ready for a vote. Three said they wanted to talk about the case for a while. One thought everyone seemed to have was unrelated to guilt or innocence, it was the impression David's father gave on the stand. "I think the family was too busy to get involved," one of the women said.

Another woman kept thinking of the time she went in Neo's to see what it was like. "These people are out of their normal element," she said. "You don't want them as your friends, you don't want them as your enemies."

David's youth was the most troubling aspect. In their minds, sixteen-year-old kids don't murder strangers just for the thrill of it. A few sensed that David, at times, became like a rattler—coiled, trapped, and striking out. There had been no mention of his disturbed past: acting tough to impress friends, shooting at strangers, trying to poison his family, and offering to kill Karen's father. Nor were they told that Dr. Stoewe and others had found that he expressed his hostility toward his family by victimizing others, making them random stand-ins for people he really wanted to hurt. Even so, one of the jurors was sure that David had never been given the help he needed.

Others thought the crime was a whim of circumstance, that David said to himself one day, "I can do whatever I want and get away with it. I've stolen, I've got a gun, and now I want to kill."

All the jurors were affected by the riddle in blood. Perhaps it did spell "I love you," but the nurse on the panel had her own idea. Suppose Nancy had recognized David from seeing him with his family somewhere and, not sure of his name, tried to write it as it sounded: BUro.

The jury foreman asked for a vote. Twelve hands.

As the jurors notified a bailiff they were ready, one of the women told the others, "I'm going home and call my children and tell them I love them."

At 2:50 P.M., O'Brien and Gevirtz entered the court, letting spectators know that a verdict had been reached. Deliberations had lasted two hours and five minutes.

David stood granite-faced as the jurors sat down. A deputy took the verdict sheets, and the clerk announced, "Guilty of first-degree murder in the death of Nancy Langert, guilty of first-degree murder in the death of Richard Langert, guilty of the intentional homicide of a fetus, guilty of home invasion."

There was not a murmur, not a creak from the spectator benches.

The judge asked each juror, "Is that then and is that now your verdict?" One by one came, "Yes, your honor." David brought a hand to his face as if the reality had at last hit him. O'Brien went to the spectators' section and hugged Joyce Bishop, and Sergeant McConnell hugged Mrs. Langert. "I wish you could have known Nancy and Richard," the short, plump woman told her as scores of strangers filed out around them.

The defense attorneys were prepared for David to

lash out at them for losing. Instead he said, "It's not your fault."

Nick Biro watched the other families leaving, then stood leaning on the crowded bench. He ran his fingers through his hair with a glassy, lost look. His eyes stayed on David, who never glanced back as he left the defense table and shambled out.

A few minutes later a deputy led Nick and Joan to a side room so that they might spend fifteen minutes with their son. For two weeks, Mrs. Biro had not let her emotions show in court. Now the trim woman with steel-gray hair had to fight against tears. As she entered the room, a deputy said, "No physical contact."

"He's my son," Joan said.

David looked up from a table and bit his lip. "It's okay," he said. Then he was silent.

The Bishops had left the courtroom crying, but they managed smiles by the time they reached the bank of elevators. Lee, however, looked stunned.

The Bishops drove that evening to the churchyard in Kenilworth not far from their home. They held umbrellas under the steady drizzle and walked through the mud and curled dead leaves. Standing before the grave marker of the two lovers, the family let them know that justice had been done.

26

Impact

Friday, December 20, 1991

THE CONVICTION HAD bridged the emotional distance between the Bishops and the Langerts. They no longer kept apart from each other in the courthouse. It was as if both families had overcome their private grief and could now share the healing. As they waited in court for David's sentencing, they shook hands and chatted until the room was called to order.

The Bishops sat bolt upright as the young man was led in. No longer caring what anyone thought of him, David briskly walked across the courtroom with his short-sleeved jail shirt flying, unbuttoned.

Rain darkened the streets surrounding the gray courthouse as Gevirtz made a last-ditch motion questioning the state's seldom-imposed mandatory term for multiple murders committed by a juvenile. But Assistant State's Attorney O'Brien, looking through his thick glasses, told Judge Singer that David "in the planning and execution of this crime has shown himself to be a criminal far beyond his years."

O'Brien reminded the court that Biro once wrote that his name is Cain and that he kills people. "Today," said the prosecutor, "is the day we remember that."

But Gevirtz said David could change in ten or twenty years. "What if he becomes a person who can benefit society?"

Judge Singer sat unmoved. Nothing could outweigh what he had read in the pre-sentence impact statements. Richard Langert's unassuming father had told of suffering increased hypertension because of the stress of so many false leads, and of having to seek counseling through the county's witness assistance program.

Joyce Bishop received informal counseling from her pastor and needed to listen to inspirational tapes and read self-help books to find meaning in life again. She and Lee not only had moved into the townhouse where the murders occurred, to feel closer to Nancy, they even ate from Nancy's china rather than their own as a way of feeling she was still with them.

Joyce still awoke at 2 and 3 A.M. some mornings and found herself unable to go back to sleep, still wondering what the last moments of Nancy's and Richard's lives must have been like. "Quite often I find myself saying out loud, 'Run, Nancy, run!' or 'No, no, no, no!' "

"I go down into that basement every day," her statement continued, "and there is not one time there that I don't hear echoes of voices and picture the terrible scene of that night of horror."

Joyce, who knew David only from his well-groomed appearance at the trial, could not imagine how this clean-cut young man could have murdered them. "There must be something that is known as the 'bad seed.' He must have been born with some kind of quirk of nature that implanted evil in him right from the beginning."

Jeanne's statement said that after her sister was murdered, she moved in with her parents because she couldn't sleep alone or with the lights out. She reported that when she went shopping and saw things she would have wanted to buy Nancy and the baby, "I wanted to cry." One day at work she received a call from an acquaintance with the same name as her sister. When Jeanne's secretary said that Nancy was on the phone, "My heart started pounding with joy. Maybe she wasn't dead! Maybe it was all a horrible mistake."

What Jeanne did not write down was that she had been so disgusted with the FBI investigation that she had given up her private law practice and accepted a lower-paying job as an assistant public defender. Instead of having a Loop office with a secretary, she now worked in a tiny room at a Chicago police station on the Northwest Side to help keep the defendants from being ground down by the system.

Judge Singer looked down from the bench and asked the defendant if he had anything to say before sentencing.

"No," David answered hoarsely.

For a month of pre-trial hearings and testimony, Singer had behaved as everyone's friendly uncle. Now he expressed his personal feelings. He said that most people who appeared before him came from broken families, poverty, and crime-ridden neighborhoods. But David, he added, "had every advantage conceivable—a cohesive family, from what I can tell. A loving family. A neighborhood not crime-ridden. Affluence rather than poverty.

"This was a murder for no other reason than the fact that the defendant wished to kill," he said, "a cold-blooded killing for a reason that remains a mystery . . . the defendant wanted to achieve some sort of infamy, some sort of notoriety from that killing."

The mandatory term he was about to impose "is a terrible sentence," Judge Singer said, but "if the sentence is ever appropriate, it is appropriate in this case. I sentence the defendant to life in prison without parole."

The words were spoken almost in a whisper. A

woman sitting among the spectators gasped so loudly that she could be heard across the room.

David leaned back in his chair, a mocking smile on his lips. A movie-assassin smile. His parents had prepared themselves for this moment, and they didn't let their faces show their feelings.

The Langerts went through the doorway without a word. Joyce Bishop, dressed in a holiday-green suit adorned with a Christmas tree pin, held a short news conference in the hall. Determined not to let her grief show, she thanked reporters for having been professional throughout the ordeal and expressed hope that the new year would be a better year for everyone.

Other reporters stopped Jeanne as she walked toward the revolving doors in the lobby. She said her family wished that, as part of the sentence, David could have been made to "sit down with us and tell us—why? How could you do this?"

How could rage become a kind of controlled madness, and three lives be taken just so a boy could boast about it to his friends?

By then the rain had stopped, and the weather was turning warmer. As people stepped outside, they exchanged "Merry Christmas" with the guards.

February 1, 1992

On the first day of February, Jeanne brought all her newspaper clippings from the murders and the trial to the Chicago law firm of Corbett and Mathews. She was acting on behalf of her family to make sure David Biro would never profit from his crimes, even though the U.S. Supreme Court had struck down New York's "Son of Sam" law preventing killers from receiving money from books about them.

Jeanne's intention was to sue not only David but his parents, holding them responsible for the actions of their son while he was still a juvenile. She also planned an unprecedented civil action that would make David's former lawyer, John Lewis, accountable for the behavior of his client in a "voluntary undertaking"—namely, holding the forged firearms owner's card in his office for safekeeping.

John Corbett, a young man with Irish good looks and a sandy blond mustache, had a reputation as a victims' rights attorney. He saw similarities to a suit filed against Laurie Dann's parents, and settled a year earlier for an undisclosed amount rumored to have been over one million dollars.

Corbett and his associate, Victoria Vhrel, immediately set to work gathering background material since they had little more than two months to file within the state's two-year time limit. They worked well into the night seven days a week, gathering records and interviewing acquaintances of the Biros.

On April 4, they held a news conference to announce a ten-million-dollar suit against Nick and Joan Biro and John Lewis. The murder of Richard and Nancy Langert had not been a sudden outburst, Corbett explained. He said the Bishop family had sufficient reason to believe that David was a sociopath, someone without a conscience. Yet instead of seeking treatment for David, he added, the Biros took him out of the Charter Barclay mental hospital and never sought follow-up care.

Jeanne insisted that the suit was about responsibility, not money. But the action raised a disturbing question: How many parents really know their children?

David's third-floor room remained as police had found it. That was Joan's way of feeling that her youngest child was still with the family. Yet the home was becoming their own prison. Neighbors who had once supported the Biros now ignored the couple out of fear of being subpoenaed. The Biros sometimes bought groceries miles away to avoid being recognized, and both Nick and his wife saw business clients pull away because of the murders.

The Biros had spent $150,000 for their son's defense, and a possible appeal could cost $200,000 more, in addition to whatever they might have to pay in the court action.

Under their homeowner's policy, their insurance company hired a lawyer from a prominent firm to represent them in the suit. But after the attorney refused to represent their son, David filed as a pauper and a lawyer was assigned to him.

In responding to charges made about their son, Nick and Joan Biro admitted the two shootings with a BB gun but denied that he had mental problems. In legal responses to the Bishops' allegations in the suit, they insisted the milk poisoning never happened.

Chief Timm announced in the fall that, at age forty-nine, he would step down in April 1993. No one would comment on whether the Langert investigation was a factor in his early retirement. Winnetka Village President Jeanne Bradner said Timm had done a good job but that "it's probably time to smell the roses. He's had some difficult issues."

Timm said he would return to college to complete his studies for a degree in criminology. No one in the Winnetka police department or the state's attorney's office could imagine a more thorough investigation of the Langert murders by a department of just two dozen officers.

Update

Judge Kathy M. Flanagan heard oral arguments on April 22, 1993, concerning the Bishops's lawsuit which tested the legal grounds for the suit against Nick and Joan Biro and David's attorney John Lewis. In October, 1993, it was now at the motion state, at which point a judge must decide if there are valid legal reasons to continue the case or dismiss it.

Responsibility, liability, and negligence were the issues. John Lewis's status as a lawyer and the charges of legal misconduct had nothing to do with the case as she saw it. Judge Flanagan's decision concerning the responsibility of the Biros was the central issue that could affect hundreds of future cases.

Nearly six months had gone by. At least half a dozen times, Jeanne Bishop called her attorney, John Corbett, and asked, "Have you any word yet?" Corbett told her to tell her family not to give up hope but that he felt uneasy. Waiting this long for a decision suggested that the ruling might be against them.

Shortly after noon on October 1, Judge Flanagan looked over her twenty-page response and made her last minute revisions. Next, she told her secretary to notify the attorneys that they could pick up her ruling in an hour.

Judge Flanagan ruled that the Biros had a duty as

parents to control the conduct of their teenage son. "It is difficult, if not impossible," she wrote, "to imagine a more fact-specific complaint concerning the prior history of the minor child." The judge also noted David's shooting of a seven-year-old boy with a BB gun and his diagnosis as "a psychopath/sociopath with dispositions toward violent, murderous and dangerous behavior."

If the Biros did not realize their son was dangerous, Flanagan held, then they should have.

The judge ruled that John Lewis was not negligent or guilty of misconduct as an attorney. But she ruled that Lewis opened himself up to civil liability when he failed to notify the police that David had threatened to break into his office. She further denied Lewis's motions to dismiss the negligence counts against him. Judge Flanagan could not find any cases in Illinois that showed grounds for legal actions against an attorney for alleged ethics violations in these types of circumstances.

Though a trial was still to come, the wheels of justice continued to turn. More people would be questioned and possibly held accountable. And the murders of Nancy and Richard and their unborn child would not end with the conviction of David Biro.